THE PORT OF DOVER

THROUGH TIME

Ian Collard

AMBERLEY

First published 2018

Amberley Publishing
The Hill, Stroud, Gloucestershire, GL5 4EP
www.amberley-books.com

ISBN 978 1 4456 7274 8 (print)
ISBN 978 1 4456 7275 5 (ebook)

British Library Cataloguing in Publication Data.
A catalogue record for this book is available from the British Library.

Origination by Amberley Publishing.
Printed in Great Britain.

Introduction

A regular ferry service was operating between Dover and Wissant around 350 BC. Over the years these small vessels became larger, being then operated by experienced seaman and propelled by sails and oars. In August 55 BC, eight vessels, escorted by galleys, sailed from a port near Boulogne. The ships contained soldiers from the Seventh and Tenth legions and were loaded with arms and provisions. It was estimated that there were approximately 10,200 men in this convoy. The Roman army landed between Deal and Walmer but were soon forced back onto their ships, which withdrew and returned to France. The following year a larger Roman convoy was despatched. When the troops were landed they made their way inland, while the fleet anchored near Richborough.

The Battle of Hastings took place in August 1066 between the Norman French army, led by William, the Duke of Normandy, and an English army, led by the Anglo-Saxon King Harold Godwinson. A large invasion fleet was gathered from Normandy by William who assembled the men at Saint-Valery-sur-Somme in preparation for the sea voyage across the English Channel. Following the landings, William's men built a wooden castle at Hastings and a fortification at Pevensey.

Around 1370 the East Brook harbour suffered from silting and was abandoned in favour of a site known as Paradise. A quay called the Wyke was built, but the problem of silting continued and this was not dealt with until 1495, when another pier was built extending south-eastward. Following the surrender of Calais in 1346, Edward III said that, 'Thenceforth, Dover was the only port to be used for the crossing to France.' However, there were few alternatives, as Folkestone and Newhaven (Meeching) were small villages and Richborough had declined in importance.

In 1583 work began on building a long wall 1,960 feet in length and a cross wall 660 feet long, incorporating a sluice, and this became the Wellington Dock. In 1606 James I granted the port a new charter and a Board of eleven men was appointed, two of whom were local – the Mayor and the Lieutenant Governor. A lock gate was added to the Great Pent in 1733 and it became a wet dock. In the late eighteenth century the Harbourmaster, James Moon, authorised the building of a wall from the cross wall to the south pier and this was completed in 1818. It was followed by the construction of a dry dock, which was opened in 1824. A report of 1845 recommended that Dover be chosen as a refuge between Chatham and Portsmouth. The Admiralty agreed and work commenced on the construction of Admiralty Pier in 1848. The lifeboat was established at Dover in 1837 and in 1850 more work was carried out on the Great Pent, creating the Commercial and Northampton quays and a slipway on the south side. It was named Wellington Dock and the outer basin became Granville Dock.

In 1816 the steamer *Majestic* crossed the English Channel with 200 passengers on board. The voyage took three and a half hours but this was no faster than some of the sailing ships of the time. *Dasher* and *Arrow* were introduced into service at Dover and joined the *Rob Roy* on the Channel service to France. *Rob Roy* was purchased by the French and was renamed *Henri Quatre* at Calais. John and William Hayward, from Dover, purchased *Sovereign* and *Monarch*, and these were placed on service to operate with the mail ships.

By 1840 the steamships were becoming the first generation of vehicle carriers and regularly sailed with carriages secured to the deck. In 1808 Thomas Telford was asked to look at future works at Folkestone, and in 1817 and 1829 further improvements were carried out. However, by 1843 the harbour was suffering from silt problems, which reduced the size of vessels able to use the facilities. The problem was resolved when the port was purchased by the South Eastern Railway, who spent a large amount of capital to alleviate the problems. Following the Napoleonic Wars, a cross-channel service resumed from Dover, which was operated by three ships that were transferred from Harwich. However, in 1835 the Post Office handed the mail service to the Admiralty, who ran it until 1854, when it was returned to private enterprise. Jenkins & Churchward of Dover paid the government £10,000 a year for the contract to operate the service from Dover.

The Lord Warden Hotel was built in Dover in 1853 and was designed by Samuel Beazley. It contained large dining rooms, a coffee room containing three large chandeliers, lounges and over 100 rooms. It was situated near the harbour of refuge and was within walking distance of the cross-channel vessels. Its opening in 1853 was celebrated by a dinner attended by 150 guests, In 1861 Dover became a Trust Port by Act of Parliament with a chairman and six trustees, representing the Admiralty, the Board of Trade, the railway companies and Dover Corporation. The Board authorised the construction of the Prince of Wales Pier, which was completed in 1902. The work on the Admiralty Pier was completed in 1871 and the London, Chatham & Dover Railway was providing a service from Dover to Calais. Vessels of the South Eastern Railway were operating from Folkestone to Boulogne and the London, Brighton & South Coast Railway from Newhaven to Dieppe. All companies were offering passengers a twelve-hour service from London to Paris.

Castalia was introduced and operated by the London, Chatham & Dover Railway but she had problems making the speed of 13 knots promised by the builders. She was eventually sold in 1884, becoming an isolation hospital on the River Thames. *Bessemer* was built at Hull by Earle's and was fitted with a saloon, which was hung on pivots. A series of hydraulic rams would be operated to ensure that the saloon would remain stable. However, the system proved unreliable and the pistons often jammed. She was later modified but soon joined *Castalia* laid up in Granville Dock. She was sold to the shipbreakers in 1879 and her saloon became a billiard room in a country house in Kent. It was later rebuilt as a lecture room for a women's horticultural college. *Calais-Douvres* was similar to *Castalia* but was built with two full hulls. She survived on the service until 1887, when she was sold and became a coal hulk on the Thames.

The *Invicta*, owned by the London, Chatham & Dover Railway, was built in 1882 and was the first Channel steamer to be lit by electricity. She operated at a speed of 18 knots and crossed from Dover to Calais in one hour and ten minutes. However, in April 1888 she went aground at Calais. By midnight the passengers were able to walk to safety along the beach and their luggage was taken off the stranded vessel by carts. *Invicta*'s generating machinery and paddle-wheels were removed and a team of men dug the sand away from around her hull. It took a week to re-float the vessel from the sandbank where she had been stranded. The *Albert Victoria* went aground in thick fog in 1893 and she became a total loss. By 1903 Hamburg-America Line passenger liners were calling at Dover on the voyage to New York.

The French vessel *Pas de Calais* was on a voyage from Calais to Dover on 26 May 1910 with 300 passengers on board. A slight bump was felt shortly after leaving the French port and the hull of a submarine rose out of the water. A boat was lowered and the crew of the *Pas de Calais* attempted to make contact with men inside the submarine. However, the submarine quickly slipped below the surface and the *Pas de Calais* returned to port.

The submarine was later discovered, holed and filled with water. There were no survivors from the collision.

During the First World War, six sets of moorings were laid down across the Straits of Dover and nine submarines were given the task to protect them. Six of these were moored to buoys and three were on patrol. Following a German attack on the British patrol boat *Attentive* on 27 August 1914, the British submarine fleet were placed on protection, rather than defensive duties. The Dover Straits were patrolled by French destroyers, as well as submarines from the Boulogne flotilla and also those from the Dover Patrol. Dover was closed as a passenger port and the cross-channel trade did not resume until 1919, when the war had ended. Most of the cross-channel traffic was sent via Folkestone and freight went through Newhaven. *Engadine, Empress* and *Riviera* were converted into seaplane carriers, while *Biarritz* and *Paris* became minelayers. *The Queen*, which was the first cross-channel steamer fitted with steam turbines, was returning empty from France to Folkestone when she was attacked by a German destroyer. Her crew took to the boats and were later landed at Dover, but the vessel sank.

The *Ville de Liege* made the first sailing to Ostend on 18 January 1919 with 332 passengers on board. Services resumed between Folkestone and Boulogne the following month but the Dover–Calais route remained closed because of the landslip blocking the railway line to Dover. The route was not finally opened until 8 January 1920. The South Eastern & Chatham, the London, Brighton & South Coast and the London & South Western railways amalgamated to form the Southern Railway in 1923. The journey from Paris to Calais was operated by the luxurious Pullman train the Fleche d'Or and this was followed by the Golden Arrow, which ran from London Victoria to Dover.

Captain Townsend chartered the *Artificer* in 1928, which was able to carry fifteen cars and twelve passengers across the Channel. However, some of the motorists had to leave their cars and travel across the Channel on the mail steamer and then reclaim their motors at the port of destination. Townsend also chartered the small *Royal Firth* later that year.

Autocarrier, the first cross-channel vessel to be specially built for the carriage of vehicles, was introduced in 1931. However, she was not a drive-through vessel as cars were craned on board, and there was room for thirty-five vehicles and 120 passengers. She was ordered as *Camberley* but was launched as *Autocarrier*, being built with a saloon, a buffet and a bathroom with hot and cold showers. When introduced she sailed from Dover at 12.15 p.m. every day and returned from Calais at 4 p.m. The fare was 10 shillings (50 pence) each way and vehicles were charged depending on the wheel-base. Captain Stuart M. Townsend purchased the ex-Admiralty minesweeper *Ford* in 1928 and she was converted to carry cars and was renamed *Forde*. The cars and buses which were carried were loaded by an 8-ton crane.

Belgian Railways & Marine operated the Ostend–Dover service. The mail service between Ostend and Dover was inaugurated on 8 April 1815, but was operated by ships flying the British flag up to 1846. There were four sailings a week in each direction, and the crossing took from five to seven hours. When the railway lines were opened between Ostend and Brussels in 1838, and between Dover and London in in 1841, the Belgian Government built a fleet of steamships, which were employed on the route. By 1848 the Belgian ships were making eight crossings and the British ships six, which made a total of fourteen crossings a week. From 1862 the service was operated by the Belgian Government alone and the following year they had seven ships operating two services each day.

By 1892 the Belgian fleet consisted of nine ships with first-class saloons aft, a large promenade deck and a number of single cabins. The *Princesse Elisabeth*, ordered in 1905, achieved 24 knots on trials, becoming the fastest ship of her class in the world. During the First World War, all the ships were used for the evacuation of Belgian refugees and crossed the Channel more than 4,000 times, carrying over 2 million soldiers and 500,000 wounded troops. In 1936 Belgian Marine converted the *Ville de Liege* into a car ferry. She carried eighty cars on covered decks and 265 passengers. She was able to embark and disembark cars without the aid of cranes, by means of mobile ramps, whatever the state of the tide and without using a special dock.

The ports of Dover and Harwich differed from all other cross-channel ports in the country in that they incorporated facilities for railway wagons and carriages to be shipped on specially designed train ferries. This facility eliminated the need to unload onto quays, cranage and other stevedoring activities. A truck loaded anywhere in Britain could be sent to any station in Europe, outside Spain and Russia, where the railway gauges were different to those in the rest of Europe. The train ferries operated from Dover to Dunkirk and Harwich to Zeebrugge. The handling of cargo was reduced to a minimum, the risk of damage or loss was slight and insurance rates were lower for goods transported in this manner, meaning it was the quickest, safest and easiest way of moving goods across the Continent. The rolling stock included covered and open, refrigerated and insulated wagons and motor car trucks. Private owners' wagons were also conveyed.

A new dock was built at Dover, in which the ship was shut off from the sea by double gates. The water level inside the dock was lowered or raised by pumps, and the rails on the ship were connected with the rails ashore by a linkspan. The journey from London to Paris was divided into three separate sections. The run from London Victoria station to Dover was too short to allow passengers to settle and rest and the sea crossing from Dover to Calais could often be very rough and uncomfortable. The longest section of the journey was that from Calais, but many passengers could not enjoy this after a crossing in rough weather. Freight carried on the route had to be loaded onto vessels and then transferred to road vehicles on arrival at ports. A train ferry had been operated by the North British Railway Company between Granton and Burntisland, in the Firth of Forth, before the Forth Bridge was built. The Harwich train ferries commenced operation in 1924 and similar operations were introduced in Germany and Sweden. However, while tides are negligible in the Baltic, there is a great difference between the high and low water mark in the English Channel.

The tides that come into the Dover Strait have all the force and power of the Atlantic Ocean behind them and there is a tidal difference of 25 feet. The linkspan between shore and ship is by a drawbridge and the huge tides at Dover and the heavy swell during rough weather made the standard drawbridge principle impracticable. Consequently, it was decided that the ferry berth and drawbridge should be placed within an enclosed dock. Engineers could control the quantity of water in this dock and it could be varied and brought to the right level by pumps, irrespective of the state of the tide.

Piles were driven into the chalk foundation but engineers were forced to abandon the work because of severe winter storms. When work commenced, concrete blocks were laid and a caisson was placed into position. However, when the pumping began it was discovered that water from outside percolated through the chalk forming the bottom of the dock faster than pumps could deal with it. The walls were coated with mud but this was unsuccessful and it was decided to build the dock without excluding the water. The task was given to George Ellson, the Chief Engineer of the Southern Railway, and he fitted a temporary caisson and used a powerful dredger to work on the chalk bottom to bring it to the required depth. This was covered by a bed of concrete 5 feet deep before the sill and gates, weighing 300 tons each, were fitted. The gates worked on horizontal hinges fixed below the dock sill. In the open position both gates would lie flat on the bottom and be hidden from view. The finished pumping chamber consisted of three sets of centrifugal pumps with a maximum capacity of 120,000 gallons of water a minute.

The connection between ship and shore at Harwich was by means of an adjustable bridge secured at the shore end by resting on the ship. The length of this bridge was governed by the rise and fall of the tide, so that at either high or low water the safe working gradient did not exceed one in twenty. The Harwich–Zeebrugge service was under the management of the London & North Eastern Railway Company, which owned the ships and the terminal installation at Harwich. The terminal at Zeebrugge was owned and operated by the Société Belgo-Anglaise des Ferryboats. The Dover–Dunkirk service was managed by the Southern Railway Company in conjunction with the ALA Steamship Company, and this was responsible for all the arrangements at Dunkirk. The train ferry service operated from Victoria station to Dover and across the Channel to Dunkirk and then to Paris. Twelve luxurious sleeping cars were built especially for this service and ticket inspections took place after eight o'clock in the morning, as the train was arriving at Paris. The train ferries also carried twenty-five cars in a large garage above the train deck.

Twickenham Ferry underwent trials in June 1934 and she was followed by *Hampton Ferry* and *Shepperton Ferry*, but the full service was not inaugurated until 1936. *Twickenham Ferry* attained 16½ knots on trials, with a coal consumption of 2.25 tons an hour. She was initially used to transport cars and lorries belonging to the British troops sent to the Saar Valley at the time of the Plebiscite in March 1935. One of the three ferries was used as a grandstand at Southampton Docks when the Cunard liner *Queen Mary* set off on her maiden voyage in May 1936. *Twickenham Ferry* was handed over to Angleterre-Lorraine-Alsace Steamship Company, which shared the operation of the service with the Southern Railway and the sleeping cars were provided by the International Sleeping Car Company, which had activities on the European continent as well as in North Africa and Asia. The first public passenger service was operated on 14 October 1936. The train left Victoria station at 10.00 p.m., arriving in Paris at 8.55 a.m. the following day. The crossing of the English Channel took three hours and fifty-five minutes on the outward passage and four hours and fifteen minutes on the homeward journey.

The Southern Railway operated from Dover to Calais, Folkestone to Boulogne, Newhaven to Dieppe and Dover to Ostend with Belgian Railways. Dover–Calais was the link for the Golden Arrow, the Brussels Pullman, the Blue Train and the Simplon Orient Express, as well as the Orient Express, the Rome Express, the Engadine Express and the Bombay Express. One of the main steamers on the route was the *Canterbury*, which was described in Southern Railway brochures:

> You will discover the harmony between these trains and the ship. The awning deck is enclosed by glass windows, making it both sheltered and light. Instead of ordinary deck chairs, there are armchairs upholstered in velvet. In addition to a large number of cabins, there are screened off alcoves. The ships also have a spacious dining saloon with accommodation for 100 people and a comfortable lounge, a buffet and a bar. The whole of the interior is of carefully selected wood, panelled and suitably decorated.

In 1938 over 50,000 people travelled by the Calais route in a summer month, and the previous year over 111,000 people passed through Folkestone, of which 32,000 were on excursions to France. The Newhaven–Dieppe route was operated by six ships and was jointly owned by the French State Railways and the Southern Railway. This service route was operated to fulfil two functions: firstly, to take people to the strip of coast that includes Pourville and Le Tréport, and secondly to provide a cheap route to Paris. Passenger traffic to Belgium increased steadily during the 1930s and all records were broken in 1937 when the total number of passengers that travelled by the Dover–Ostend route was 778,961. This was an increase of 110,000 over the previous year.

In a paper on 'Ships of the Narrow Seas', A. C. Hardy, BSc AMINA describes the characteristics required by vessels employed on routes around the coast of the British Isles prior to the Second World War:

> The voyage varies all the way from the one-hour route between Dover and Calais up to nearly five hours on the Parkeston/Flushing route. Some of the fastest speeds are found on the Newhaven/Dieppe route, where a speed of 25 knots is available, if required. Some of the biggest ships are on the Dover/Ostend route, maintained by the Belgian State Railways, while the smallest craft are those running on the morning and evening service between Larne and Stranraer. In a nutshell, the characteristics required are extreme seaworthiness and an ability to make quick turn-arounds. There must be a large lounge space for passengers, ample dining and smoking room accommodation, and one or two special cabins for use during rough weather, these being either of the individual type let at a supplement or of the open berth type. However interchangeable day and night service ships are of comparable type to the day service vessels, and serve the Channel Islands and the Holyhead/Dublin routes. The problem is to provide ample lounging and deck space for passengers during the day, coupled with ample cabin accommodation for night.

On 3 September 1939 Britain declared war on Germany and two days later the British Expeditionary Force landed in France. In June the following year British and French troops were cornered by the advancing German army near Dunkirk. Between 26 May and 3 June more than 330,000 troops were rescued from the beaches by the 'little ships', as they became affectionately known. Vice-Admiral Bertram Ramsey controlled Operation Dynamo from a bunker within Dover Cliffs and Dover was the busiest of the ports during the evacuation. Dover suffered sustained bombing and shelling by guns based on the other side of the Channel. During the hostilities, 216 civilians lost their lives and 10,056 properties were damaged in the town. At the end of the war three flotillas of minesweepers arrived to help clear the mines. Most of the seafront premises were damaged and the destroyer HMS *Codrington* was beached, while the western entrance was closed by the sunken blockships *Minnie de Larrinaga, Spanish Prince* and *War Sepoy.*

The Southern Railway lost eight ships, which included the *Brighton* and *Maid of Kent.* Twelve of their vessels had survived the war but it was not until April 1946 that a regular ferry service could commence from the Admiralty Pier. The Belgian Marine Administration lost the *Prince Leopold* and *Prince Philippe,* and *Prince Baudouin* reopened the Ostend–Dover service on 24 July 1946.The crossing actually celebrated the centenary of that service. *Cote d'Argent* and *Cote d'Azur* were badly damaged in 1940 and abandoned at the French ports. They were taken over by the Germans and renamed *Ostmark* and *Elsass* respectively, and both later sank. *Londres* resumed service on the Dieppe–Newhaven service on 11 April 1947, and was later joined by *Arromanches*. *Falaise* was launched on 25 October 1946 for the Southampton–St Malo route, but was designed to operate on any of the Southern Railway services.

The train ferry service to Dunkirk was also able to recommence in December 1946. The western entrance to the harbour was not opened until 1960, when all wrecks and obstructions had been cleared, and *Spanish Prince* remained in place until 2010, when the wreck was finally lifted. In August 1946 *Dinard* was sent to the Tyne and was converted by Palmers to carry cars, which were craned on and off of the vessel. She replaced the *Autocarrier* and entered service on the Folkestone and Dover services in July the following year.

The rail and shipping services of British Railways were nationalised on 1 January 1948 and the services at Dover came under the British Transport Commission, Railway Executive – Southern Region. The British Railways Board was created on 1 January 1953. Belgian Marine introduced the *Prince Philippe* and *Koning Albert*, but lost the *Prinses Astrid* on 22 June 1949. She was on a voyage from Ostend to Dover and collided with an uncleared mine. Five of her crew lost their lives, but all of the passengers were saved. She was beached on a sandbank but later broke into two and sank. The *Prinses Josephine Charlotte* was sold and the name transferred to a new vessel.

On 14 December 1951 *Lord Warden* was launched by William Denny & Bothers at Dumbarton. She was designed as British Rail's first specially designed car ferry, with an electric, not hydraulic, stern door. She undertook trials on 28 April 1952 and was delivered for the Boulogne route from Dover. However, cars were craned on and off the vessel for the first year in service as the car ramp was not ready. She was a true 'Dover' vessel and spent most of her career based at the port. On 15 June 1953 she was present at the Coronation Spithead Review and then returned to Dover to inaugurate the new roll-on/roll-off car ferry service.

Maid of Orleans entered service on the Dover–Calais route on 23 June 1949 and *Brighton* sailed on her maiden voyage from Newhaven to Dieppe in 1950, while *Cote d'Azur* was introduced in 1951, followed by the *Lisieux* in 1953. *Normannia* was completed in 1952 and replaced the *Hantonia* on the Southampton–Le Havre service. *Roi Leopold III* was introduced in 1956, *Koningen Elisabeth* in October 1957 and the *Reine Astrid* in the following May. *Artevelde* entered service in 1958 and *Prinses Paola*, built in 1966, was the last conventional passenger ferry to be built for the Ostend–Dover route. The French vessel *Compiègne* was introduced in 1958 and *Maid of Kent* was introduced in May of the following year.

When Townsend Brothers disposed of *Forde*, they acquired the *Halladale*, which was an ex-frigate. She was converted to carry vehicles and a car ferry terminal was opened in 1953 in the Camber area of the port. *Autocarrier* sailed on her final voyage on 6 August 1954 and was towed across the Channel to Ghent, where she was broken up. However, the name *Autocarrier* was given to the General Steam Navigation Company vessel *Royal Sovereign*, which was built in 1937. She was acquired by Townsend Car Ferries in 1966 and was converted into a freight carrier. She was able to carry twenty-four lorries and trailers, plus their drivers.

Townsend Ferries went public in 1957, and 51 per cent of the shares were bought by Roland Wickenden. Townsend Ferries had a turnover of around £100,000 a year and had captured 5 per cent of the Cross-Channel business. The company was merged with the Norwegian company Thoreson Ferries, who operated services from Southampton to Cherbourg with a new vessel that was specially built for the route. They had purchased the

Atlantic Steam Navigation Company (Transport Ferry Service) from the United Kingdom Government. In 1966 the monopoly that had operated on the Dover–Ostend service was broken when Townsend Ferries also provided sailings on this route.

In 1962, some 7,500 vessels totalling upward of 7½ million tons net register entered the harbour at Dover. Over 3 million passengers passed through the port – three times as many as any other seaport in the United Kingdom. The port dealt with 440,000 accompanied motor vehicles and 1.2 million tons of general cargo, including 41,000 commercial motor vehicles; in all, 56 per cent of the passenger traffic by sea between the United Kingdom and the Continent passed through the port, as did 40 per cent of the passenger traffic by sea between the United Kingdom and the rest of the world. At this time Dover Harbour comprised 850 acres, of which 650 acres were water with a depth of up to 30 feet, providing facilities for ocean-going, cross-channel and coastal shipping. The port undertook a complete modernisation in 1962, which included the opportunity for the removal of a variety of out-of-date warehouses and other buildings. These were replaced with an entirely new layout and transit accommodation. New electric cranes were installed plus improved road and rail facilities to ensure a rapid turn-around for vessels.

George Hammond & Company Limited were established over 250 years ago as shipbrokers and general ship's agents. Hammond's also provided insurance services, passenger agents, marine surveyors, clearing and forwarding agents, as well as being engaged in stevedoring. In 1962, the principal cargoes were wood pulp and timber from Scandinavia, tomatoes from the Canary Islands, fruit from the Mediterranean and boxboards from Portugal.

The new car ferry *Free Enterprise* was introduced in 1962 and was followed by *Free Enterprise II* in 1965, *Free Enterprise III* in 1966, *Free Enterprise IV* in 1969, *Free Enterprise V* in 1970, *Free Enterprise VI* in 1972, *Free Enterprise VII* in 1973, *Free Enterprise VIII* in 1974, *Herald of Free Enterprise* in 1980, *Pride of Dover* in 1987 and both *Pride of Free Enterprise* and *Spirit of Free Enterprise* in 1980. Sealink introduced *St Anselm* and *St Christopher* in 1980 while SNCF introduced *Cote d'Azur* in 1981 and *Champs Elysées* three years later.

In 1966 British Rail formed a wholly owned subsidiary named Seaspeed and operated a service between Southampton and Cowes with SR.N6-type hovercraft. A service from Dover to Calais was also provided by Townsend Car Ferries by SR.N6 craft, but following several technical incidents the project was abandoned. A new service was provided by Seaspeed from Dover and the craft could accommodate 250 passengers and thirty cars.

In November 1969 it was announced that British Rail's Shipping & International Services Division would be renamed Sealink. The aim was to move to a fleet that would be utilised year-round with container ships and multi-purchase vessels, such as the new *Vortigern.* British Rail had pooled services with the French National Railways (SNCF), who operated *Compiègne* and *Chantilly* on the Dover–Calais service. British Rail operated the *Lord Warden, Maid of Kent, Normannia* on the route to Boulogne. Sealink UK Limited was formed in 1978 as a wholly owned subsidiary of the British Railways Board.

In July 1984 Sealink was sold to the Bermuda-based Sea Containers Limited, led by James B. Sherwood. The company was renamed Sealink British Ferries in 1991. The Swedish shipping Group Stena Line purchased 8 per cent of Sea Containers shares in March 1989 and they eventually took over the control of the company on 31 May 1990. Stena acquired Sealink ferries and ports for £259 million but Hoverspeed, the Isle of Wight services, the share in the Isle of Man Steam Packet and the ports of Folkestone, Newhaven and Heysham were all retained by Sea Containers Limited. The ships operated as Sealink Stena Line and Stena Sealink Line until 1 January 1996, when the company became Stena Line.

P&O introduced the *Lion* to a service from Dover to Boulogne, which was operated by Normandy Ferries, who also provided services from Southampton to Le Havre. *Lion* had been operating on the Ardrossan–Belfast route but the sustainability and profitability of the service had been damaged by the Troubles in Northern Ireland. *NF Tiger* was also introduced to the route by P&O in 1978 and *NF Panther* followed the year after. P&O ferry operations in Dover were sold to European Ferries in 1985. *Lion* was sold but the Boulogne service continued with *NF Tiger* and *NF Panther*, which were painted in Townsend Thoresen's colours. Both vessels continued in service until 1986, when they were replaced by *Free Enterprise IV* and *Free Enterprise V*.

While leaving the port of Zeebrugge on the night of 6 March 1987, the *Herald of Free Enterprise* took on water through the open door of the car deck. The sea immediately flooded the deck, which affected the stability of the vessel and she sank, with 193 people losing their lives. The immediate cause was directed to a member of crew who was responsible for closing the bow doors but a general culture of poor communication in the company was also blamed for the tragedy. *Herald of Free Enterprise* was salvaged and was towed to Taiwan, where she was broken up. The sinking was the worst disaster involving a British ship since the sinking of His Majesty's Yacht *Iolaire* on 1 January 1919, near Stornoway, when 205 out of the 280 people aboard lost their lives.

On 19 January 1987 P&O took over the European Ferries Group, who were trading as Townsend Thoresen. The group operated services from Dover, Portsmouth, Felixstowe and Cairnryan, and also included the ports of Felixstowe and Larne in Northern Ireland. The services were renamed P&O European Ferries on 22 October and operated routes from Dover, Felixstowe and Portsmouth. The Dover ships were given 'Pride' names and between 1991 and 1993 four more vessels were added to the fleet, with *Pride of Burgundy* being introduced in April 1993. The Zeebrugge route was closed in 1991 and the Boulogne route followed two years later. In 1997 P&O became the sole owner of North Sea Ferries and the group was later divided into P&O Portsmouth, P&O North Sea and a joint venture between P&O and the Stena Line, known as P&O Stena Line, in Dover. In August 2002 P&O acquired Stena Line's 40 per cent share of P&OSL for £150 million, and it was merged with the Portsmouth and North Sea operations under the P&O Ferries Limited brand. The Zeebrugge service was closed in 2002 and the Fleetwood–Larne route was sold to the Stena Line Group in 2004, together with the *European Leader*, *European Pioneer* and *European Seafarer*. An experimental Mostyn–Dublin service had also been introduced, but this was closed in 2004.

With the increasing popularity of cruising in the United Kingdom, Dover Harbour Board decided to provide a cruise terminal at the Marine station building, and this was opened in 1993. A second berth was added in 2000, which included a new purpose-built facility allowing two ships of up to 260 metres in length to be berthed at the Admiralty Pier. Since then the port has been able to attract many of the largest cruise lines to use Dover, either as a cruise base or a port of call.

Stena Line introduced the *Stena Empereur* on the Dover–Calais route in August 1996. The vessel was previously operated by Stena in Scandinavia and she replaced the smaller *Stena Challenger*, which was transferred to the Holyhead-Dublin service. *Stena Empereur* entered service following an £8 million refit.

In 1996 the French Government made some FFr 200 million available to ship-owners in the form of investment and aid towards modernisation and restructuring. The French ferry operators had already received a large share of the sum and the ship-owners feared that the government would be tempted to increase this share at the expense of other shipping companies in response to the deteriorating financial situation of the French ferry operations. The situation was blamed on the opening of the tunnel, which corresponded to a 50 per cent increase in capacity on the Channel, for the collapse of ferry prices and the heavy operating deficits of Brittany Ferries and SeaFrance. SeaFrance was formed when the link between SNCF and Stena, under the Sealink banner, was broken up at the end of 1995. The Central Committee of French Shipowners was also concerned over the reduction in aid.

P&O blamed the increased competition from Eurotunnel for a slump in its cross-channel ferry traffic. The number of cars carried by the company fell by almost a quarter in the first three months of 1996 compared to the same period in 1995. P&O said vehicle crossings on the Dover–Calais route fell to 292,780 from 380,391, a drop of 23 per cent, while passenger numbers fell to 1.86 million from 2.3 million. During the same period Eurotunnel doubled its share of the tourist traffic market from 20 to 40 per cent.

Norfolk Line started a service from Dover to Dunkirk in 2000. The Maersk Company Limited, a subsidiary of A. P. Møller, acquired Norfolk Line in 1985. In 2005 the renamed Norfolkline took over Norse Merchant Ferries with their services in the Irish Sea, and established a new route between Felixstowe, North Killingholme and Vlaardingen in 2006. *Maersk Delft, Maersk Dover* and *Maersk Dunkerque* were built in 2005/06. In July/August 2010 they were renamed *Delft Seaways, Dover Seaways* and *Dunkerque Seaways,* operating for DFDS Seaways France.

In March 2006 P&O Ferries, P&O Estates and P&O Maritime Services were sold to Dubai World. On 8 August 2008 the company placed an order for two new ships for the Dover–Calais service. They were named *Spirit of Britain* and *Spirit of France* and are the largest ferries operating in the English Channel. *Spirit of Britain* entered service on 21 January 2011 and *Spirit of France* on 9 February the following year. Following the delivery of these two ships the *Pride of Calais* and *Pride of Dover* were withdrawn and broken up at Aliaga in Turkey. Transmanche Ferries operated between Dieppe and Dover and Dover and Boulogne for LD Lines. *SeaFrance Cezanne, SeaFrance Manet* and *SeaFrance Renoir* were withdrawn and sailings by *Nord Pas-de-Calais* were reduced. In 2015 P&O Ferries operated services from Dover to Calais, Hull to Rotterdam and Zeebrugge, Liverpool to Dublin and Larne to Troon and Cairnryan.

SeaFrance spent the whole of 2011 in administration and the company was up for sale. The company was declared bankrupt on 16 November and it was liquidated in January, 2012, when the fleet was put up for sale. Norman Spirit inaugurated the DFD Seaways/LD Lines joint service between Dover and Calais on 12 February 2012. The service was 82 per cent owned by DFDS and 18 per cent by Louis Dreyfus Armateurs. MyFerryLink was established and owned by Eurotunnel but it was decided by the British Competition and Markets Authority in 2015 that the service should cease and Eurotunnel should sell the company. The Société Coopérative et Participative (SCOP) appealed against the ruling and Eurotunnel said that it was ceasing its involvement with the SCOP. DFDS announced on 7 June 2014 that it had made a request to purchase or charter the *Rodin* and *Berlioz* from July the following year. The *Nord Pas-de-Calais* would be retained by Eurotunnel and be used to transport goods that could not be accommodated through the tunnel. The *Rodin* and *Berlioz* were sold to DFDS and re-entered service on the Dover–Calais route as the *Cote des Dunes* and *Cote des Flandres* respectively. *Nord Pas-de-Calais* was chartered to FRS Iberia and was renamed *Al Andalus Express.*

In 2013, following two years of decline, the number of short-sea international ferry journeys increased by 4 per cent to 20.5 million. Dover remained the busiest United Kingdom sea port, carrying 12.7 million short-sea international ferry passengers. This was a 7 per cent annual increase but it remained 20 per cent lower than ten years previously. In 2012 more passengers travelled internationally via the Channel Tunnel than ferries for the first time. However, in 2013 ferries accounted for 1.7 million (9 per cent) more international journeys than the Channel Tunnel. Passenger traffic on domestic sea crossings has steadily declined over the last decade. However, the number of passengers travelling by ferry from Great Britain to Northern Ireland and the Channel Islands increased to 2.1 and 0.4 million respectively.

The total number of international short-sea passengers travelling through British ports decreased by 1 per cent from 21.3 million in 2014 to 21.0 million in 2015. Passenger numbers at Thames, Kent and West Coast port groups declined by 2 per cent. Dover–Calais remained the busiest short-sea route, handling 47 per cent of all international short-sea passengers, but declined by 9 per cent to 9.8 million compared with the previous year. The volume of international short-sea passengers on the Dover–Dunkirk route increased by 27 per cent from 2.5 million in 2014 to 3.2 million in 2015. In 2015 the number of passengers travelling via the Channel Tunnel decreased by 1 per cent to 20.9 million, which is marginally fewer than the number of sea passengers. Since opening in 1994, the trends in the number of passengers travelling by the Channel Tunnel and by sea have steadily merged. France remained the most popular country of destination, with the Irish Republic being the second.

In 2016 *Delft Seaways, Dover Seaways* and *Dunkerque Seaways* operated on the Dover–Dunkirk service and *Calais Seaways, Cote Des Flanders* and *Cote Des Dunes* operated on the Dover–Calais route. *Pride of Burgundy, Pride of Canterbury, Pride of Kent, Spirit of Britain* and *Spirit of Kent* served on the Dover–Calais route.

The Port of Dover specialises in the handling, storage and freight forwarding of temperature-controlled commodities, and is ideally situated for the fast shipment of perishable goods by both sea and road. The port offers a minimum deviation for reefer ships and fast onward journeys to all other parts of Europe. The port is connected to the M2 and M20 motorways, which connect to the M25 London orbital route, giving fast access to central London and other parts of the United Kingdom. Dover Cargo Terminal offers 24-hour access, with no locks or tidal restrictions and a minimum quay water depth of 8.5 metres. Consequently, ships can berth at any time, day or night. The terminal also offers a dedicated 215-metre berth plus two further 200-metre berths. It has two Terex Gottwald harbour mobile cranes, two Terex Telescopic road mobile cranes and forklifts, container handlers and tugmaster units. There is temperature-controlled storage for 7,500 pallets and a car and truck lifting platform. The Port of Dover Cargo Limited performs a wide range of stevedoring and freight forwarding for customers importing and exporting goods through the port.

Moreover, the Port of Dover has successfully achieved government approval to develop the Western Docks, which will transform the waterfront with a new marina pier and marina curve to ultimately attract a host of shops, bars, cafes and restaurants. It will relocate and further develop the cargo business with a new cargo terminal and a distribution centre. The scheme will also create greater space within the Eastern Docks for ferry traffic and create much-needed, quality employment opportunities for local people.

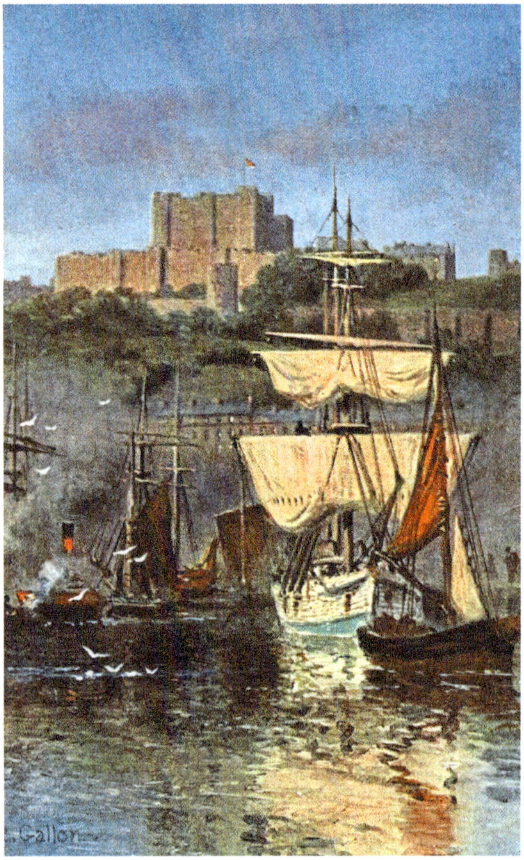

Left: Dover Harbour.

Below: *The Queen* leaving Dover.

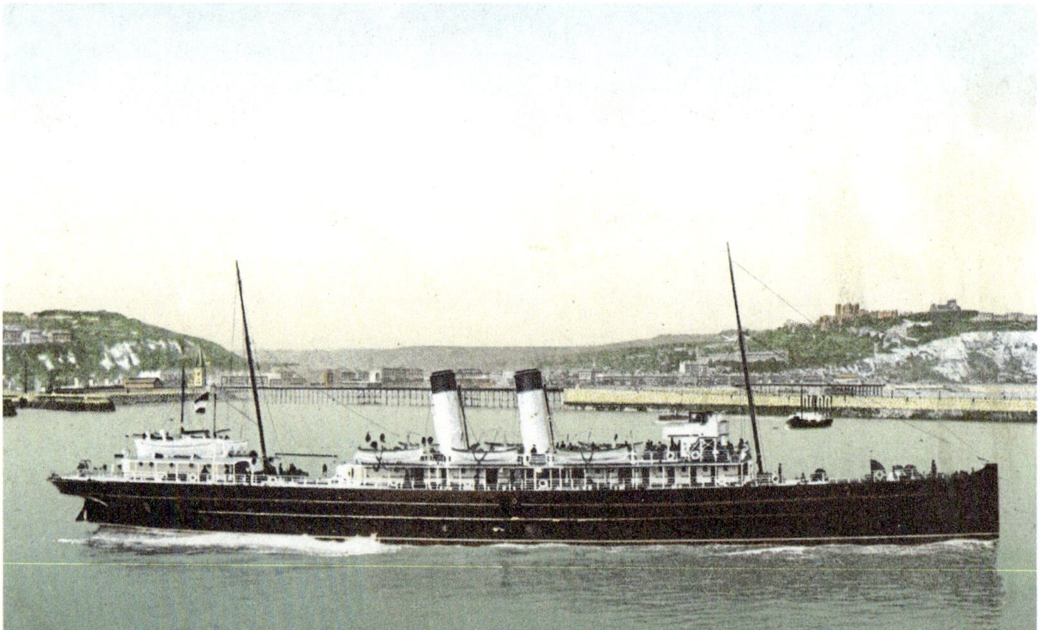

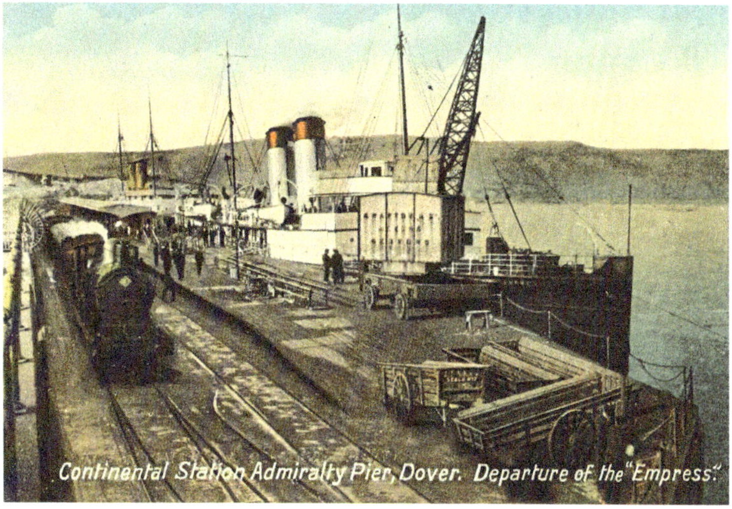

Empress departs from Admiralty Pier.

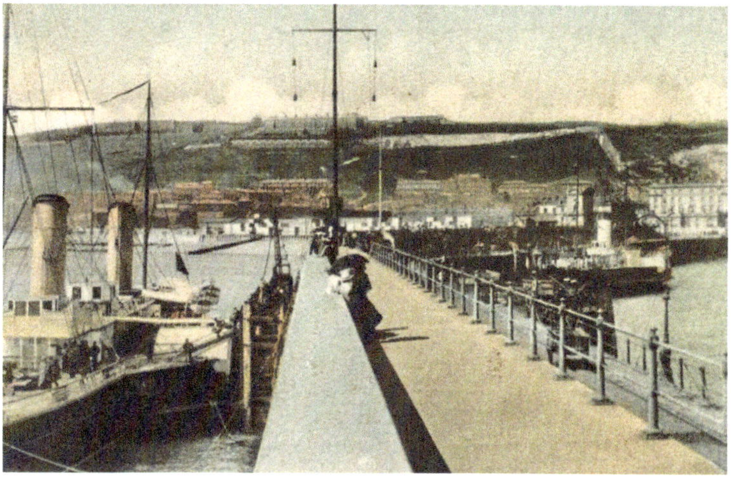

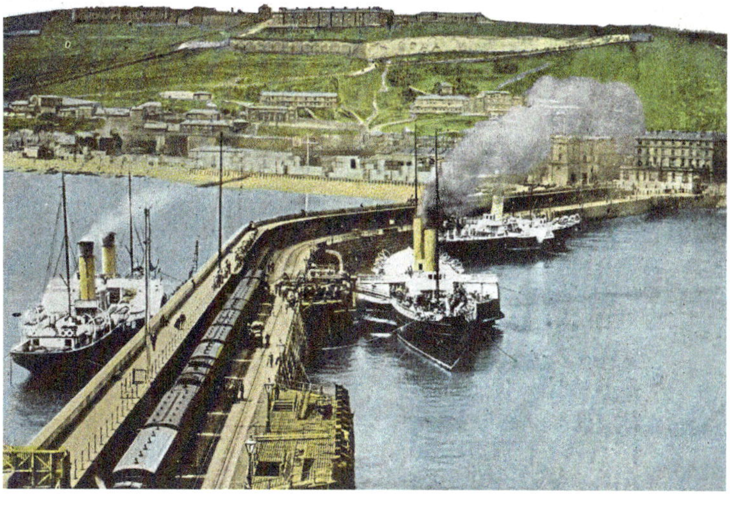

Admiralty Pier in 1905.

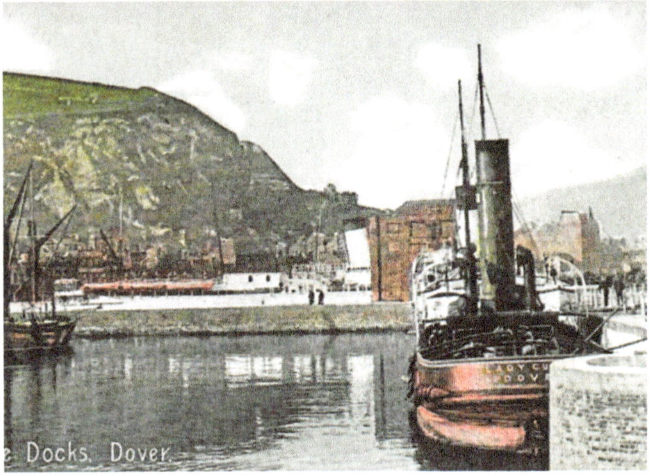

Granville Docks, Dover.

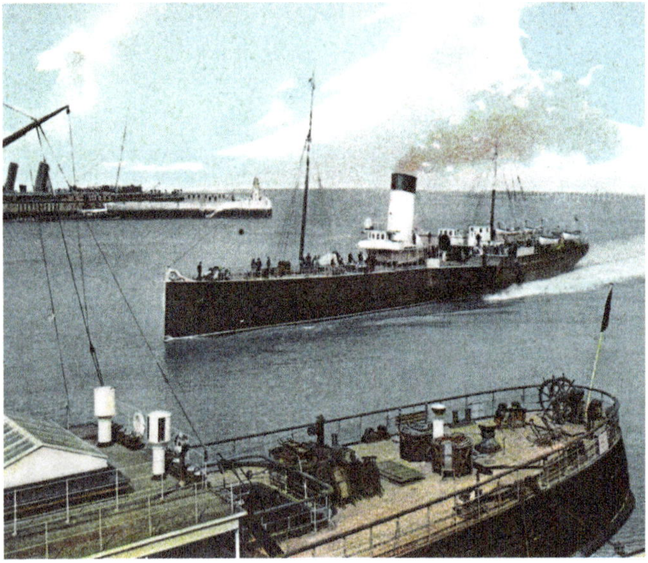

The London, Chatham & Dover steamer *Lord Warden/ Dover Calais* at Pas de Calais.

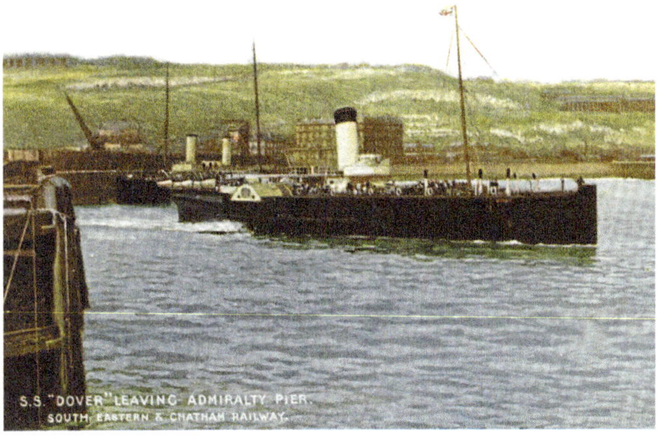

***Dover*, 1896, 979 grt. 85.34 x 10.67 x 4.08 metres. 18 knots.** b. William Denny & Brothers, Dumbarton. Paddle steamer, nine floats, three-cylinder triple expansion, 491 NHP, four single boilers, 150 Psi by builder. Passengers: 200 berths, 700 day. London, Chatham & Dover Railway Company.

She sailed on her maiden voyage from Dover to Calais on 2 February 1896. In 1911 she was sold to Stavanger Skibs-Ophugnings, Stavanger, and was broken up.

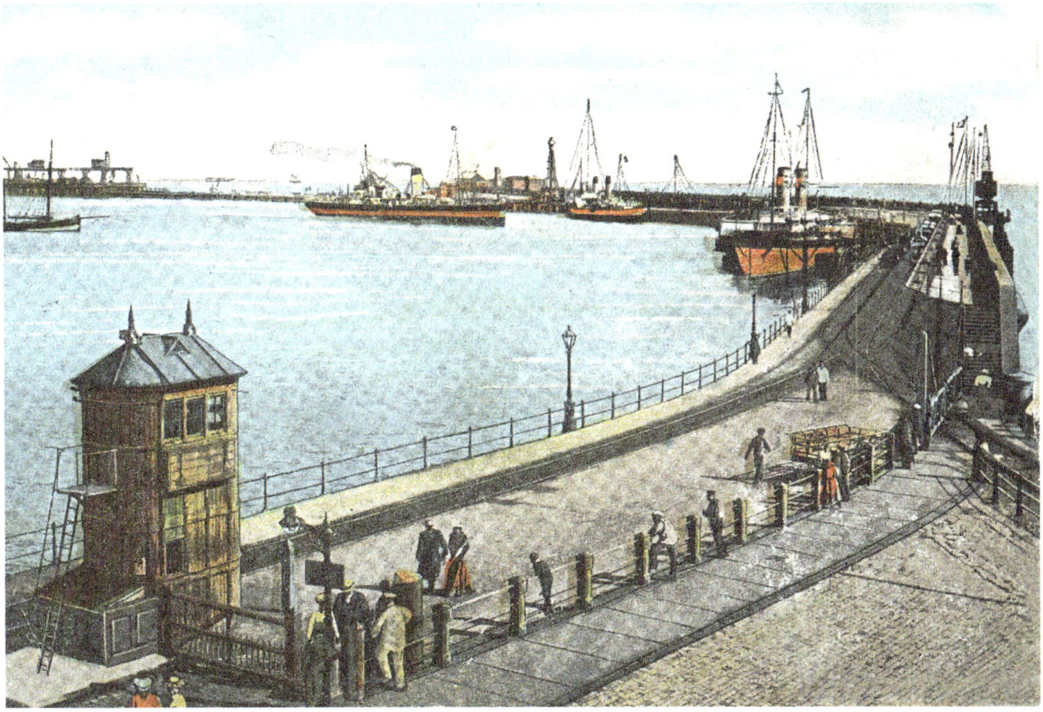

Above: Admiralty Pier, Dover.

Below: *Dover* (1896, 979 grt) at Dover.

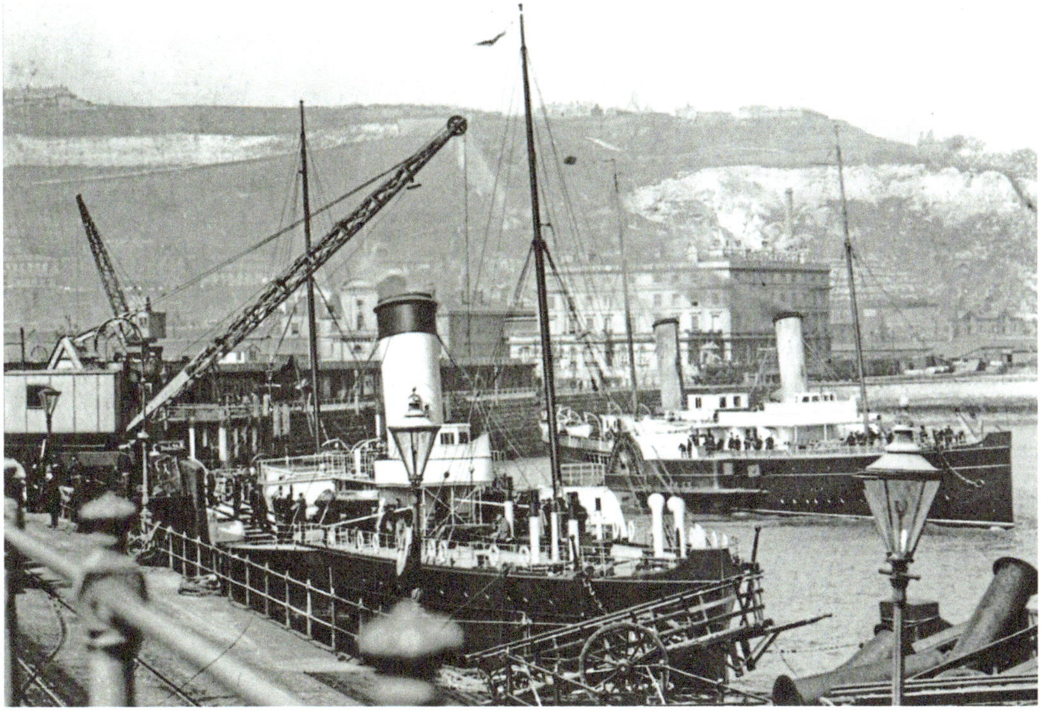

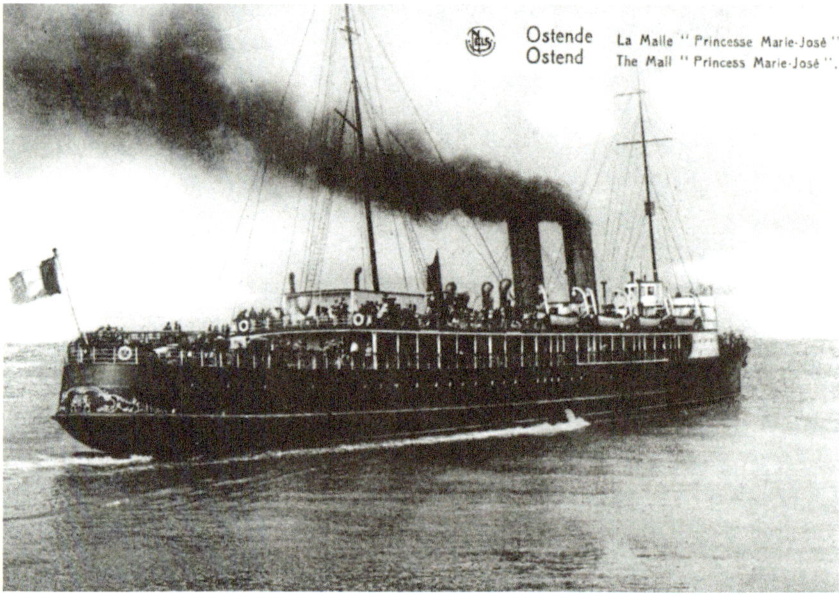

Above: *Prinsesse Marie-Jose,* 1923, 1,821 grt. 110 x 13 x 7 metres. 23 knots.
b. Cockerill of Hoboken (Yard No. 579). Four Parsons/Cockerill single reduction steam turbines in two independent sets, each working one of the twin screws, 13,500 SHP. Passengers: 1,200. Belgium Marine Administration.

Below: *Jan Breydel,* 1909, 1,767 grt. 108.81 x 13 metres. 24 knots.
b. Cockerill, Hoboken (Yard No. 493). Passengers: 1,100. Belgium Marine Administration.

Between 1914 and 1918, *Jan Breydel* assisted with the evacuation of troops from Ostend to France and England and transported wounded servicemen from France to England. On 1 January 1919 she helped with the repatriation of troops to Britain and on 9 June 1919 she returned to commercial service. On 24 September 1921, on a voyage from Ostend to Dover in thick fog, she collided with the Norwegian vessel *Selina,* which sank in five minutes.

On 4 November 1931 she was sold for scrap, and she was broken up the following year.

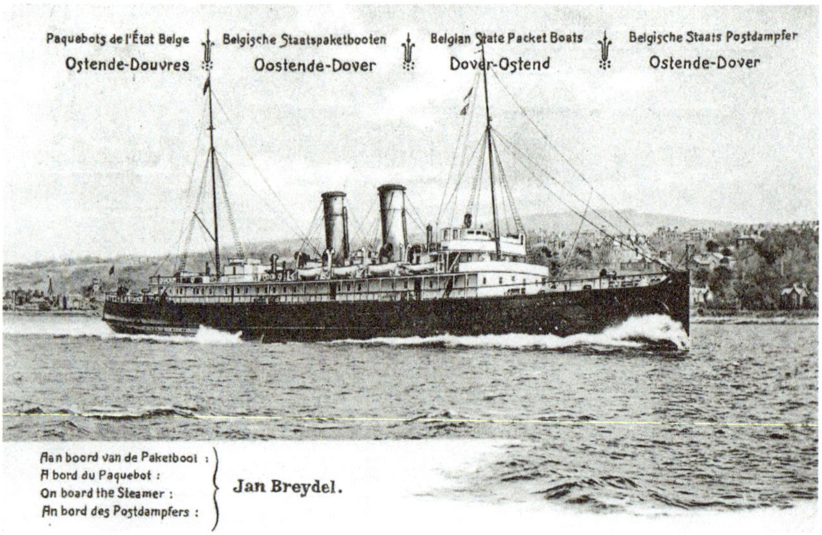

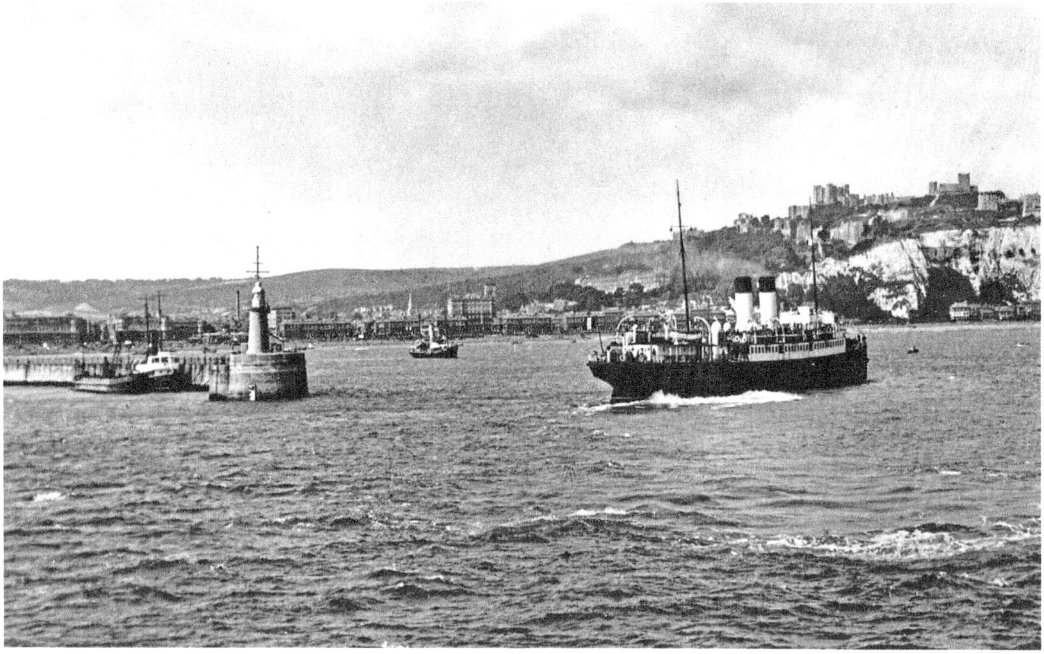

Above: Dover Harbour.

Below: Luggage is loaded onto the mail ship at Dover.

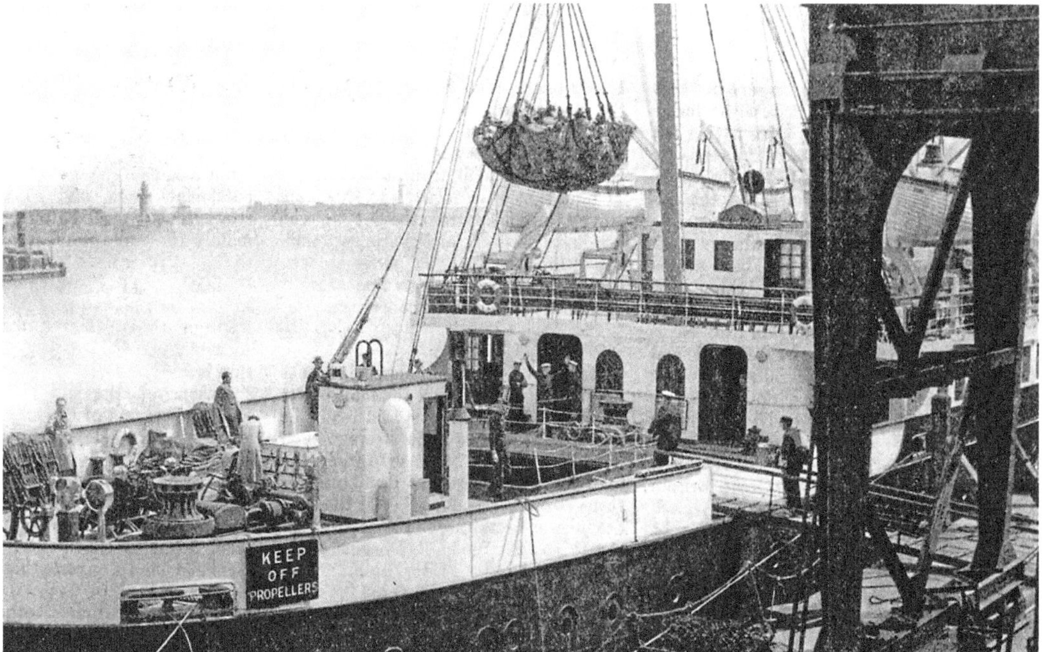

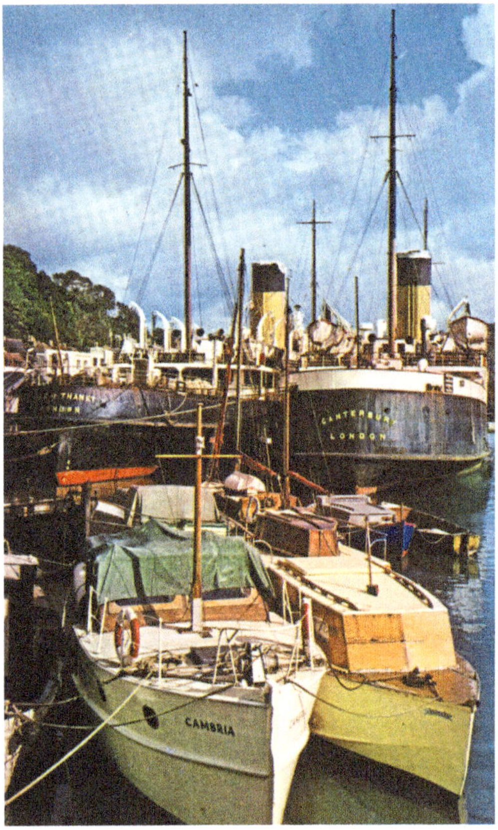

Left: *Isle of Thanet* (1925, 2,701 grt) and *Canterbury* (1929, 2,912 grt) are seen laid up at Dover.

Below: *Versailles*, 1919, 1,903 grt. 91.6 x 10.5 x 7 metres. 24 knots.

b. Les Forges et Chantiers de la Méditerranée, Le Havre. Twin screw, two single Parsons turbines, 14,000 SHP by builder.

In 1919 work was suspended on her construction due to the First World War. She was completed in 1921 with the London, Brighton & South Coast Railway Company as her manager and from 1 January 1923 she was managed by the Southern Railway.

In 1928 her promenade deck was plated over and she was converted to burn oil by her builder in March of the following year. At the outbreak of the Second World War in 1939 she was taken over by the French Navy and was captured by German forces in August 1940. In March 1941 she was converted into a minelayer and became a naval accommodation ship in July 1942. She returned to her owners in June 1945, was declared uneconomic to repair, and was later scrapped.

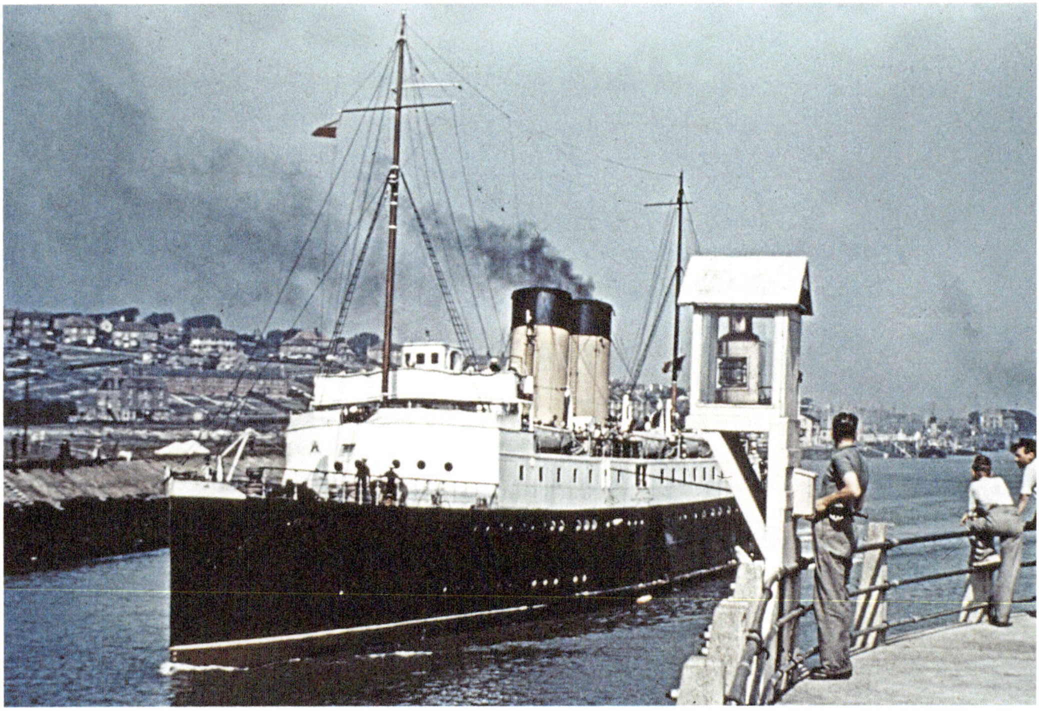

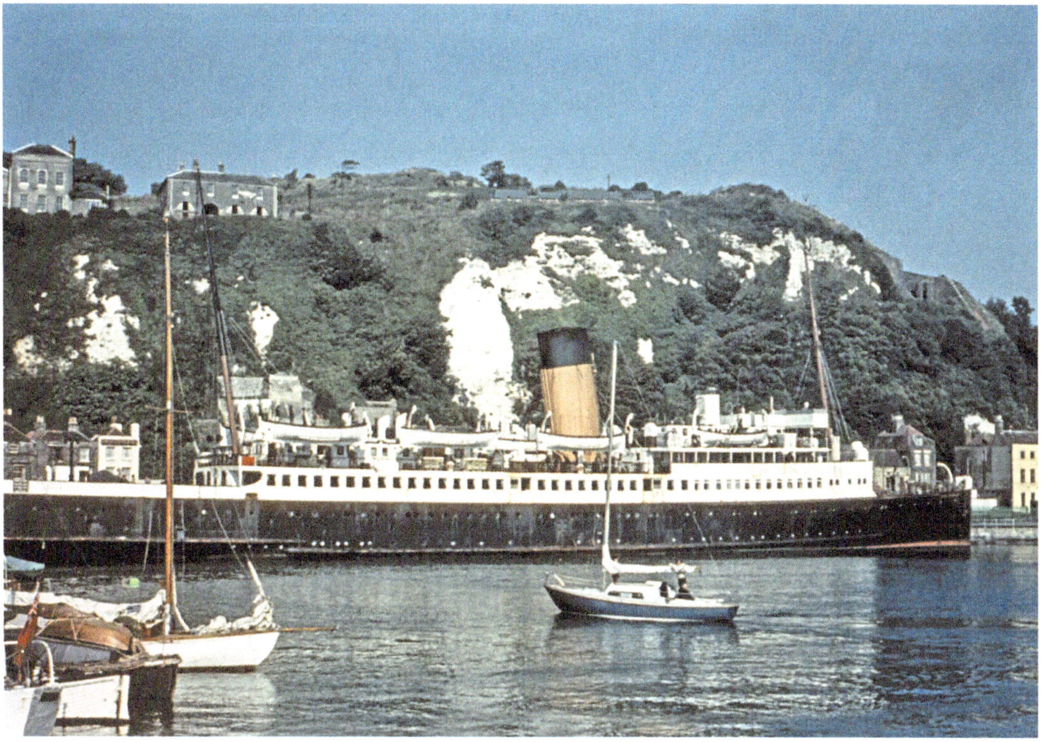

Canterbury, 1929, 2,912 grt. 100.28 x 14.32 metres. 23 knots.
b. William Denny & Brothers Limited, Dumbarton. Yard No. 1218.
Twin screw, 2x2 Parsons Turbines, 930 NHP, four Babcock & Wilcox boilers by builder.
Passengers: 800 first-class only. Southern Railway.

She was ordered for the new Dover–Calais Golden Arrow service on 23 February 1928, with accommodation for 400 passengers in first class only. Launched on 13 December 1928, she attained a speed of 22.15 knots when on trial on 2 March 1929. She was delivered at Southampton on 15 March, and arrived at Dover on 29 April. She sailed on her maiden voyage on 17 May and during the following month her port-engine lubricating pump seized. As a result, she was out of service for over four weeks.

In 1931–32, accommodation for second-class passengers was fitted, and on 3 September 1939, while en route to Dover from Calais, war was declared. The Port of Dover was immediately closed and she was diverted to Folkestone. On 6 September 1939 she was requisitioned as a troop transport and became the British Expeditionary Force leave ship on 8 December.

In May 1940 she transported troops from the Hook of Holland, Cherbourg, Boulogne, Calais and Dunkirk, later moving to Scapa Flow as a tender and then to Rosyth as a Fleet Air Arm target ship. In 1942 she was converted to a Landing Ship Infantry and was fitted with six assault craft.

On 6 June 1944 she was at the Normandy landings, being based at Portland, and on 7 December 1944 she was trooping on the Dover–Ostend route.

In February 1946 she arrived on the Tyne to be refitted and prepared for commercial service. On 15 April 1946 she returned to the Dover–Calais Golden Arrow route and in November 1946 she was replaced by *Invicta*, moving instead to the Folkestone–Calais service.

On 1 January 1948 she transferred to the British Transport Commission, operating on the Folkestone–Boulogne route. Her last sailing, on the Boulogne–Folkestone service, took place on 27 September 1964, and she was laid up at Dover. She was towed to Antwerp on 29 July 1965 and was broken up by Union de Remorquage.

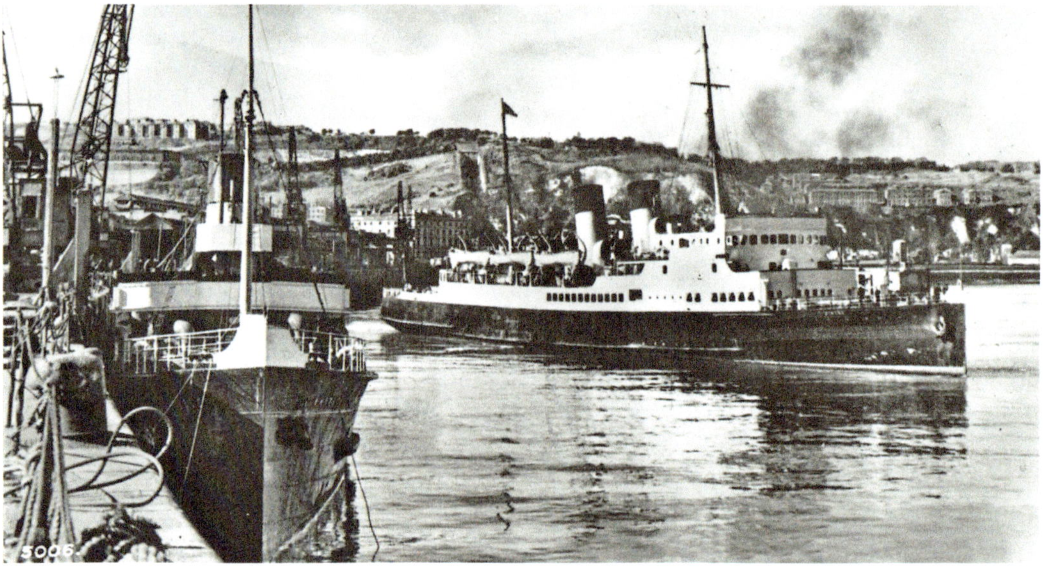

Dinard, **1924, 2,291 grt. 99.06 x 12.53 x 4.24 metres. 18 knots.**
b. William Denny & Brothers, Dumbarton, Twin screw, 2x2 turbines, 433 NHP, one single and one double boiler by builder. Passengers: 1,300 (324 first-class berths, in cabins, 118 second-class berths in saloons aft). Southern Railway.

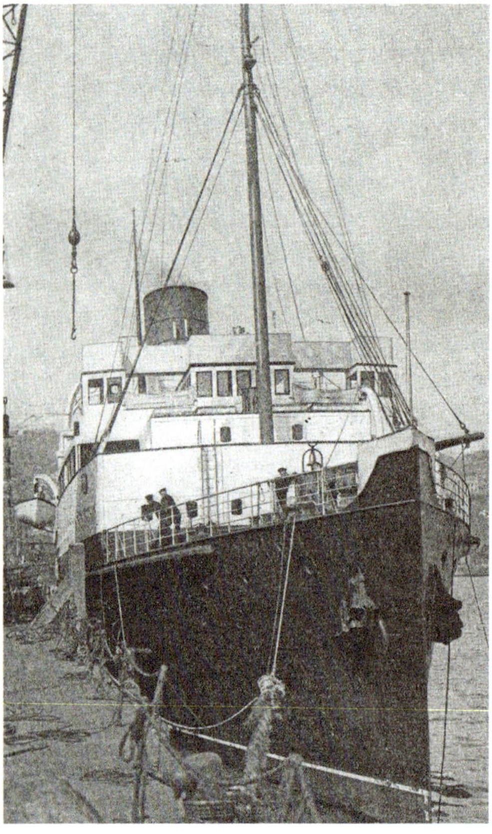

Maid of Kent, **1925, 2,386 grt. 102.11 x 13.75 x 5.21 metres.**
b. William Denny & Brothers, Dumbarton. Twin screw, 2x2 single compound Parsons turbines, 800 NHP, five Babcock & Wilcox boilers by builder.
Passengers: 1,000 first class, 400 second class. Southern Railway.

She was launched on 5 August 1925 and delivered at Southampton for the Dover–Calais service on 26 October. She was designed to act as standby vessel when *Canterbury* was not available for the Golden Arrow service. In November of her first year in service she collided with Calais East Pier and was sent to Southampton for repairs. In March the following year she was carried against the southern breakwater at Dover, which ripped holes in her hull. In 1934 she conveyed Princess Marina of Greece to the United Kingdom for her marriage to Prince George, the Duke of Kent.

In 1940 she became HM *Hospital Ship No. 21* and was placed on the Dieppe–Newhaven route. On 21 May that year she was bombed by German aircraft and sank at Dieppe, near Brighton. Her hull was later raised by the Germans and sank at sea.

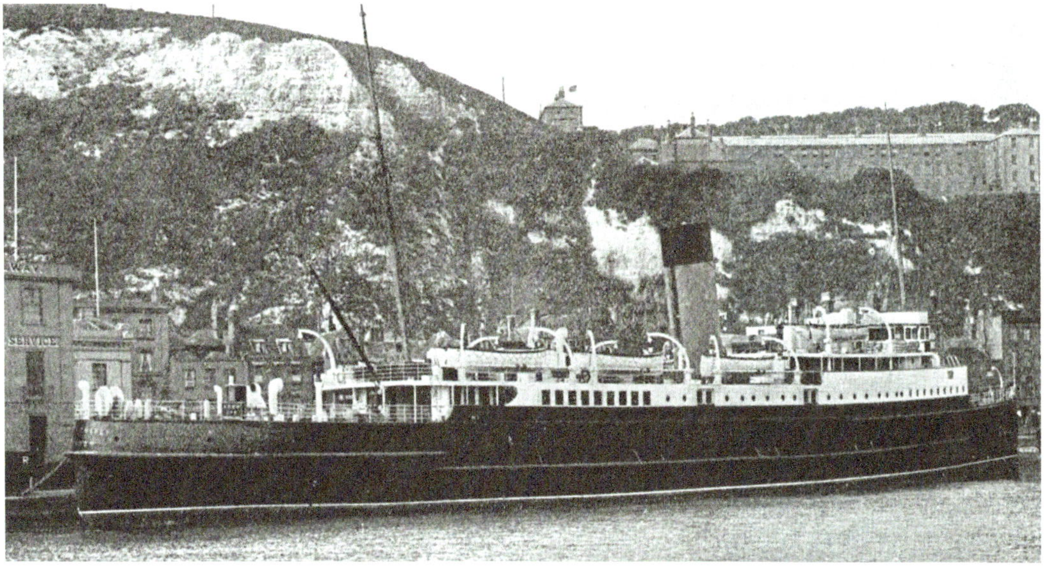

***Isle of Thanet*, 1925, 102.11 x 13.75 x 5.21 metres.**
b. William Denny & Brothers, Dumbarton. Twin screw, 2x2 single compound Parsons turbines, 800 NHP, five Babcock & Wilcox boilers by builder. Passengers: 1,000 first class, 400 second class. Southern Railway.

She was delivered at Southampton on 13 July 1925 as the company's first single-funnelled turbine steamer on the route, and sailed on her maiden voyage from Dover to Calais on 25 July. She also operated on the Folkestone–Boulogne route at times. In November 1934 she collided with the Admiralty Pier in strong winds and damaged her bow and bow rudder, with the result that she was out of service for twenty-eight days. She collided with the Western Breakwater at Boulogne in fog in February 1937, and in January 1938 she was blown into the quay at Folkestone, causing considerable damage to her starboard quarter.

In 1939 she was employed on the Southampton–St Malo service and carried the first RAF Wing Southampton–Le Havre service on 1 September. Following this she was converted to HM *Hospital Ship No. 22* at Newhaven and operated sailings from that port to Dieppe and Cherbourg. She returned to Dover on 23 May and was sent to Dunkirk to transport wounded soldiers back to England. Two days later she was again at Dunkirk, berthed alongside *Canterbury*, and embarked 600 wounded soldiers. She sailed from the port at 01.20 for Dover and then Newhaven. On 27 May she was ordered back from another voyage to Dunkirk and at Dover she collided with the *Ocean Reward*. Later that day she attempted to berth at Dunkirk but was fired upon by the Germans and was forced to return to Dover. She was at Southampton on service to Cherbourg on 5 June when France fell. She was decommissioned as a Hospital Ship on 29 July and converted to a submarine target ship at Preston. In 1943 she was at Dundee as a Fleet Air Arm navigator's training ship and returned to Southampton to be converted into a Landing Ship Infantry (H), Pennant 4.262. In 1944 she was based at Southampton and made two voyages with troops to Normandy on 6 June. In 1945 she was refitted as a troop ship and served on the Newhaven–Dieppe route, operating as a passenger vessel on that service the following year. On 1 July 1947 she opened the Folkestone–Boulogne service and the Folkestone-Calais route on 8 May 1948.

In the following years she was placed on Dover, Folkestone and Southampton routes. In August 1963 she experienced engine problems over the Bank Holiday weekend and was replaced by *Lord Warden*. Her final sailing from Folkestone was on 15 September and she arrived at Wellington Dock, Dover, the following day, where she was laid up. On 10 June 1964 she left in tow of United Towing's Headman for Blyth and was broken up by Hughes, Bolckow & Company (Metal Industries).

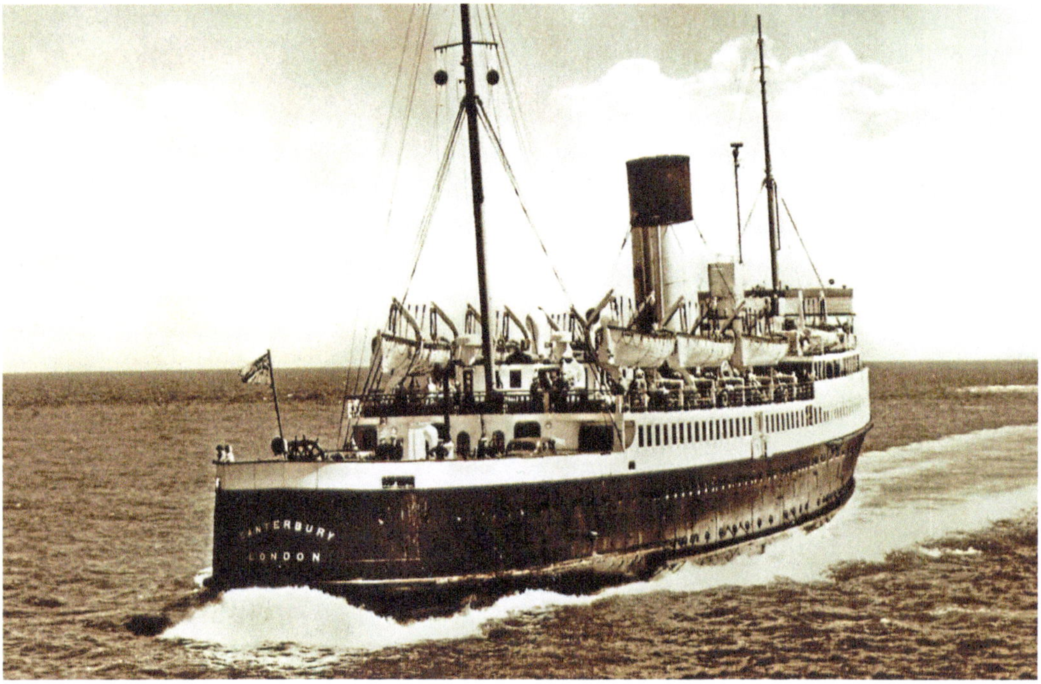

Above: *Canterbury* enters Dover Harbour astern.

Below: Parsons Marine Geared Turbines advertisement.

Parsons
MARINE GEARED
Turbines

SUITABLE FOR ALL CLASSES OF PASSENGER and CARGO VESSELS and for ALL TYPES OF WARSHIPS

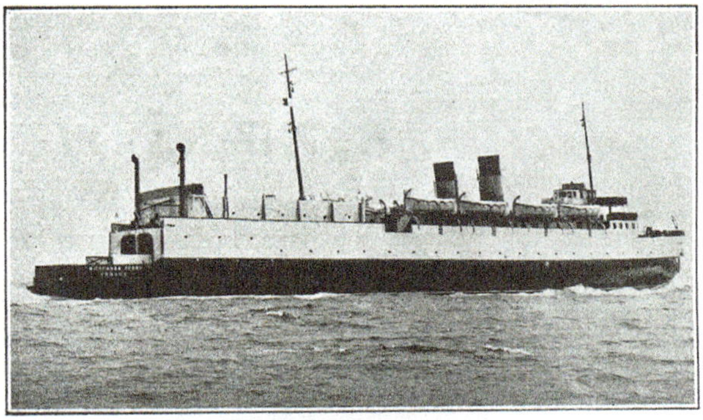

The Southern Railway Ferry " Twickenham Ferry," fitted with geared turbines manufactured by :—

THE PARSONS MARINE STEAM TURBINE CO. LTD.

TURBINIA WORKS, WALLSEND-ON-TYNE

Telegraphic Address : " TURBINIA, WALLSEND." Telephone No. 63261, WALLSEND

LONDON OFFICE : - - 56, VICTORIA STREET, S.W.1

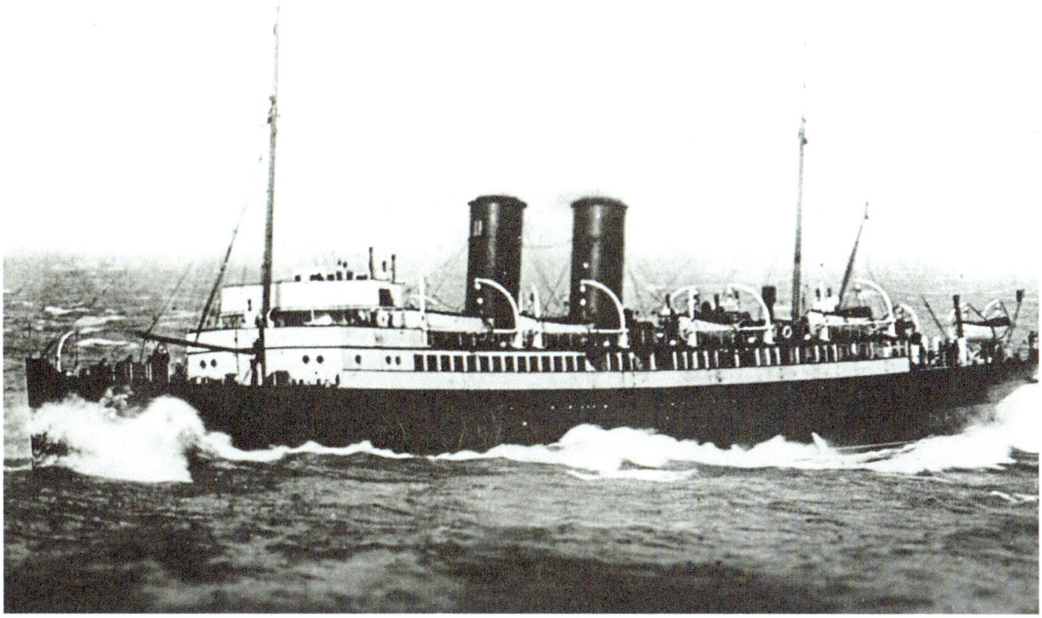

Maid of Orleans, 1918, 2,384 grt. 103.63 x 12.8 x 7.31 metres. 23 knots.
b. William Denny & Brothers, Dumbarton. Twin screw, 2x2 Parsons single turbines, 859 NHP, six Babcock and Wilcox boilers by builder. Passengers: 130 first class, 1,200 second class.

She was ordered in August 1914 but work was stopped the following year as her turbines were needed by the Royal Navy.

She was finally launched on 4 March 1918 and delivered in August that year.

In January 1923 she was transferred to the Southern Railway and in May the following year carried the King and Queen of Romania on their state visit to London.

In 1940 she evacuated Dutch citizens from Rotterdam and carried troops from the Dunkirk evacuation.

On 5 August 1943 she carried Winston Churchill and his staff out to the *Queen Mary* in the Clyde, when on his way to the Quebec Conference.

She took part in the Normandy operations in June 1944, and was torpedoed by *U998* in the English Channel and sank on 28 June that year.

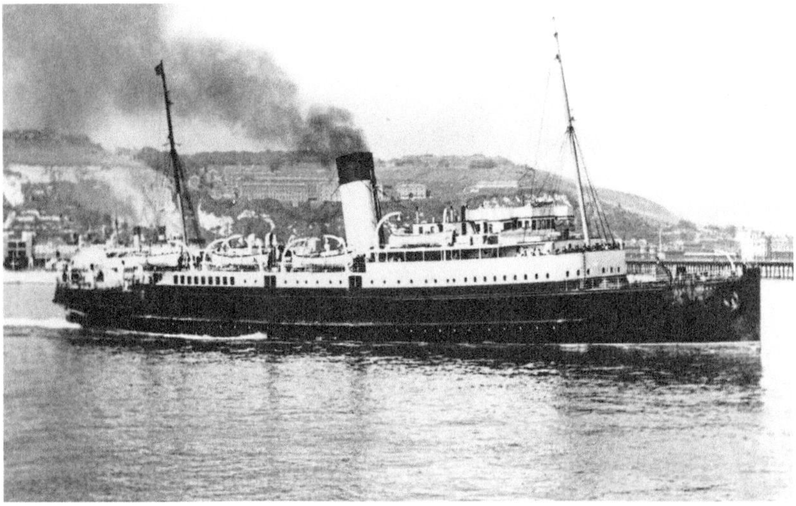

Isle of Thanet.

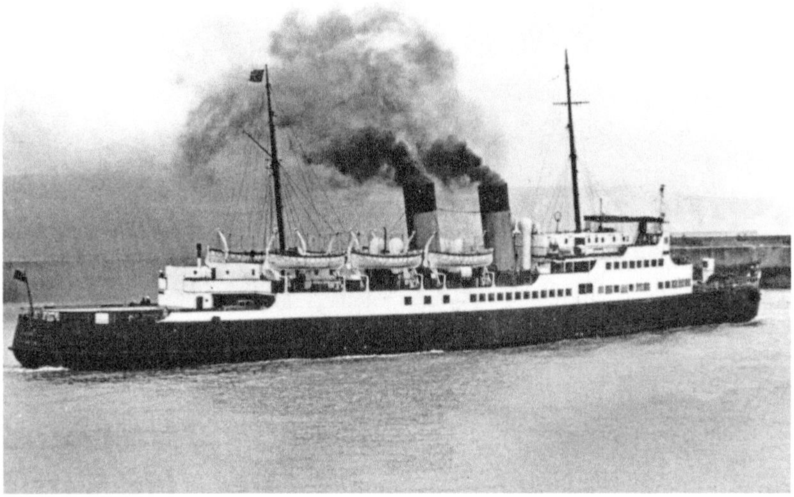

Dinard (1924, 2,291 grt).

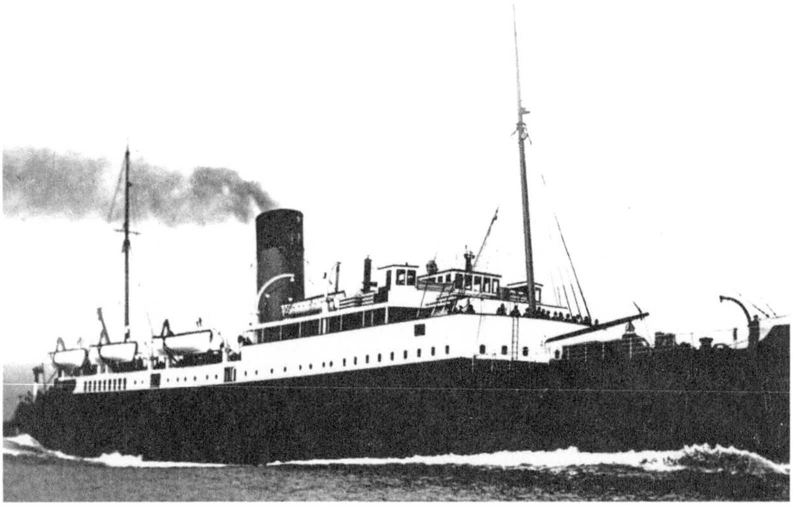

Maid of Kent (1925, 2,386 grt).

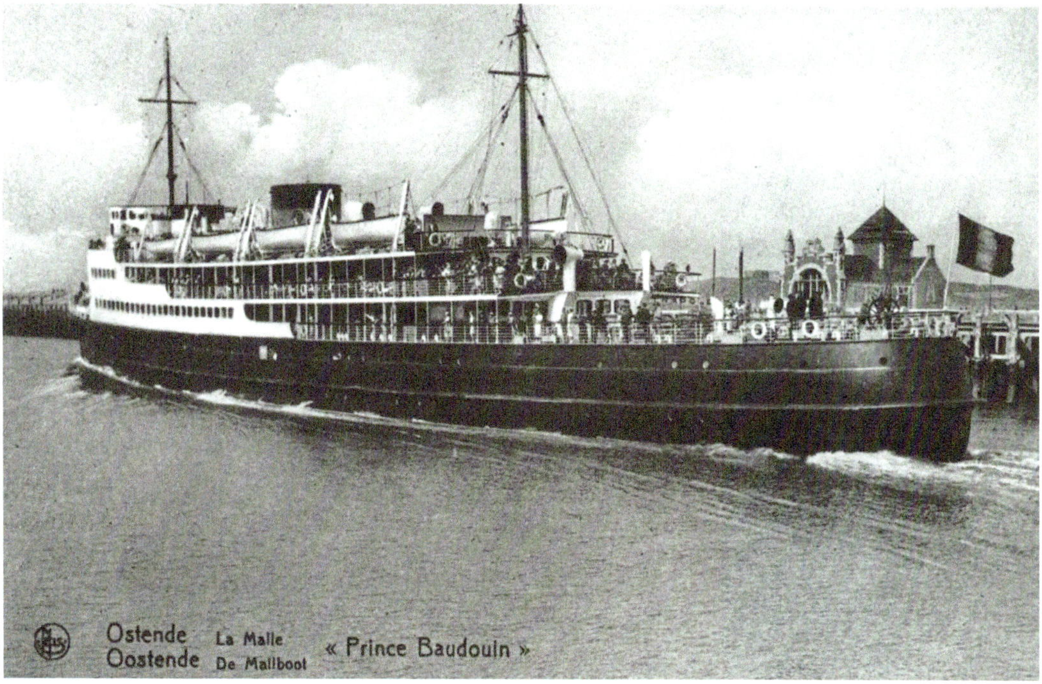

Prince Baudouin (2), 1934, 3,050 grt. 113.60 x 14.97 x 6.52 metres. 24 knots.
b. Cockeill, Hoboken. Two Sulzer-twelve-cylinder 8,500 HP diesel engines.
Passengers: 1,829. Belgium Marine Administration.

She was launched on 16 September 1933; however, problems were experienced with her engines and she was taken out of service on 27 October 1934 and several specialised teams worked on the engines at the builders. Following successful trials she re-entered service on 26 November. On 18 May 1940 she left Ostend for Le Havre and Southampton, where she was handed over to the British Admiralty. She participated in the transport of British troops between Brest, Southampton and Cherbourg on 28 May and St Malo in early June. It was intended that she would be converted to a torpedo hunter in July, but this was cancelled, and she remained at Southampton until October. However, on leaving the port on 1 November, she collided with two ships, the *Mahsud* and the *Graslin*. She remained at Gareloch until May 1941, when she was converted to a supply ship.

From 13 August to 2 December 1941 she was crewed by the General Steam Navigation Company and operated as a supply and transport of troops. In January 1943 she was converted to a Landing Ship Infantry and renamed HMS *Prince Baudouin*. On 6 June 1944 she landed troops on Omaha Beach and then proceeded to Naples, Sicily and Gibraltar. She was disarmed at Greenock in October 1944 and was then sent to Cockerill, returning to service in July 1946 on the Ostend–Dover and Folkestone routes. On 11 October 1945 she was returned to the company and was converted and refurbished by Cockerill's.

A special sailing operated on 24 July 1946 to celebrate the 100th anniversary of the Ostend line. However, *Prince Baudouin* did not return to commercial service until 11 October 1945 – the day that the Port of Dover opened again for commercial traffic.

She was taken out of service in 1963 and was used as accommodation and offices. She arrived at Ghent on 6 September 1967 and was broken up.

VERY **CHEAP RATES**

FOR THE CONVEYANCE OF

YOUR MOTOR CAR

TO THE CONTINENT—*VIA* DOVER/OSTEND

BY THE MOTOR-CAR FERRY "LONDON-ISTANBUL" OR PASSENGER SERVICES

FOR FULL PARTICULARS APPLY FOR FOLDER NO. 9 (free) TO:

THE BELGIAN RAILWAYS & MARINE,

99, REGENT STREET,

PICCADILLY CIRCUS, LONDON, W.1

(TELEPHONE: **REG**ENT **5992/3**)

Above: A Belgian Railways & Marine advertisement from 1938.

Below: The car ferry terminal.

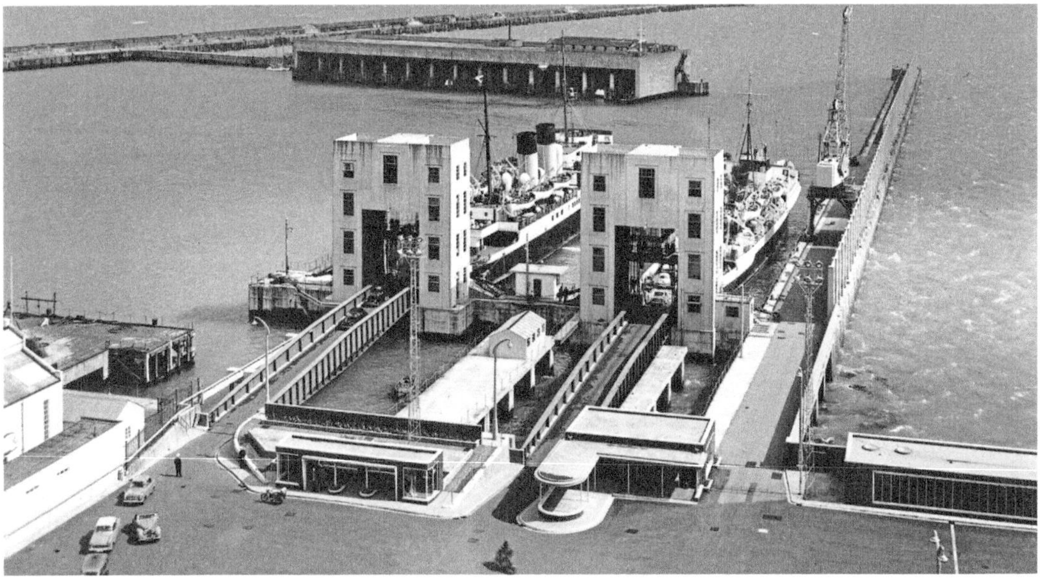

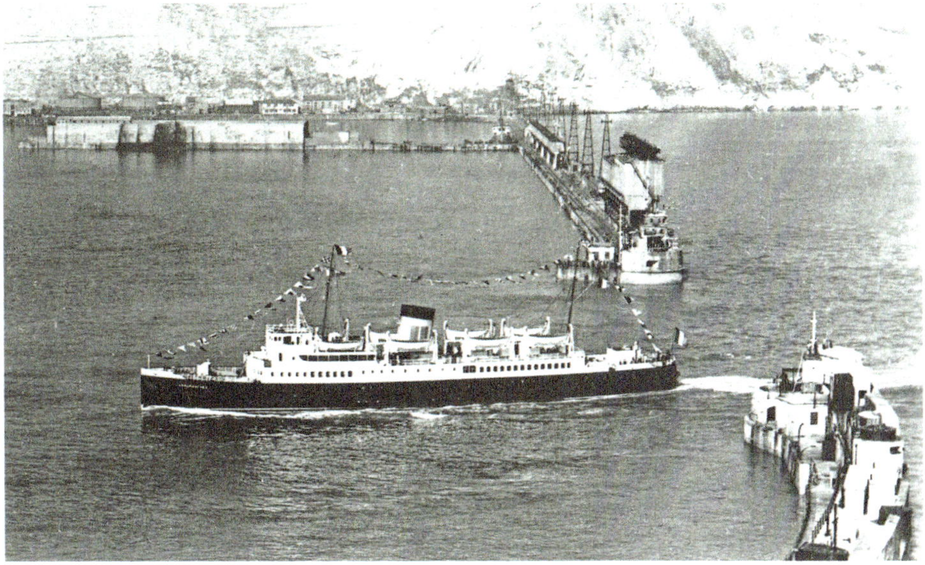

Above: The President of France, Vincent Auriol, arriving at Dover aboard *Arromanches* (1947, 2,404 grt) in March 1950. As *Arromanches* approached Dover Harbour, four 25 lb guns fired a salute, which was followed by a salute of twenty-six guns from HMS *Vanguard*. The Duke of Gloucester, representing the King, went onboard to greet the President. The party then proceeded to London Victoria station by train.

Arromanches was laid down as *Newhaven* at Forges et Chantiers de la Méditerranée in 1939 and was taken over by the Germans in 1940, who renamed her *Vichy*. She was launched in March 1946 as *Arromanches* and entered service in October the following year on the Dieppe–Newhaven route.

On 8 July 1964 she was grounded off Newhaven in a gale and was later re-floated. She was withdrawn the following year and was sold to Petros M. Nomikos of Piraeus, who renamed her *Leto* for the service from Piraeus to Tinos and Mykonos. In October 1970 she damaged her rudder in a gale and ran aground on Tinos.

Below: *Isle of Thanet* (1925, 2,701 grt).

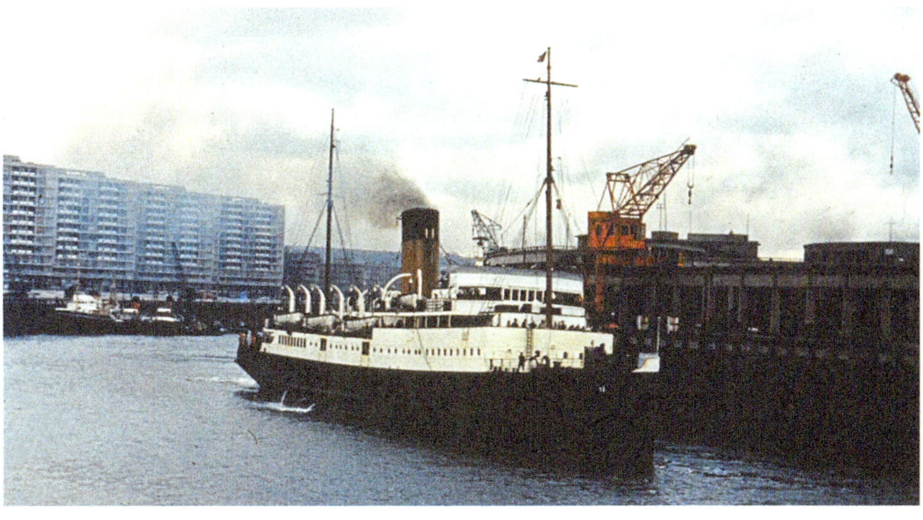

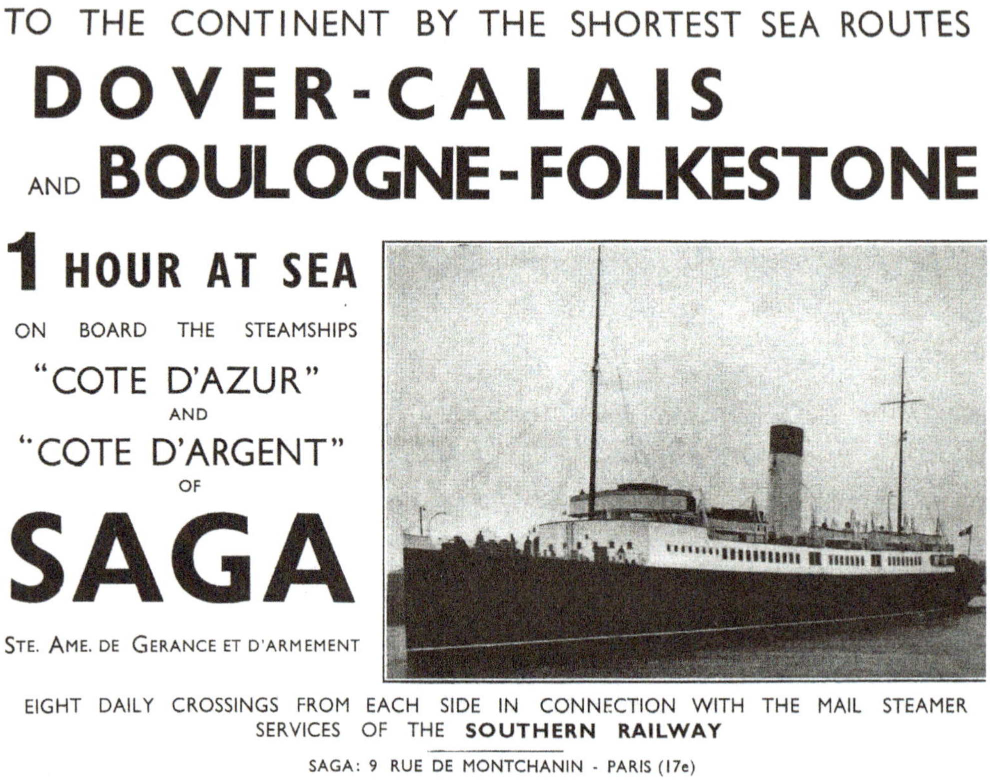

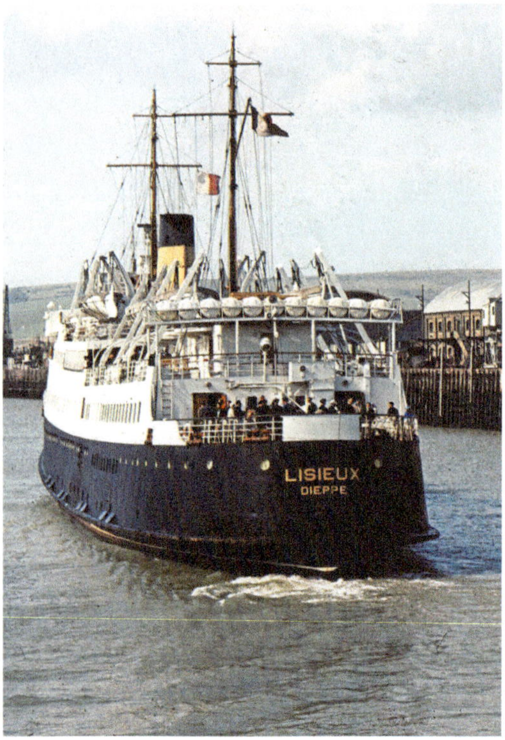

Above: A SAGA advertisement from 1938.

***Left*: *Lisieux*, 1952, 2,943 grt. 95.49 x 13.01 x 7.1 metres. 22 knots.**
b. Forges et Chantiers de la Méditerranée SA, Le Havre. Twin screw, two Parsons turbines, 22,000 SHP by builder.

She was delivered to SNCF in 1952 for the Dieppe–Newhaven route and operated on the Weymouth/Jersey–St Malo service in 1960. She was sold to Petros M. Nomikos, Piraeus, in 1966 and was renamed *Apollon* for the Piraeus–Mykonos daily service. Purchased by Agapitos Brothers, Piraeus, in 1977, she suffered boiler failure in 1980 and was laid up at Perama. She arrived at Eleusis on 12 October 1982 and was broken up.

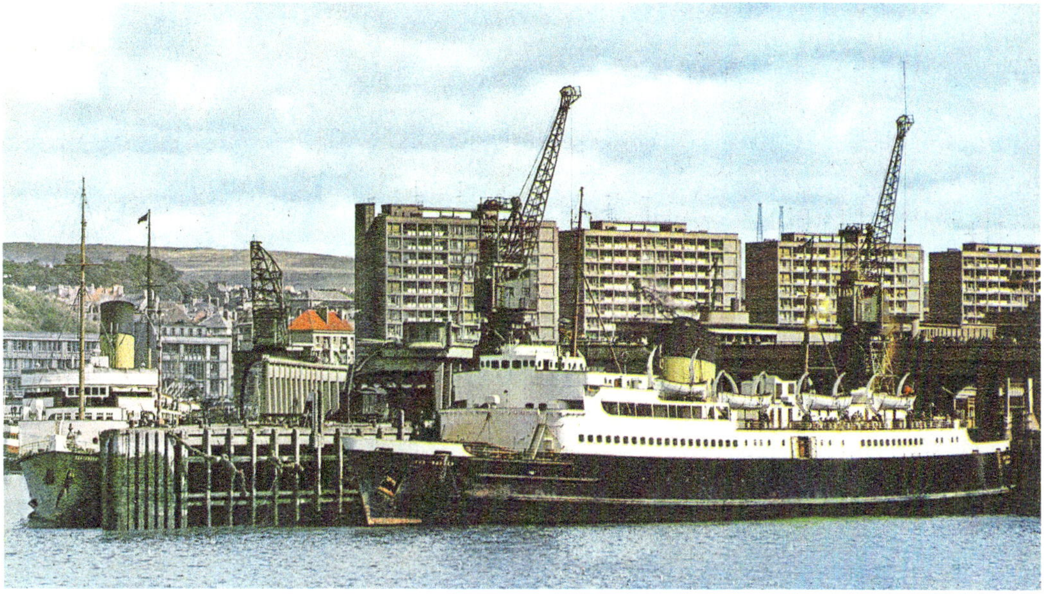

Above: *Canterbury* (1929, 2,912 grt) and *Lord Warden* (1952, 3,333 grt).

Below: *Autocarrier*, 1931, 822 grt. 15 knots.

b. D. & W. Henderson & Company Limited, Glasgow. Twin screw, two four-cylinder triple expansion, 154 NHP by builder. Southern Railway.

She was launched on 5 February 1931 as *Camberley* and was modified for the carriage of thirty to thirty-five vehicles. In 1940 she assisted in the evacuation of the Channel Islands and was later used as a troop transport and entertainment ship at Scapa Flow. She transported the residents of Alderney back home following their exile in Britain during the hostilities. She operated on various routes in 1946 and 1947 and was replaced on Dover–Calais by the *Dinard*. On 6 April 1954 she left Dover in tow for Ghent, where she was broken up.

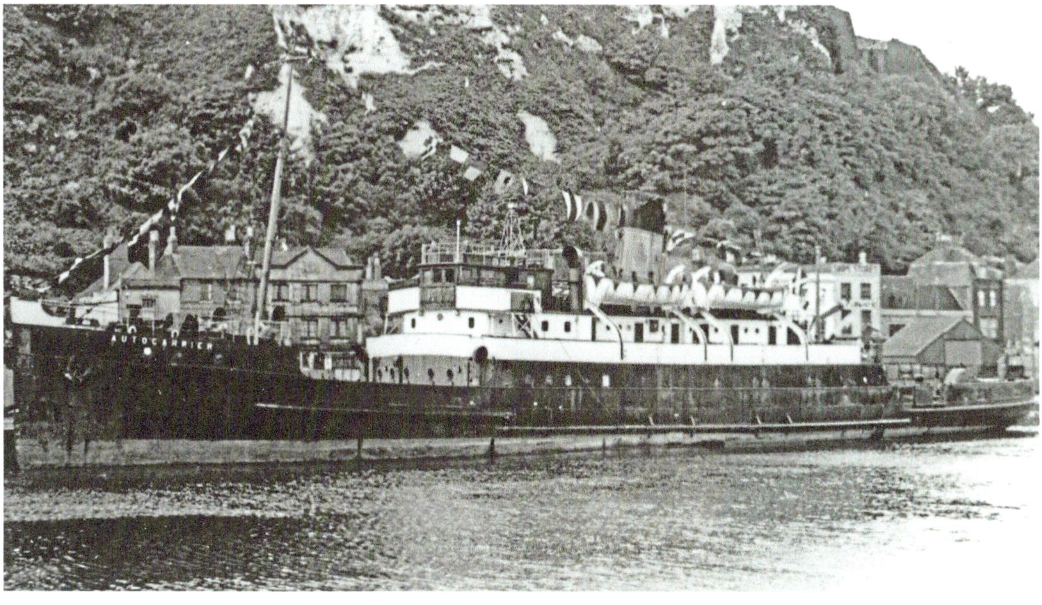

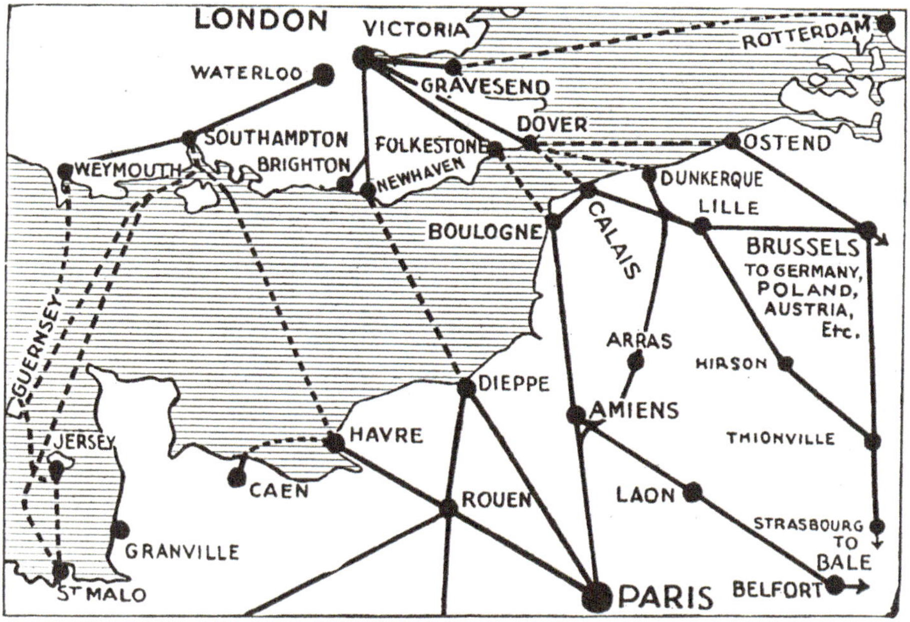

Above: Southern Region routes as of 1938.

Below: *Halladale*, 1944, 1,441 grt. 91.90 x 11.19 metres. 20 knots.

b. A. & J. Inglis Limited, Pointhouse, Glasgow. Four Parsons steam turbines, single reduction gearing, each set of turbines connected to two screw shafts.

A Formal Royal Naval 'River' Class frigate, she was purchased by Townsend Brothers Ferries Limited in 1949 as a replacement for *Forde*. She was converted into a car ferry by the Cork Dockyard Company at Rushbrooke, Cork. She inaugurated the car ramp at Calais on 27 June 1951, which allowed cars to be driven on and off of the vessel by the ramp that was lowered onto the vessel.

She made her last trip from Calais to Dover on 5 November 1961 and was sold to W. Rostedt of Finland, being renamed *Norden* and becoming *Turist Expressen* the following year. She was sold to Venezuela interests in 1962, becoming *Ferrymar III*, and was broken up in 1987.

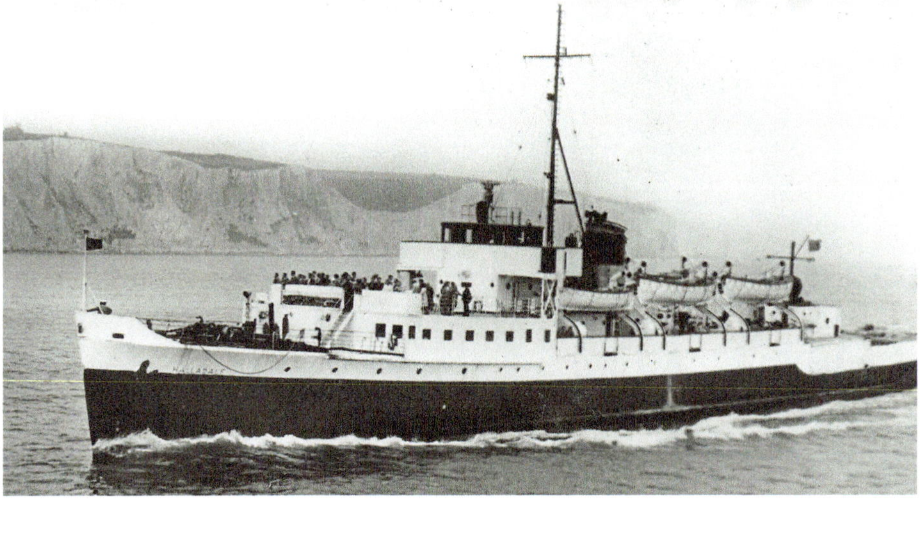

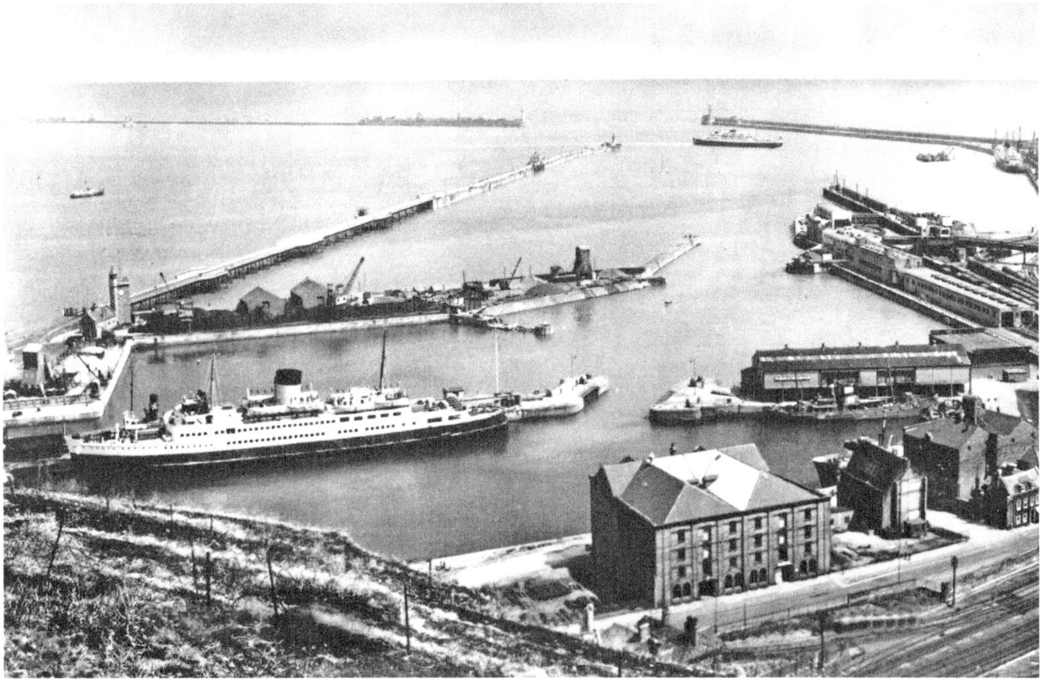

Above: Dover Harbour.

Below: *Prince Baudouin (2)* (1934, 3,050 grt).

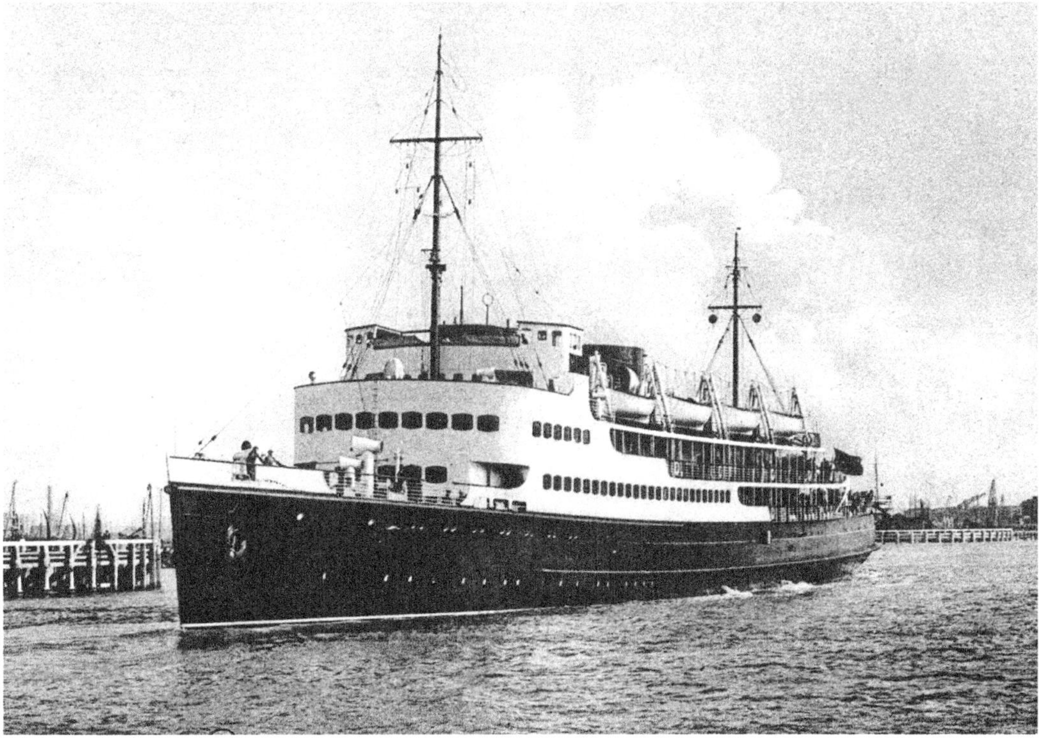

Passenger and Railway Diesel-motor Ferry "Saint-Germain" built 1951 for the Dover-Dunkirk service for the Société Nationale des Chemins de Fer Français.

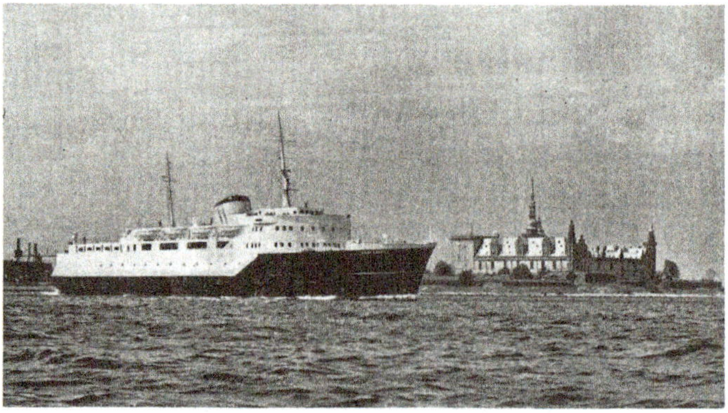

BUILDING - REPAIRING

APPLY TO

HELSINGØR SKIBSVÆRFT OG MASKINBYGGERI A/S

ELSINORE SHIPBUILDING AND ENGINEERING COMPANY LIMITED

ELSINORE — DENMARK

PASSENGER VESSELS · FRUIT VESSELS · CARGO VESSELS · FERRIES
DIESEL AND STEAM ENGINES · ELSINORE EXHAUST STEAM TURBINE SYSTEM

Telephone: Elsinore 1400 Telegrams: Shipbuilding, Elsinore

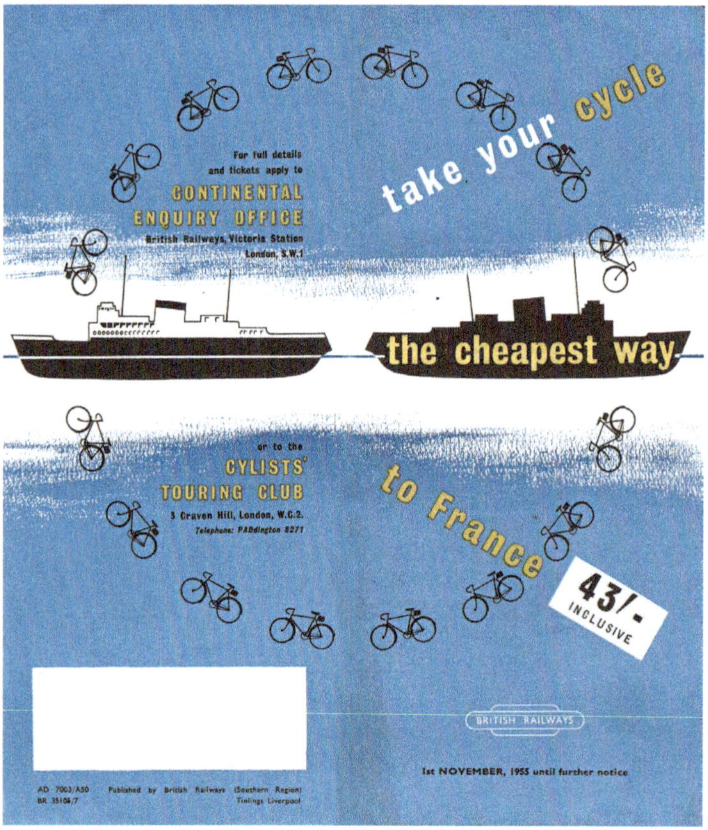

Above: An advertisement for Helsingør Skibsværft og Maskinbyggeri A/S featuring *Saint-Germain*.

Left: A 'Take your cycle to France' brochure from 1955.

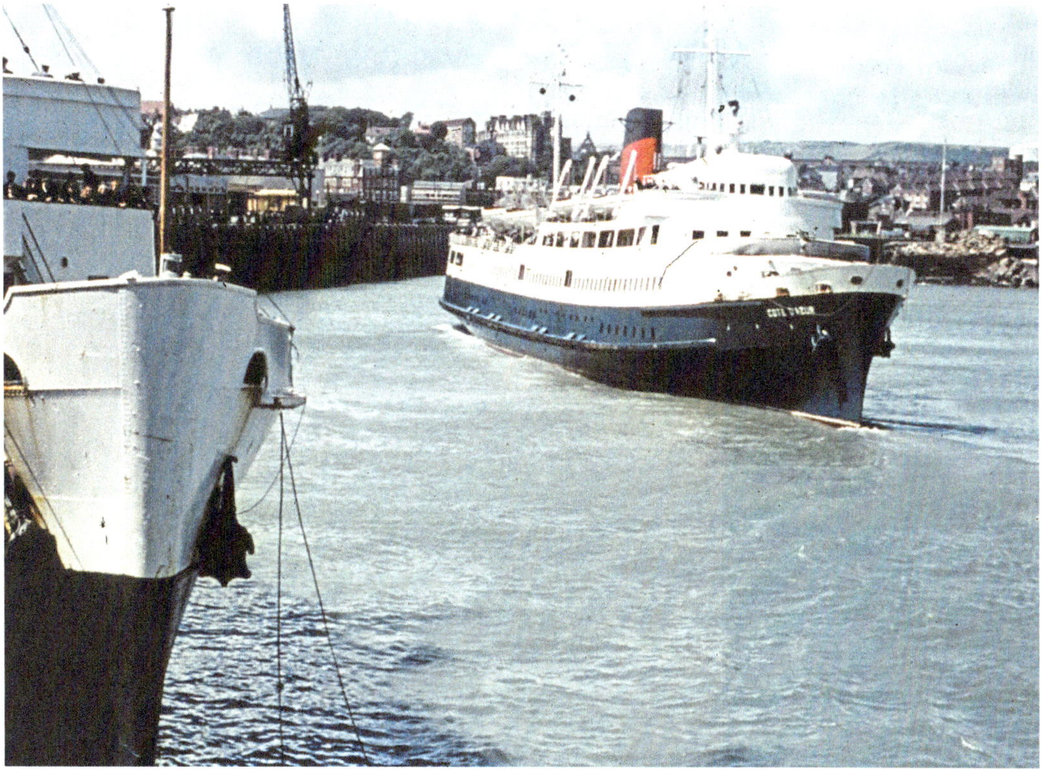

Above and below: *Cote D'Azur (2)* (1951, 4,037 grt).

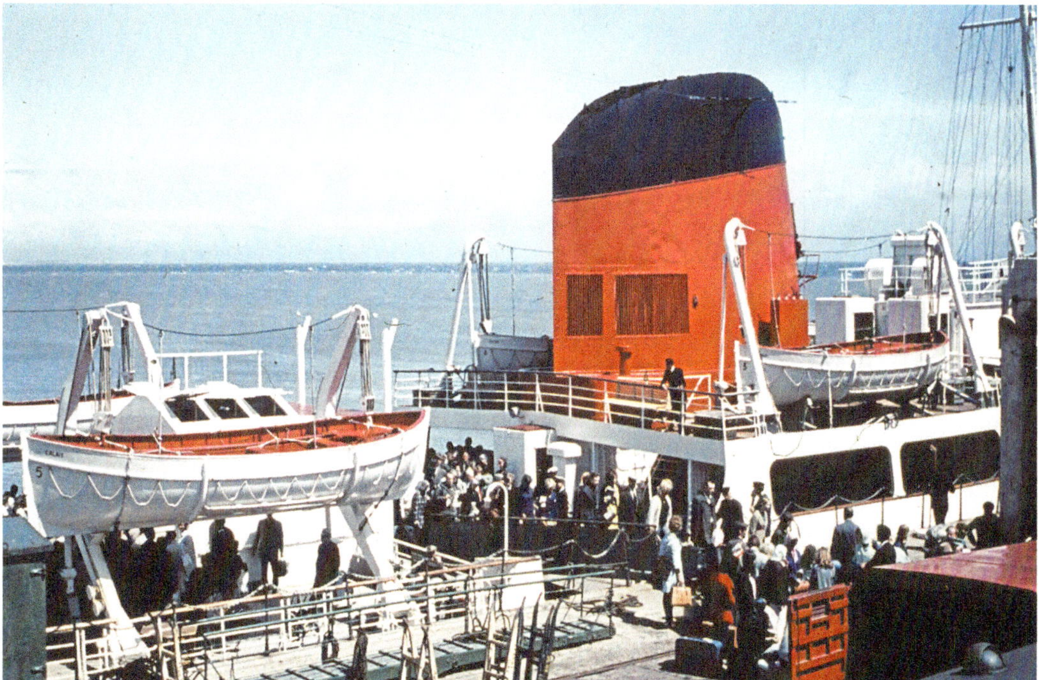

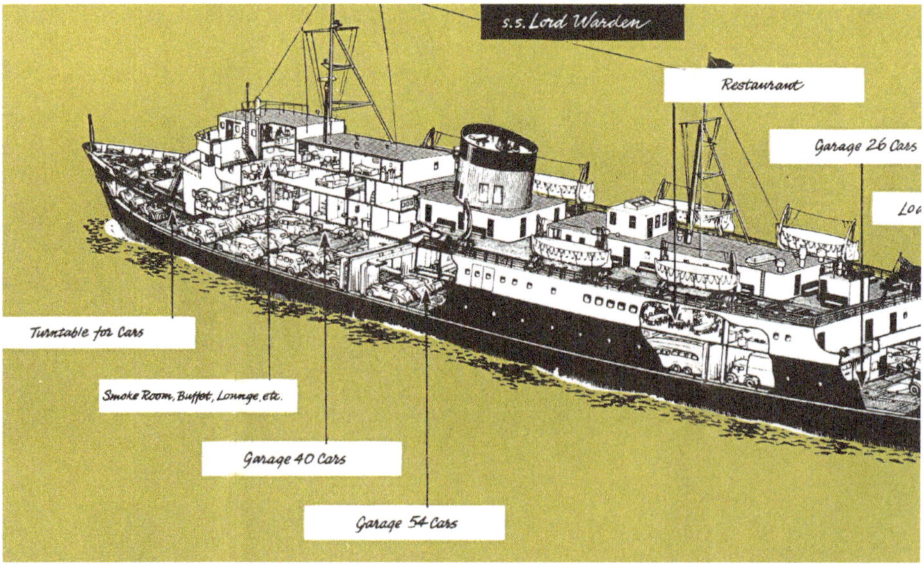

Lord Warden, 1952, 3,333 grt. 110.37 x 18.5 metres. 20 knots.
b. William Denny & Brothers Limited, Dumbarton. Yard No. 1455. Twin screw, two turbines, 8,000 SHP, two Babcock & Wilcox boilers by builder. British Transport Commission, Southern Region.

She was launched on 14 December 1951 as British Railways' first drive-on/drive-off car ferry, with electrically operated, rather than hydraulic, stern doors. She sailed on her maiden voyage from Dover to Boulogne on 16 June 1952. As the facilities were not yet ready, cars were craned onboard at Dover, but were driven off at Boulogne. On 15 June 1953 she was present at the Coronation Spithead Review, prior to the ramp becoming available at Dover. In 1956 her funnel was fitted with a new top to alleviate fumes when going astern. In May and October 1968 she was used as a 'Back Britain' exhibition ship at Copenhagen, Gothenburg, Stockholm, Helsinki and Oslo. On 7 April 1971 she operated on the Holyhead–Dun Laoghaire route when *Holyhead Ferry 1* was sent to Fishguard.

On 1 January 1979 she was transferred to Sealink UK Limited and after operating at Holyhead she was sent to Newhaven, where she was laid up. On 19 November she was sold to Ahmed Mohamed Baaboud of Jeddah, becoming *Al Zaher*. Following work on her by Thornycroft, she left Southampton on 2 January 1980 for Jeddah, carrying a cargo of sheep on the Port Sudan–Jeddah section of the voyage. On 25 April 1981 she arrived at Gadani Beach and was broken up by Karim Shipbreaking Industries.

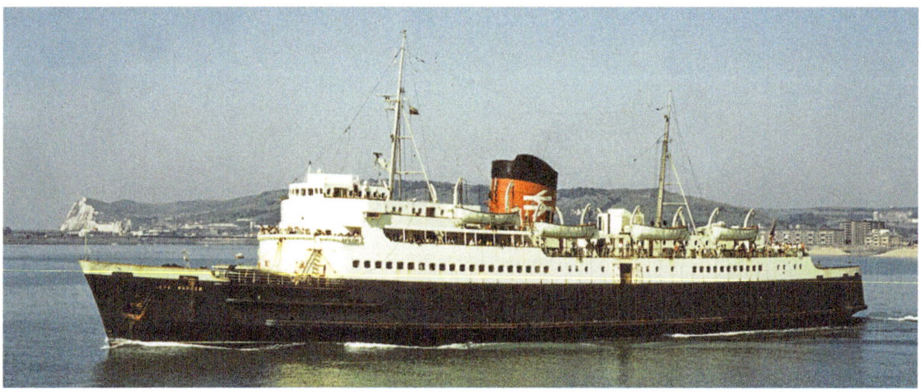

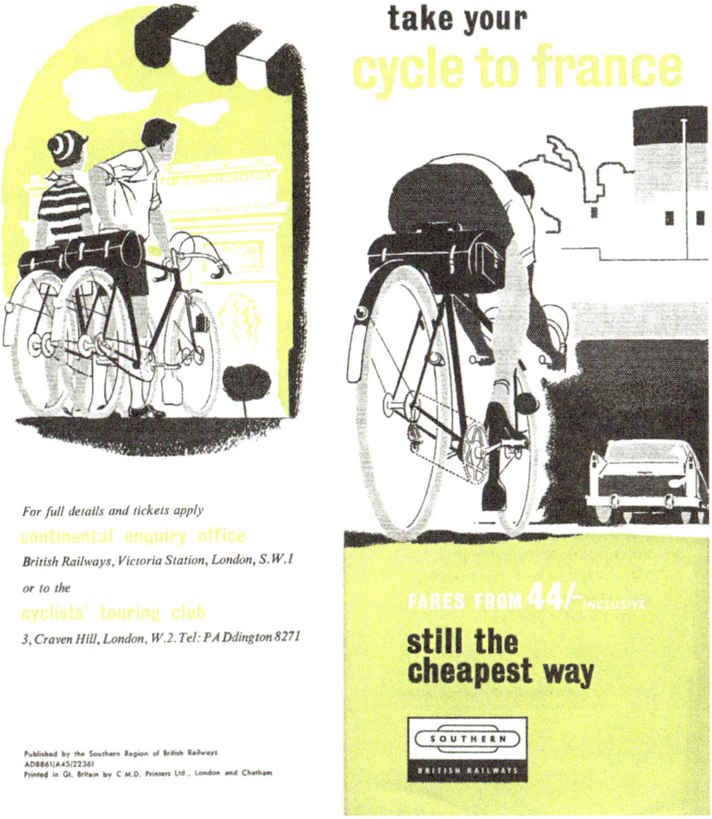

Right: A 'Take your cycle to France' brochure from 1961.

Below: *Falaise*, 1946, 3,710 grt. 94.64 x 15.1 metres. 20½ knots. b. William Denny & Brothers Limited, Dumbarton. Yard No. 1400. Twin screw, 2x2 stage Parsons turbines, two Foster Wheeler boilers by builder. Southern Railway.

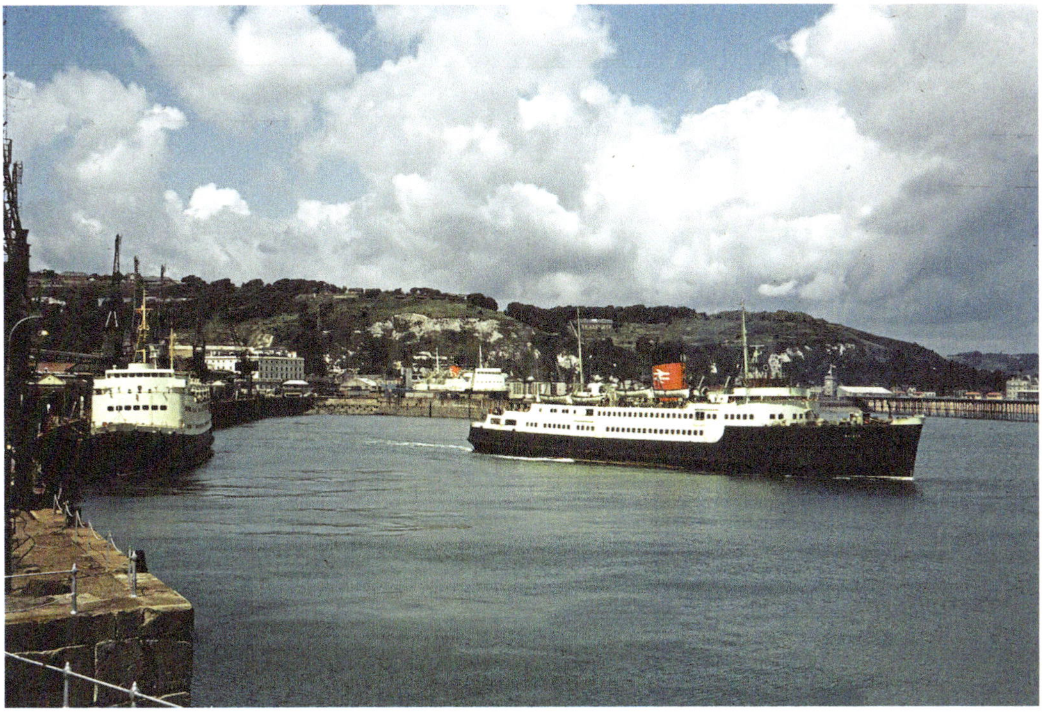

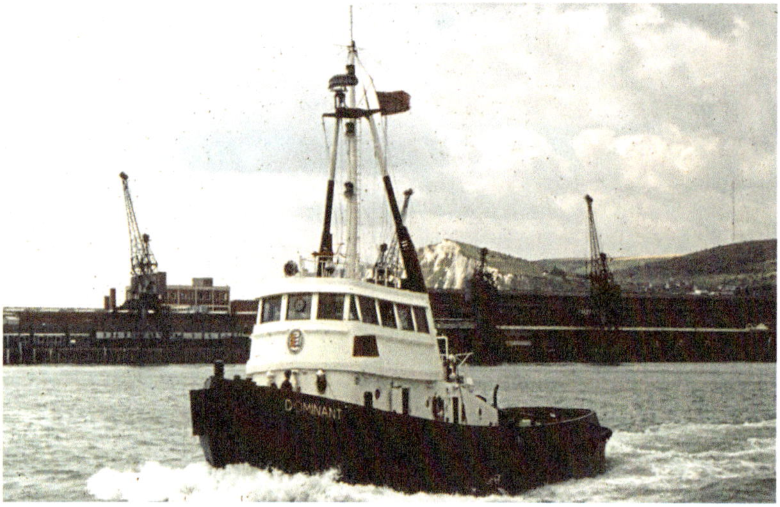

Above: The tug *Dominant* (1958, 161 grt).

Below: _Twickenham Ferry_, 1934, 2,839 grt. 105.7 x 18.5 metres. 16½ knots.
b. Swan, Hunter & Wigham Richardson Limited, Newcastle. Yard No. 1446. Twin screw, 2x2 turbines, 4,500 IHP, four automatic Yarrow boilers by Parsons Marine Steam Turbine Company. Southern Railway.

She was designed and built as a train and car ferry with accommodation for twelve sleeping cars or forty rail wagons, plus twenty-five cars in the upper deck garage. Delivered for the Dover–Dunkirk service, the introduction of which was delayed because of engineering problems at Dover, she operated the first Dover–Dunkirk night crossing on 6 October and was transferred to SA de Nav. Angleterre-Lorraine-Alsace (ALA) ownership. On 25 August 1939 the service was suspended and she was converted into a minelayer, becoming HMS *Twickenham*. In 1940 she operated on the English Channel and was later transferred to the Stranraer–Larne service. In July she was fitted with large gantries, an eighty-four-trolley crane and a stern ramp to enable her and her two sisters to deliver railway stock to places where the infrastructure had been destroyed.

In 1945 she returned to ALA ownership and was converted to burn oil two years later. In January 1974 she was replaced by *St Eloi* but continued in service to complete a large order for railway wagons for Yugoslavia. Her final sailing was on 5 May. She was sold later that month and was broken up by Steelnorte SA at San Esteban de Pravia.

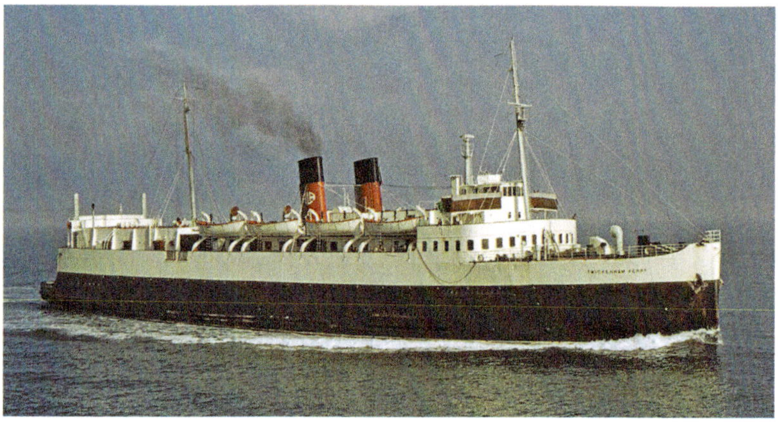

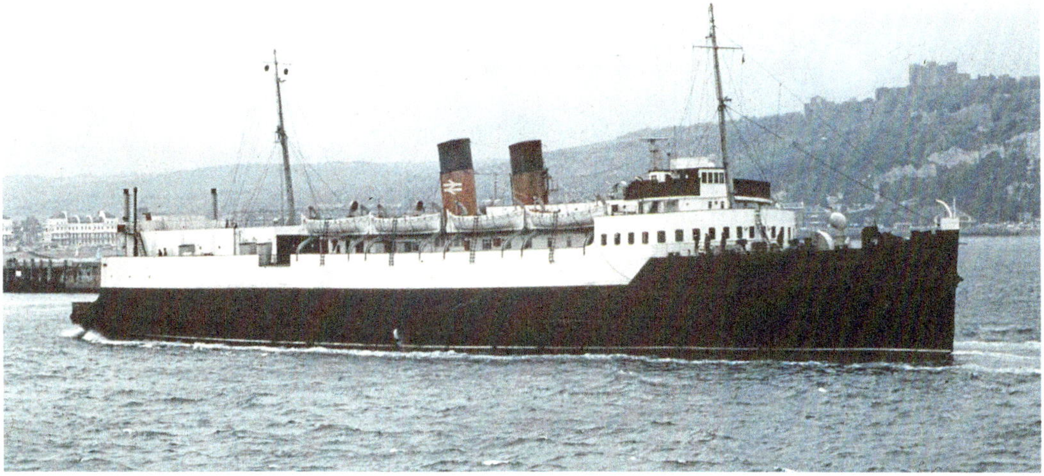

***Above*: *Shepperton Ferry*, 1935, 2,839 grt. 105.7 x 18.5 metres. 16½ knots.**
b. Swan, Hunter & Wigham Richardson Limited, Newcastle. Yard No. 1446. Twin screw, 2x2 turbines, 4,500 IHP, four automatic Yarrow boilers by Parsons Marine Steam Turbine Company. Southern Railway.

She operated as a minelayer in the Straits of Dover as HMS *Shepperton* in 1939, and assisted in the evacuation of the Channel Islands in 1940. Following this she reverted back to minelaying for a short period before transferring to the Stranraer–Larne route. At the end of hostilities she reopened the Dover–Dunkirk route on 19 February 1946 and was converted to burn oil later that year.

She relieved the *Caledonian Princess* on the Stranraer–Larne service in 1964, during her annual overhaul. Her final sailing took place on 25 August 1972 and she was then laid up at Wellington Dock, Dover. She left Dover in tow on 12 September and arrived at Bilbao on 19 September, where she was broken up.

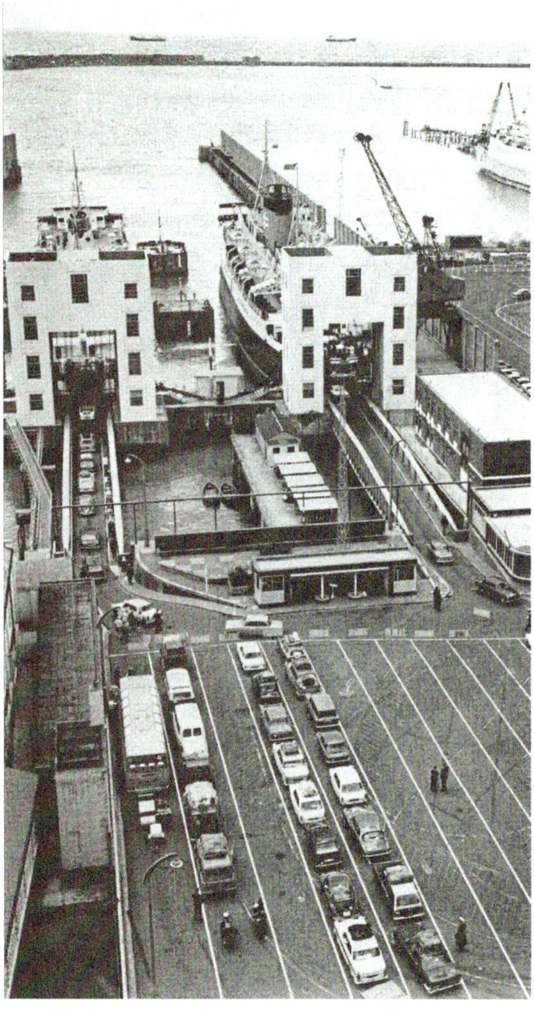

Right: Car ferry berths in 1968.

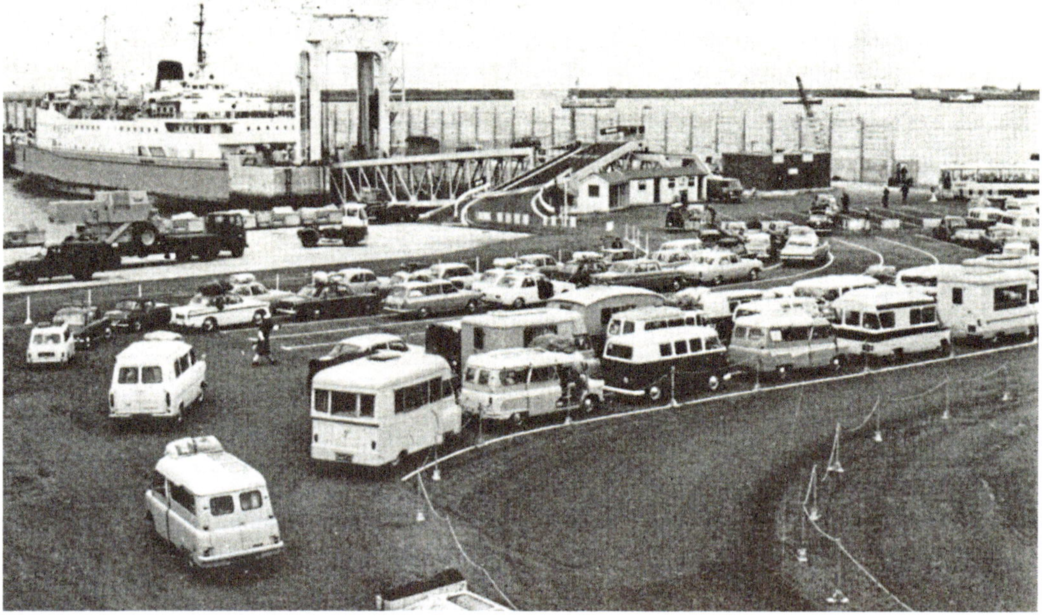

Above: *Free Enterprise III* (1966, 4,657 grt) loading vehicles in 1969.

Below: A Townsend brochure from 1968.

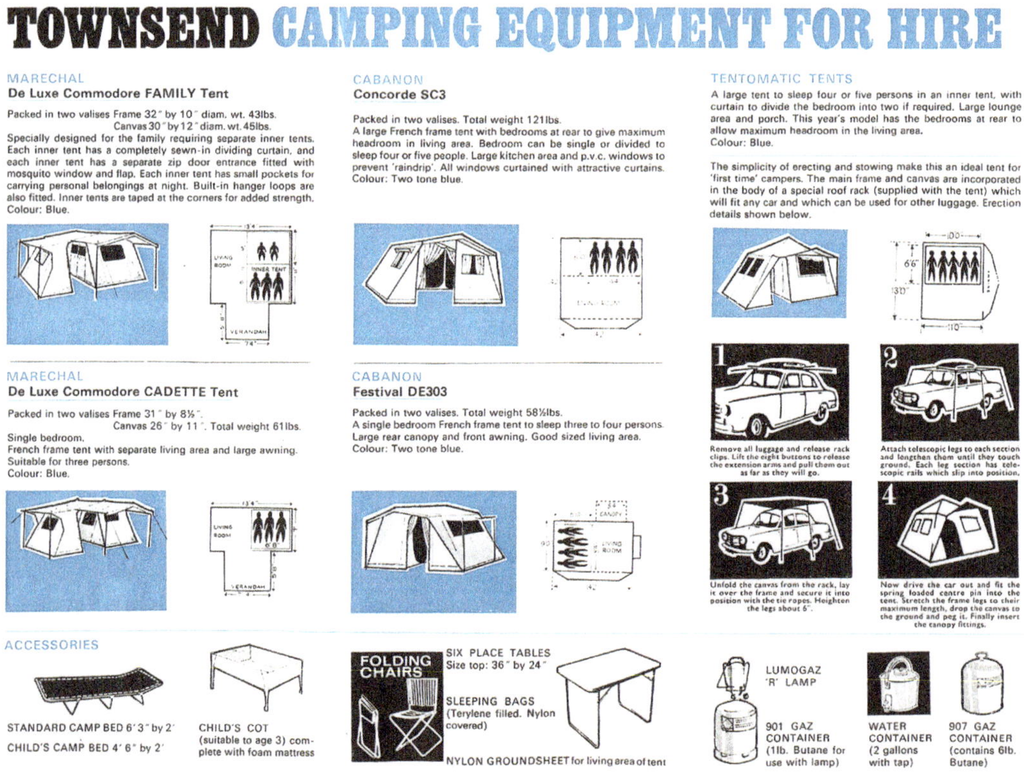

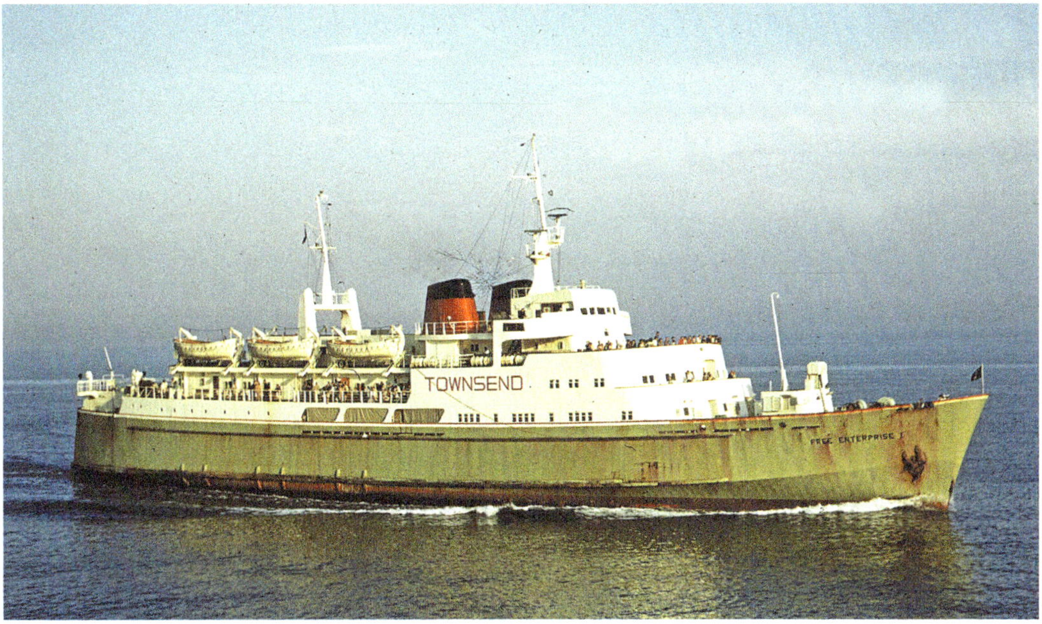

Above: Free Enterprise I, 1962, 2,607 grt. 96.5 x 16.4 metres.

b. NV Werft Gusto, Schiedam, Holland. Yard No. 424. Townsend Brothers, Ferries Limited.

She was launched as *Free Enterprise* on 2 February 1962, becoming *Free Enterprise I* in 1964. In 1980 she was sold, becoming *Kimolos*. She became *Ergina* in 1993, *Ventouris* in 1994, *Methodia II* in 1995, *Kallisti* in 1996, *Okeanis* in 2005 and *Oceanis* in 2013. She arrived at Aliaga on 3 June 2013 and was broken up.

Below: Normannia, 1952, 3,543 grt. 94.24 x 14.69 x 5.33 metres. 19 knots.

b. William Denny & Brothers, Dumbarton. Twin screw, two Pametrada turbines, 8,000 SHP, two Foster-Wheeler boilers by builder. Southern Region.

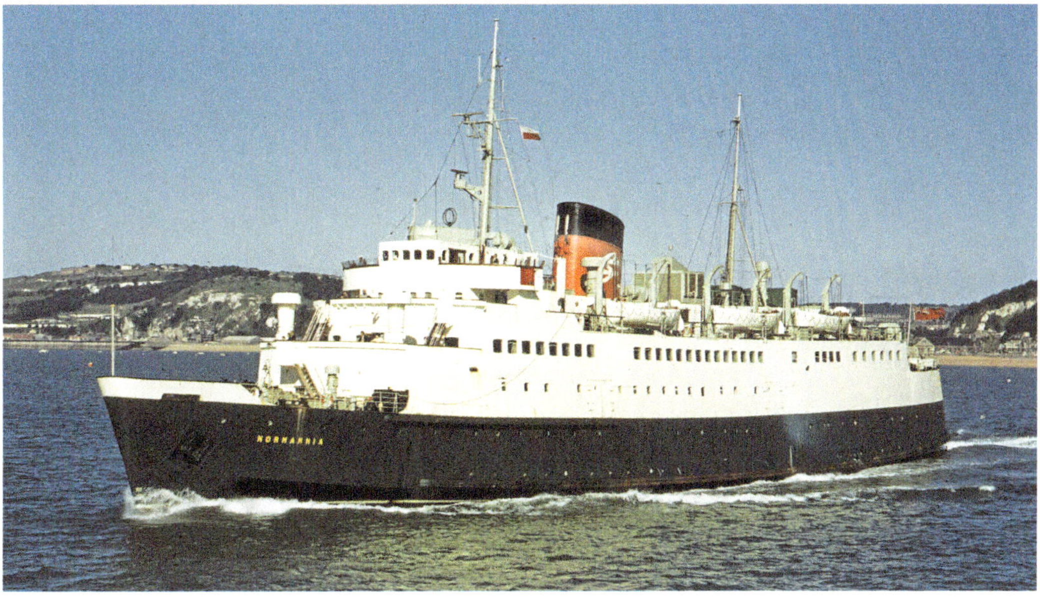

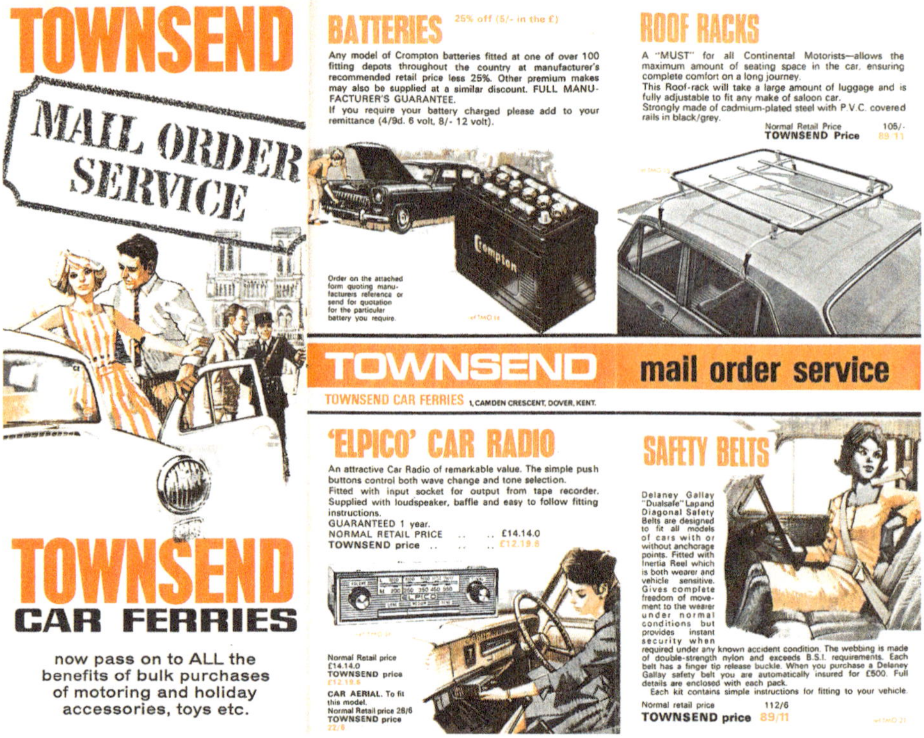

Above and below: A Townsend brochure from 1967.

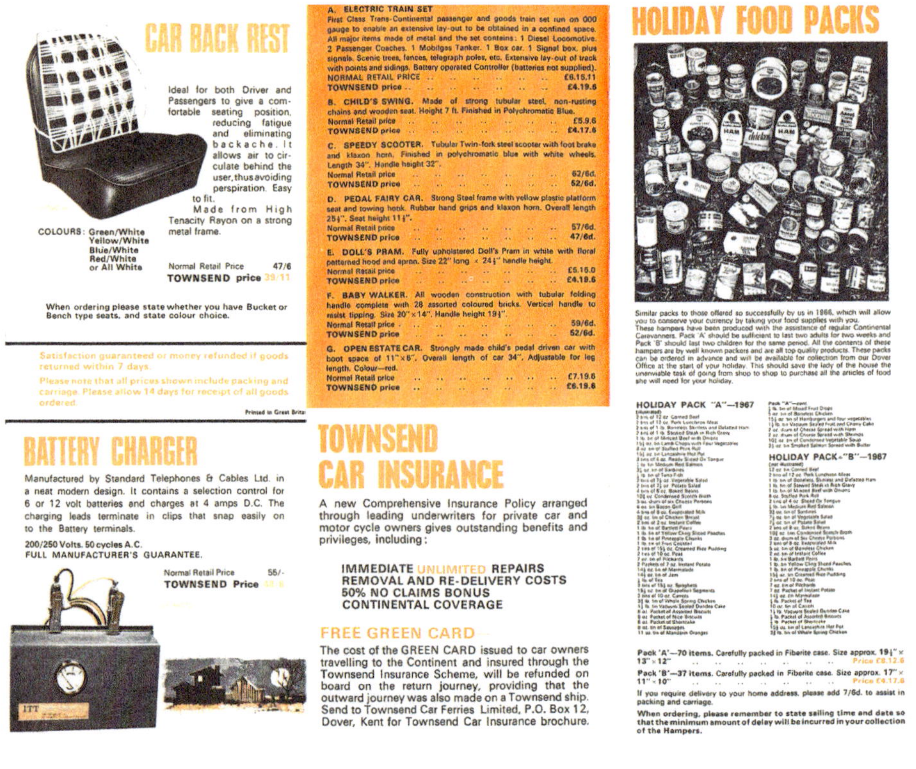

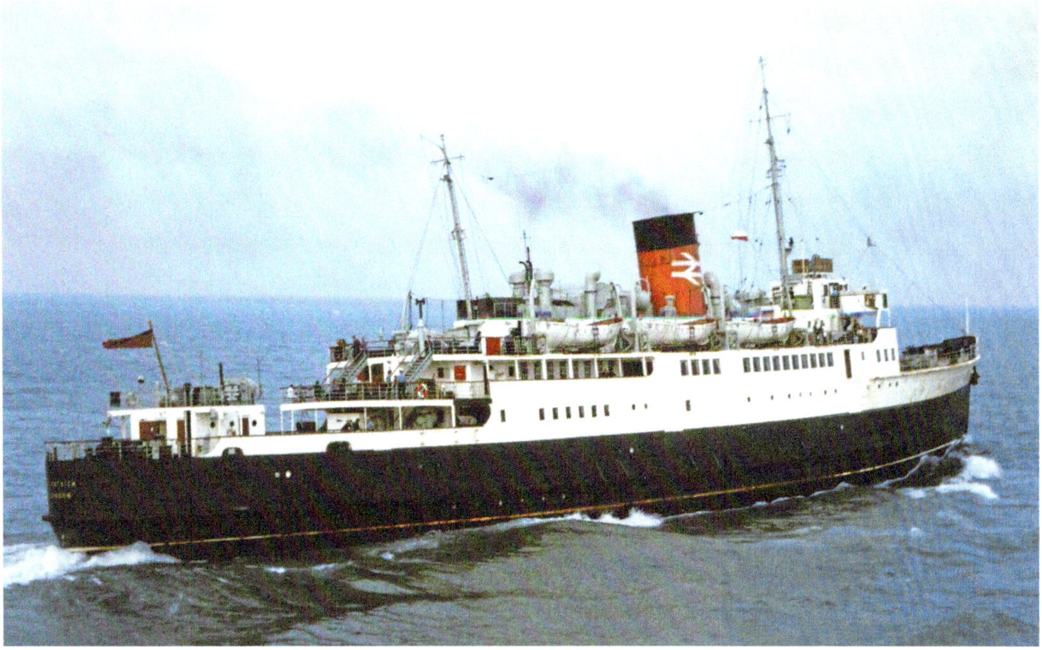

Above: ***St Patrick*, 1948, 3,482 grt. 97.9 x 14.69 metres. 20 knots.**
b. Cammell Laird & Company Limited, Birkenhead. Twin screw, 2x2 Parsons steam turbines, 8,500 BHP, three Babcock & Wilcox boilers by builder. Western Region, Fishguard & Rosslare Railway & Harbour Company.

Below: *Christopher M* (1956, 1,035 grt) in the Channel off Dover.

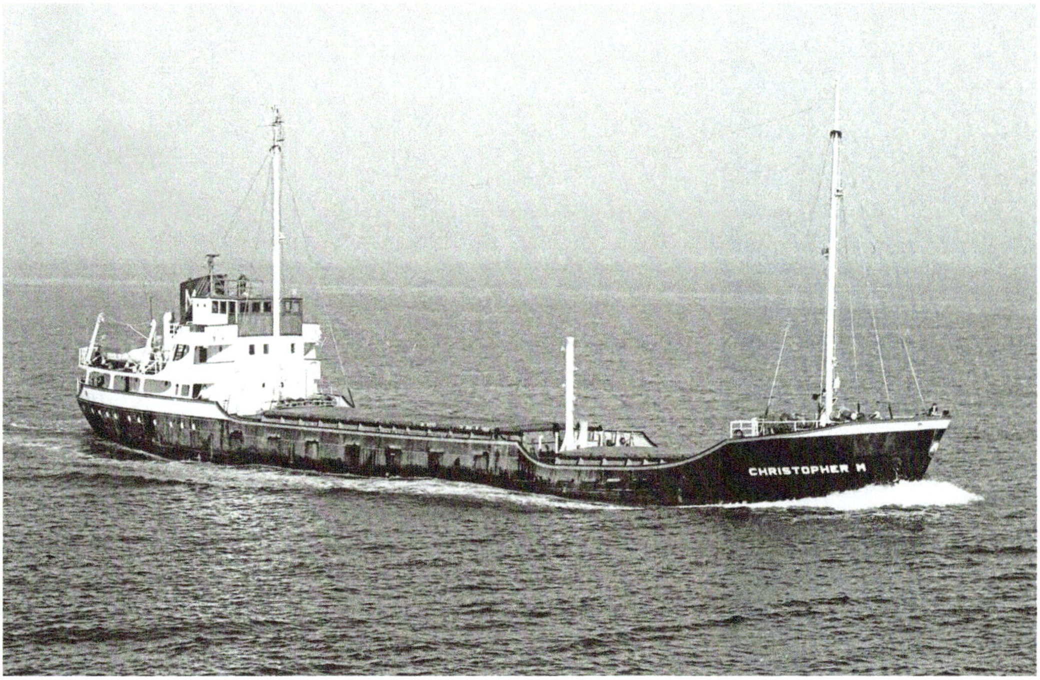

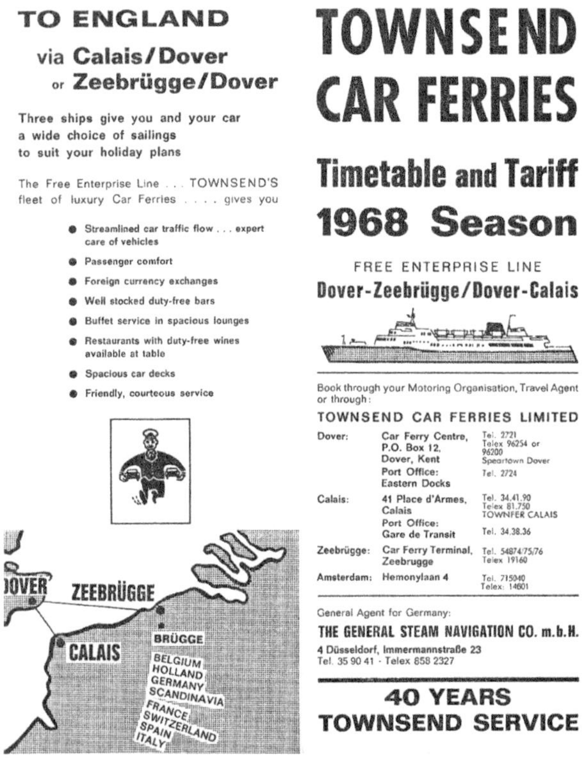

1968 Townsend Car Ferries timetable.

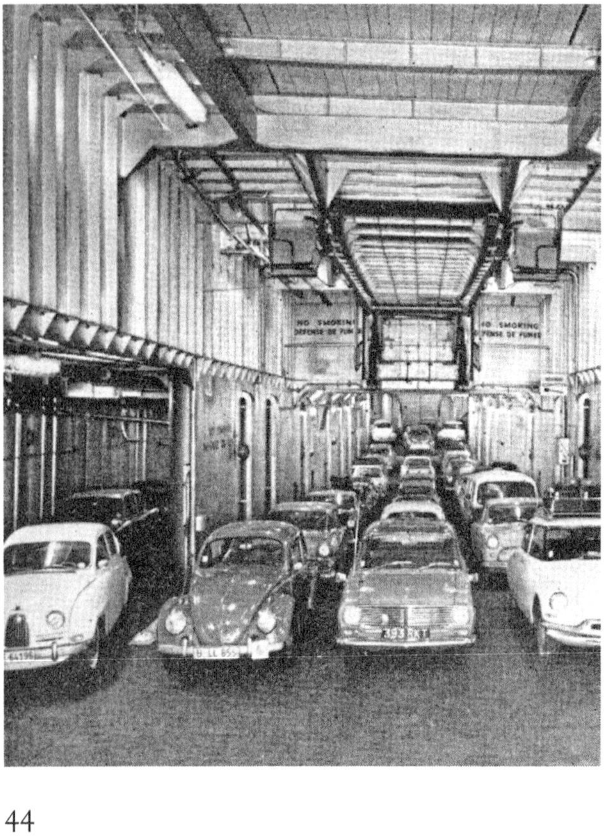

Car deck on *Free Enterprise* (1962, 2,607 grt).

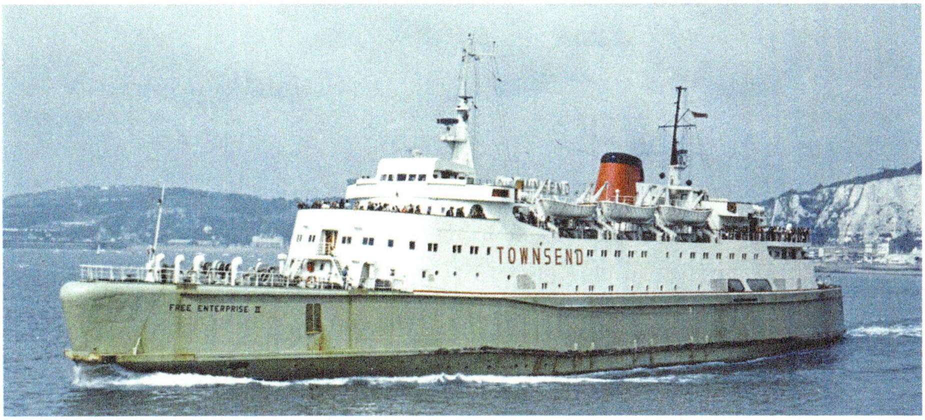

Above: *Free Enterprise II* (1965, 5,956 grt).

Below: *Invicta*, 1939, 4,178 grt. 117.19 x 15.27 metres. 22 knots.
b. William Denny & Brothers Limited, Dumbarton. Yard No. 1344. Twin screw, 2x2 two stage Parsons turbines, 1,100 NHP, two Yarrow boilers by builder. Southern Railway.

She was ordered on 13 February 1939 for the Golden Arrow service to replace *Canterbury* and operated one return trip each day. She was launched on 14 December and was delivered on 1 July the following year. However, she was laid up at anchor for ten months before being requisitioned by the Admiralty and was fitted with de-gaussing equipment by Barclay Curle. She was commissioned on 19 August and transported Canadian troops to Dieppe during Operation Jubilee. In June 1944 she participated in the Normandy invasion and was decommissioned in December the following year.

In 1946 she was operating on Southern Region services, replacing *Canterbury* on the Golden Arrow service on 15 October. She held the distinction of being the largest English Channel ship until the arrival of *Prinses Paola* in 1966. During her 1947 overhaul her original stabilisers were finally fitted, and on 1 January 1948 she was transferred to the British Transport Commission. Early in 1965 she introduced the new British Rail livery on the Dover–Calais service. However, in July 1972 she was replaced on the Golden Arrow service by the *Maid of Orleans*, taking her final sailing on 8 August before being laid up at Newhaven. On 21 September she left in tow of Michel Petersen for Rotterdam, where she was broken up.

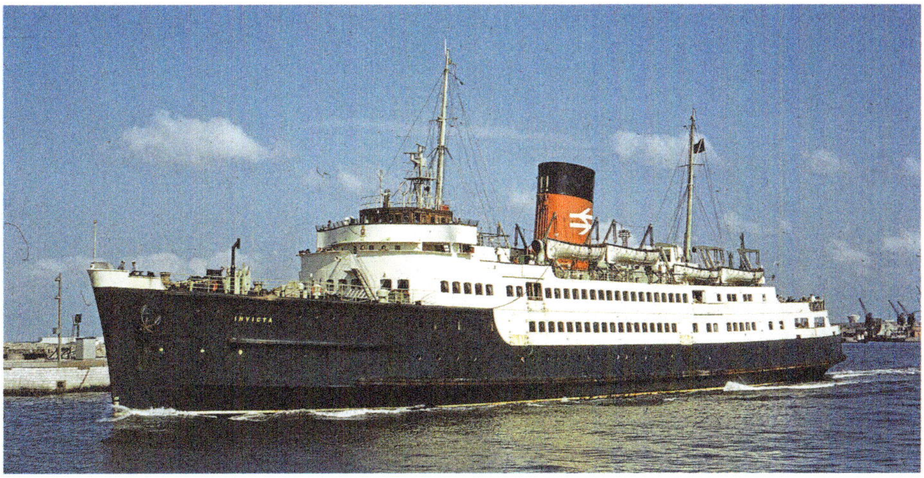

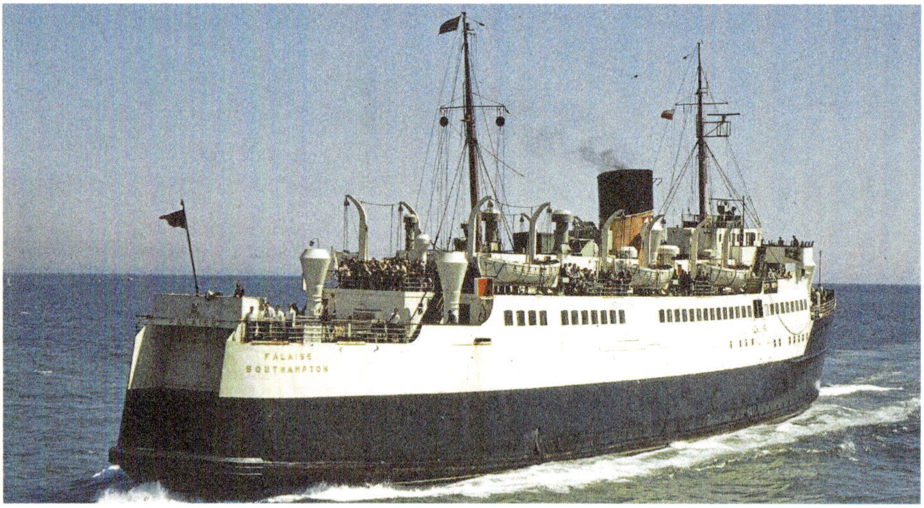

Above: *Falaise*, 1946, 3,710 grt. 94.64 x 15.1 metres. 20½ knots.
b. William Denny & Brothers Limited, Dumbarton. Yard No. 1400. Twin screw, 2x2 stage Parsons turbines, two Foster Wheeler boilers, 450 Psi by builder. Southern Railway.

Launched on 25 October 1946 and delivered for the Southampton–St Malo service, she was the Southern Region's first post-war new build and could operate on any of their routes. She was transferred to the British Transport Commission on 1 January 1948. In 1964 she was converted to a car ferry and took the first dedicated car ferry sailing from Newhaven to Dieppe on 1 June. In June 1973 she operated the first drive-on/drive-off service to Jersey. The following year she suffered engine problems and was replaced by *Svea Drott*, until *Normannia* was available. On 24 December she left Holyhead in tow of the tug *Fairplay XII* for Bilbao, where she was broken up.

Below: A Dover–Ostend, Harwich–Ostend advertisement for 1969.

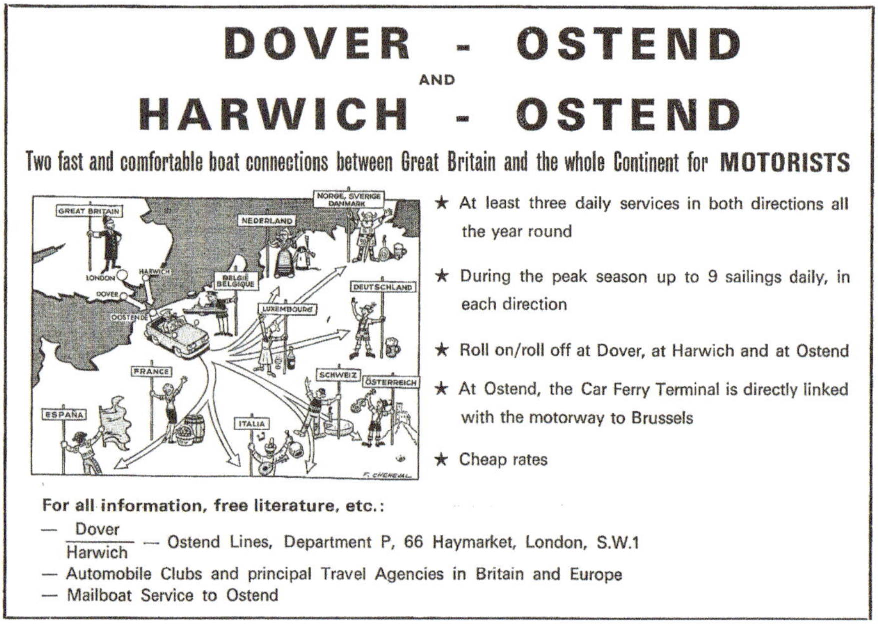

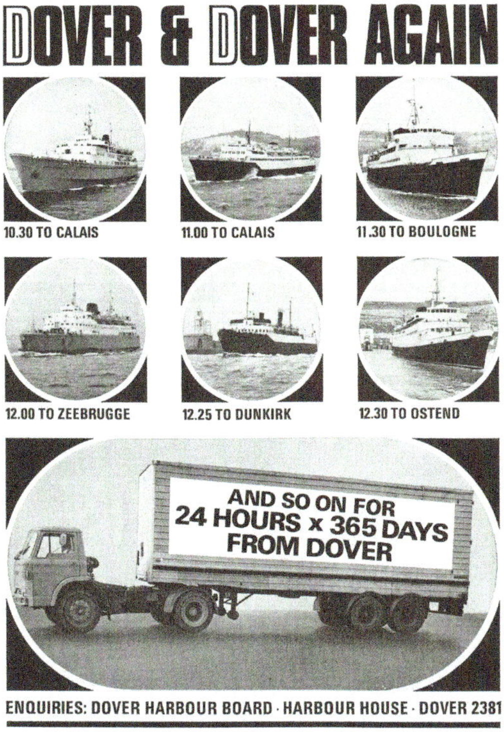

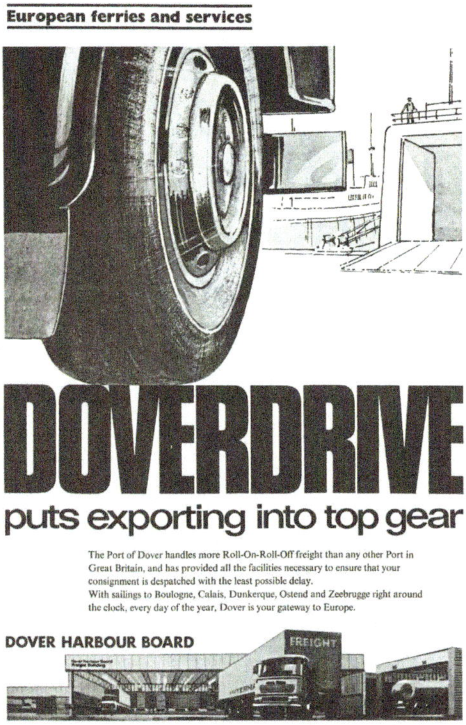

Above left: A Dover Harbour Board advertisement for 1969.

Above right: A Dover Harbour Board advertisement for 1976.

Below: Dover Harbour.

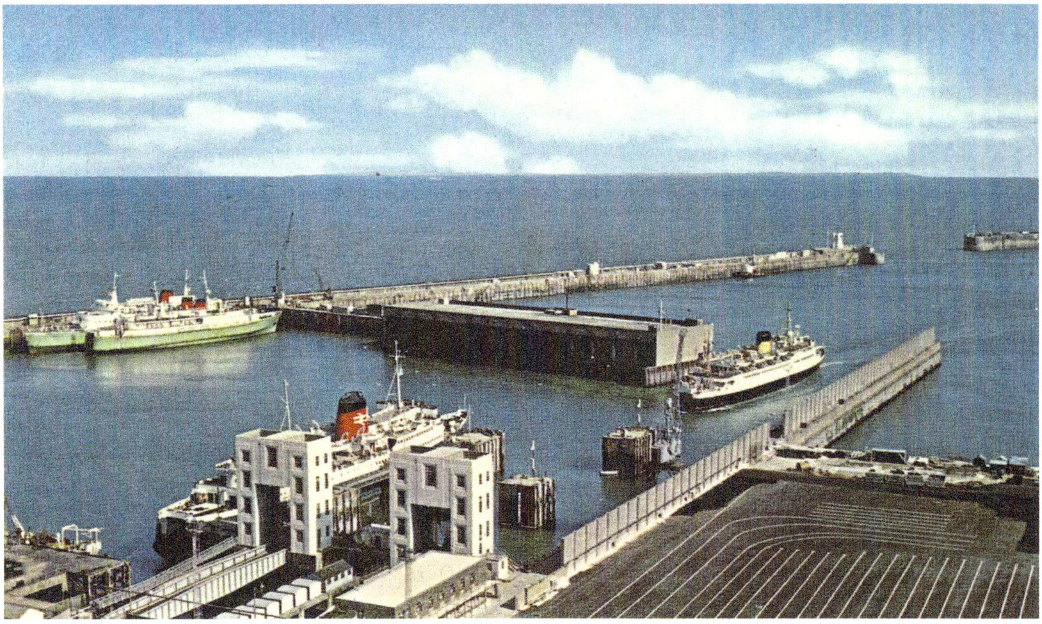

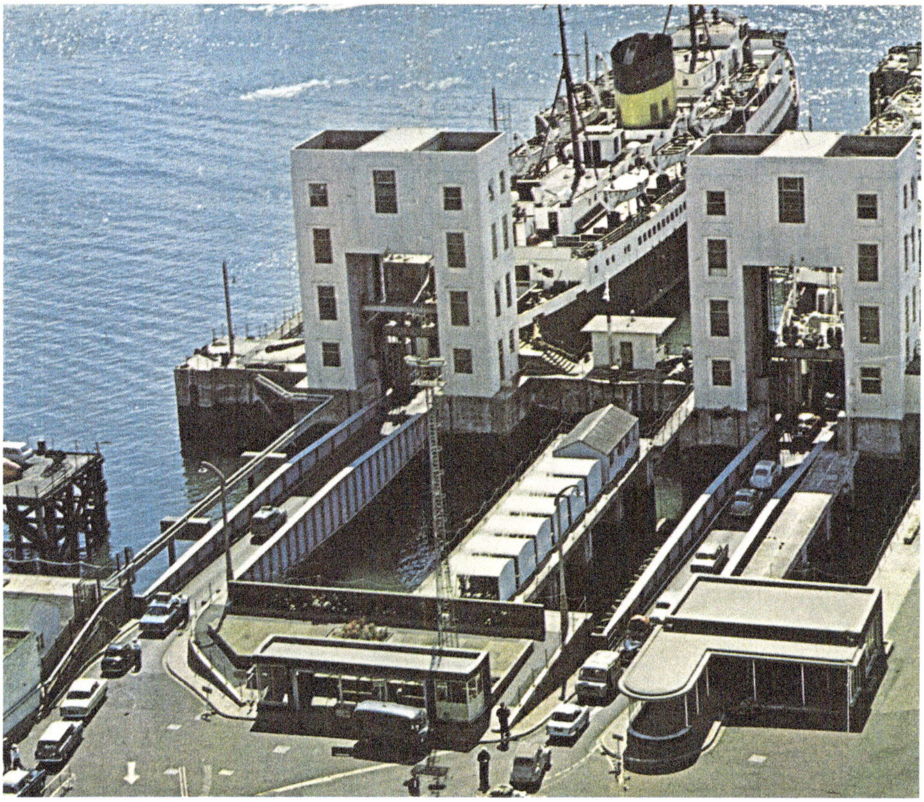

Above: Car ferry berths in 1964.

Below: Dover Eastern Docks in 1969.

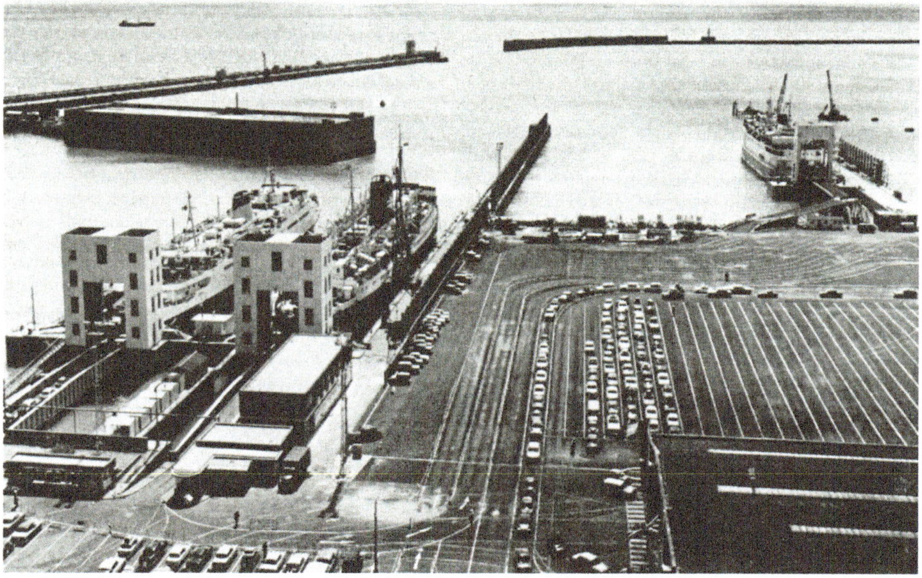

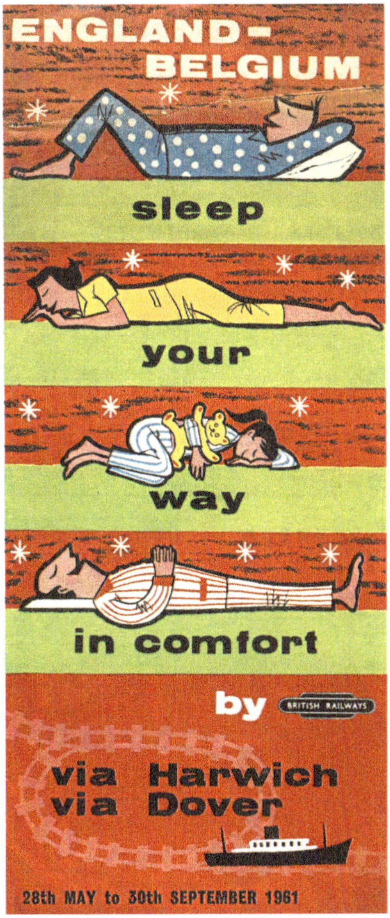

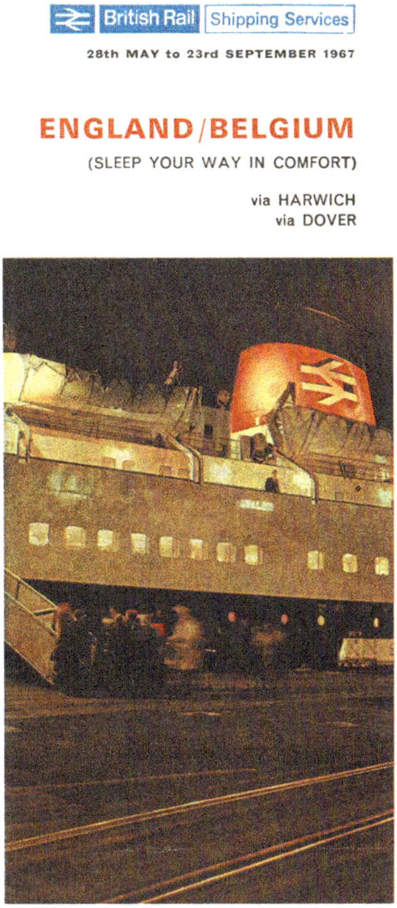

Above left: A Harwich/Dover brochure for 1961.

Above right: A Harwich/Dover brochure for 1967.

Below: ***Compiègne***, **1958, 3,467 grt. 115.03 x 18.35 x 6.4 metres. 20 knots.**
b. Chargeurs Réunis Loire-Normandie, Rouen. Twin screw, controllable pitch, oil, two sixteen-cylinder Pielstick 4s.sa, 9,000 SHP by Soc. Gen. de Construction Mécanique. SNCF, Southern Region as managers.

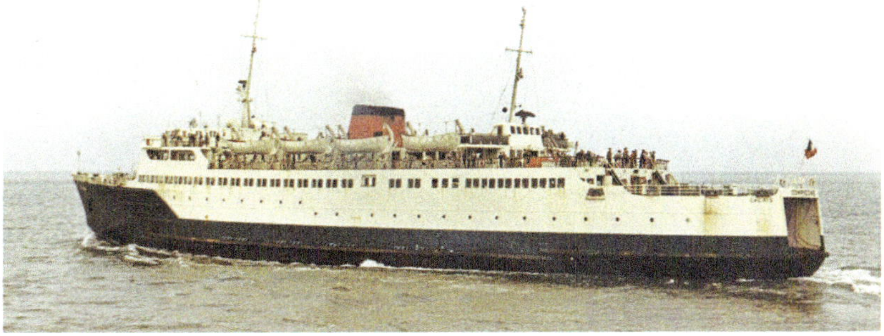

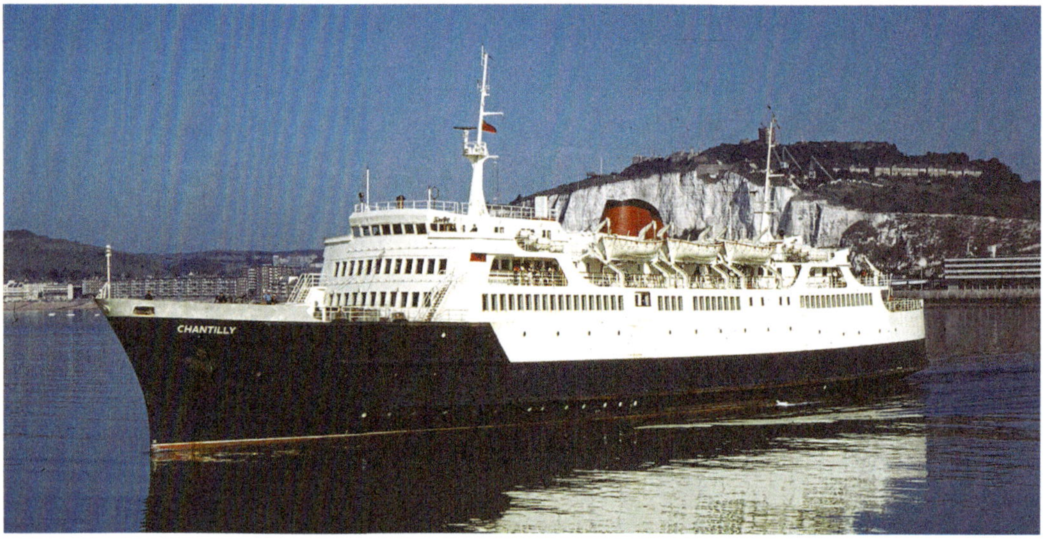

Above: **Chantilly, 1966, 3,400 grt. 109.9 x 17.8 metres.**
b. Dubigeon-Normandie, Nantes-Chantenay. Yard No. 822.

Soc. Nationale des Chemins de Fer Français. Twin reversible screw, two Pielstick Vee oil, two twelve-cylinder, 9,300 BHP by Ateliers & Chantiers de Nantes.

She was launched on 9 November 1965 for cross-channel services from France to England. In 1987 she was sold and renamed *Olympia*, followed by *Europa Link* in 1990, *Baltavia* in 1993 and *Al Salam 93* in 1996. She was broken up in 2003.

Below: **Saint-Germain, 1951, 3,400 grt. 115.76 x 18.44 x 6.19 metres. 18½ knots.**
b. Helsingør Skibs of Mask. A/S., Elsinore. Twin screw, oil, two nine-cylinder B&W 2s.sa, 6,400 BHP by builder. Soc. Nationale des Chemins de Fer Français.

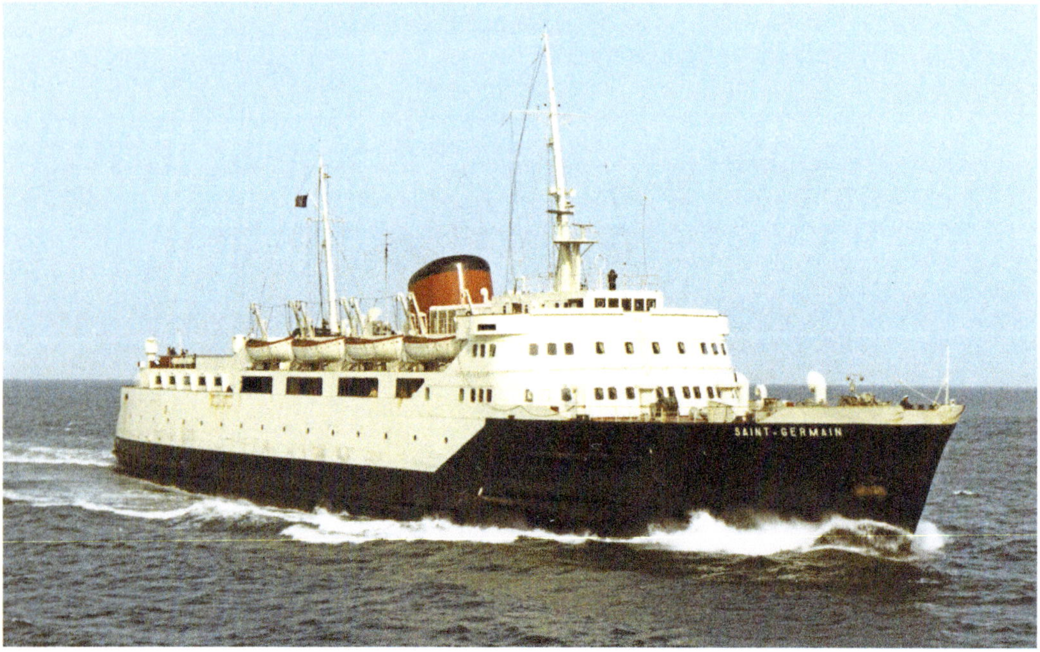

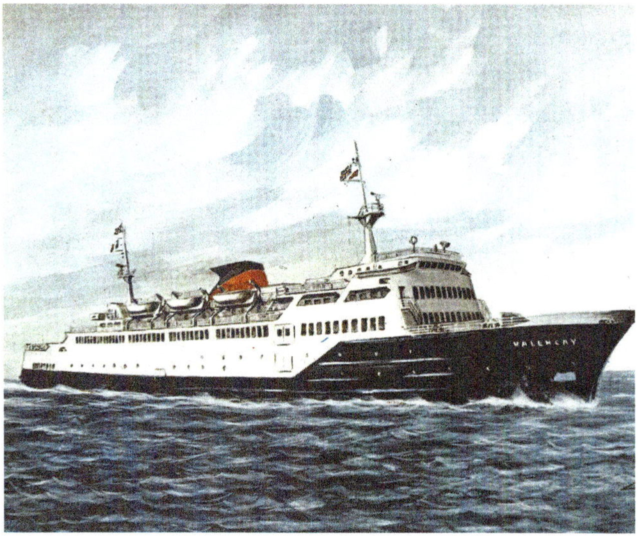

An artist's impression of *Villandry*, which was issued prior to her introduction in 1965.

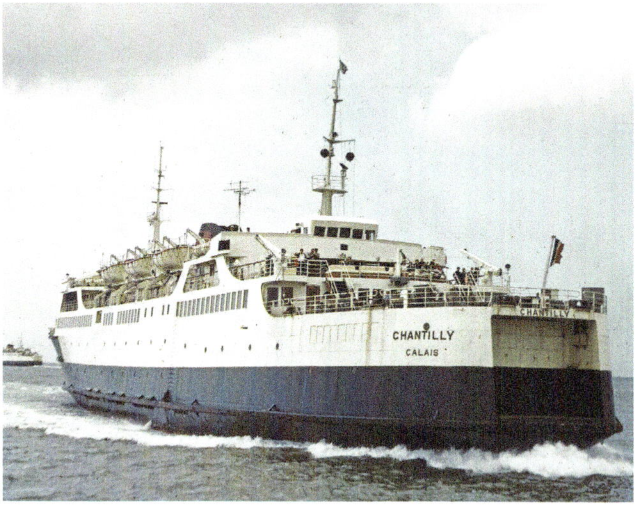

Chantilly (1965, 3,400 grt).

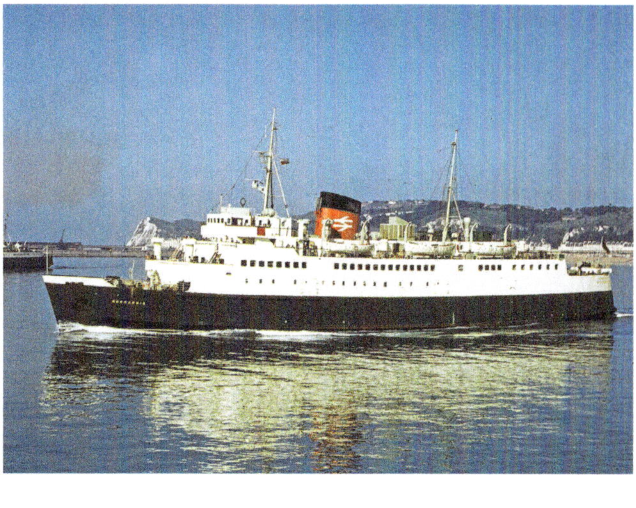

Normannia (1952, 3,543 grt) and *Lord Warden* (1952, 3,333 grt) at Dover.

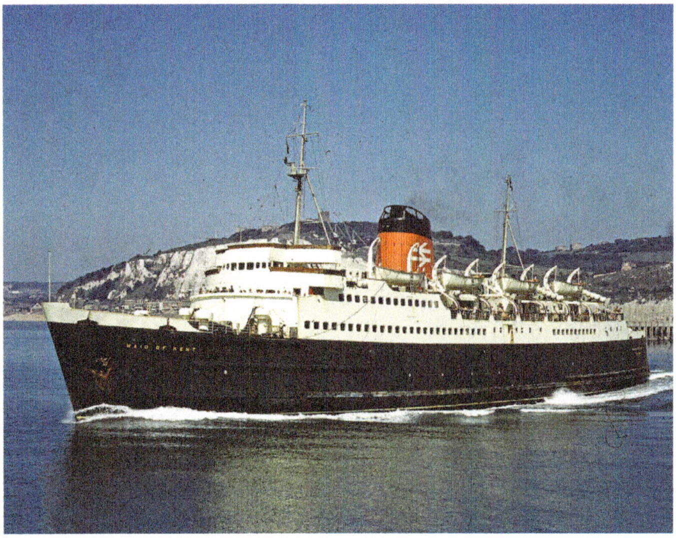

***Maid of Kent*, 1959, 4,413 grt. 113.7 x 18.4 metres. 20 knots.**
b. William Denny & Brothers Limited, Dumbarton. Yard No. 1492. Twin screw, two Pametrada turbines, 11,500 SHP, two Babcock & Wilcox boilers by builder. British Transport Commission, Southern Region.

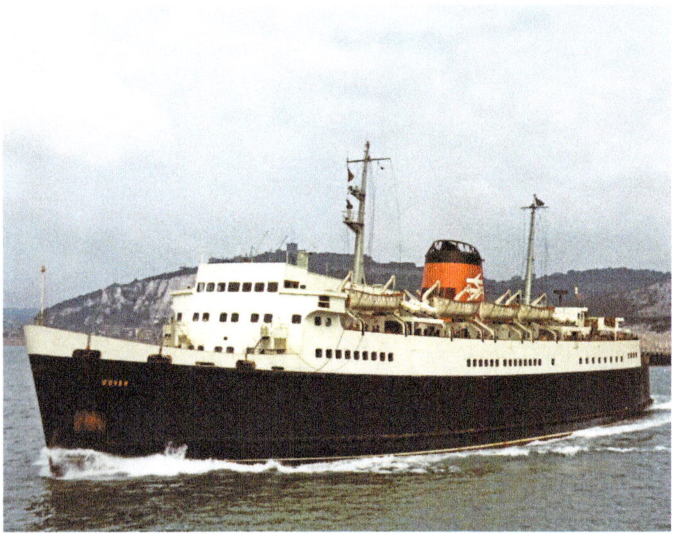

***Dover*, 1965, 3,602 grt. 112.47 x 16.76 x 10.52 metres. 19½ knots.**
b. Swan, Hunter & Wigham Richardson Limited, Newcastle. Twin screw, two turbines, 12,000 BHP, two boilers by Wallsend Slipway & Engineering Company. British Transport Commission, Southern Region.

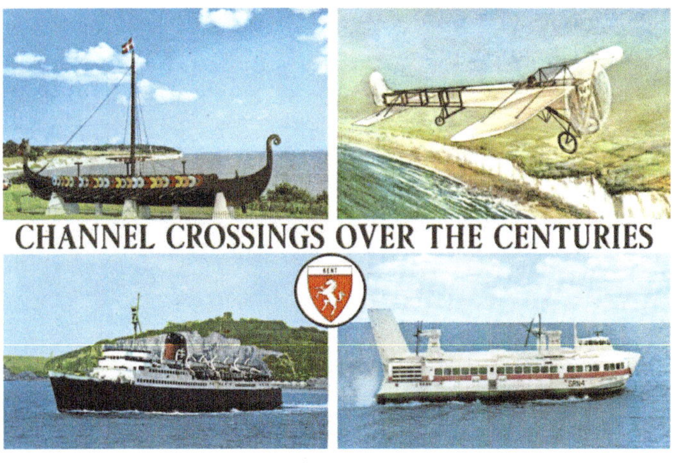

'Channel crossings over the centuries' postcard.

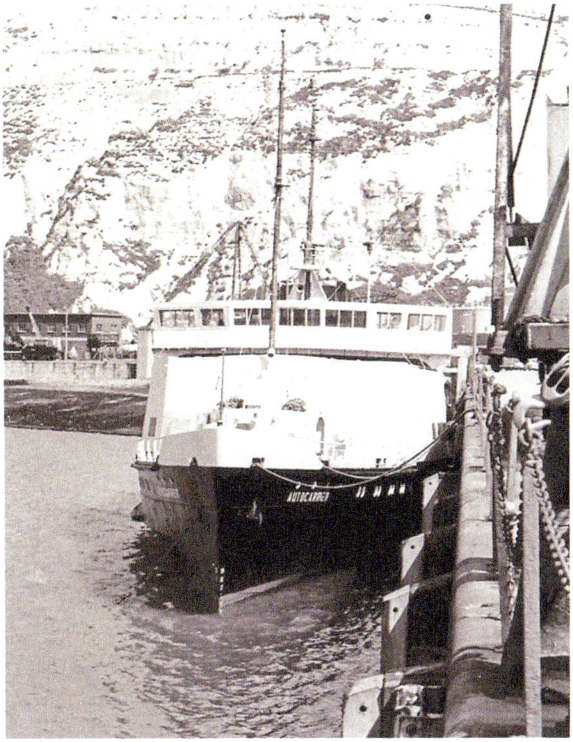

***Autocarrier*, 1948, 1,851 grt.**
87.99 x 16.1 metres.
b. William Denny & Brothers, Dumbarton. Two twelve-cylinder, Sulzer, two-stroke single acting diesels.

She was built as *Royal Sovereign* for the General Steam Navigation Company to operate coastal cruises from the Thames and across the Channel to France. In 1967 she was purchased by the Stanhope Shipping Company (Townsend Ferries) and was rebuilt as a roll-on/roll-off vessel by Verschure & Company at Amsterdam, being renamed *Autocarrier*. In service at Dover until she was sold, she left the port on 15 October 1973 for Italy as the *Ischia*. She was broken up at Aliaga in 2008.

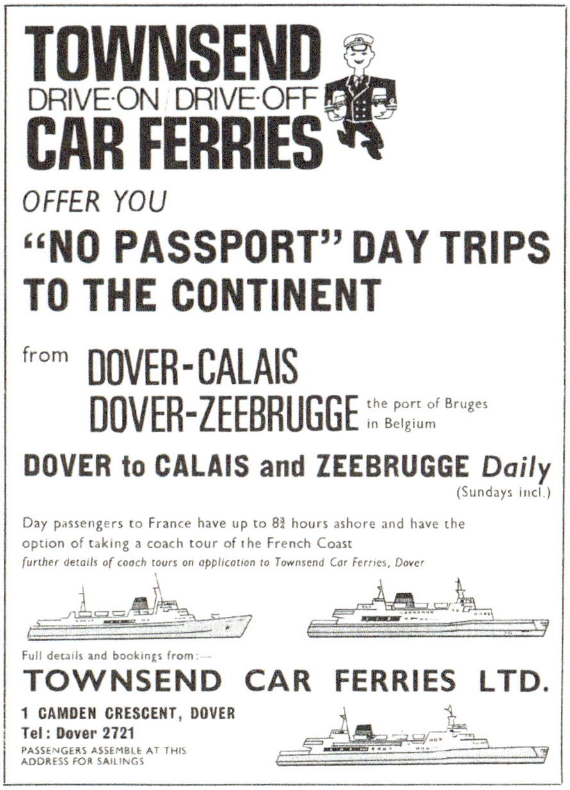

Townsend Car Ferries' '"No passport" day trips to the Continent' leaflet for 1969.

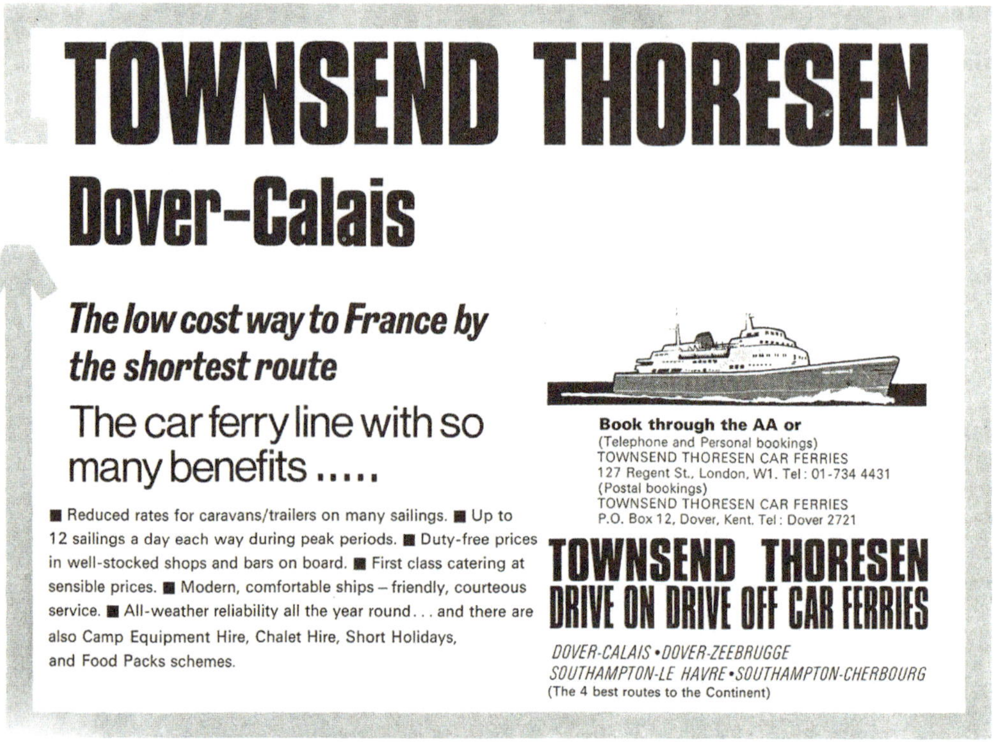

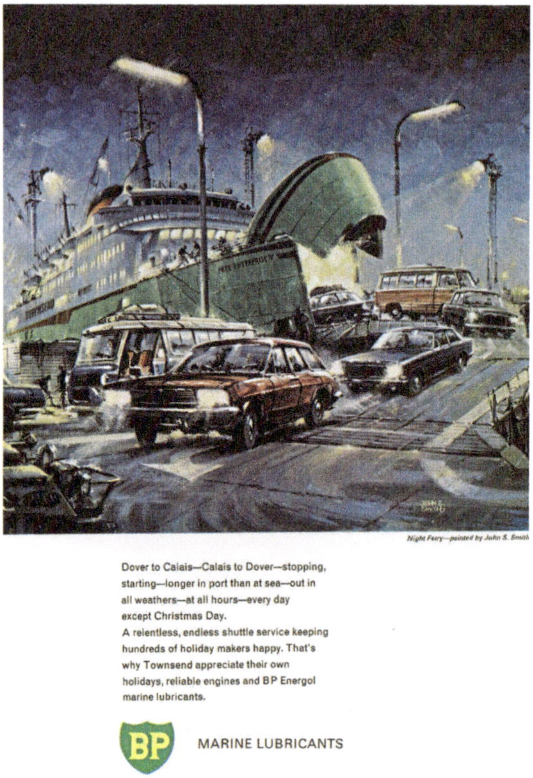

Above: A Townsend Thoresen advertisement for 1970.

Left: A BP advertisement for 1969.

Right: A Dover–Ostend advertisement for 1970.

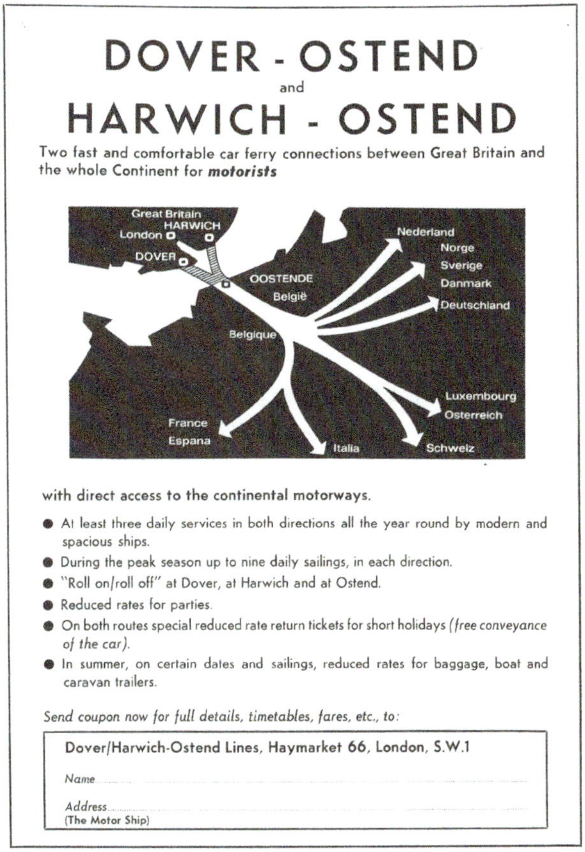

Below: *Free Enterprise* (1962, 2,607 grt) and *Chantilly* (1966, 3,400 grt) at Calais.

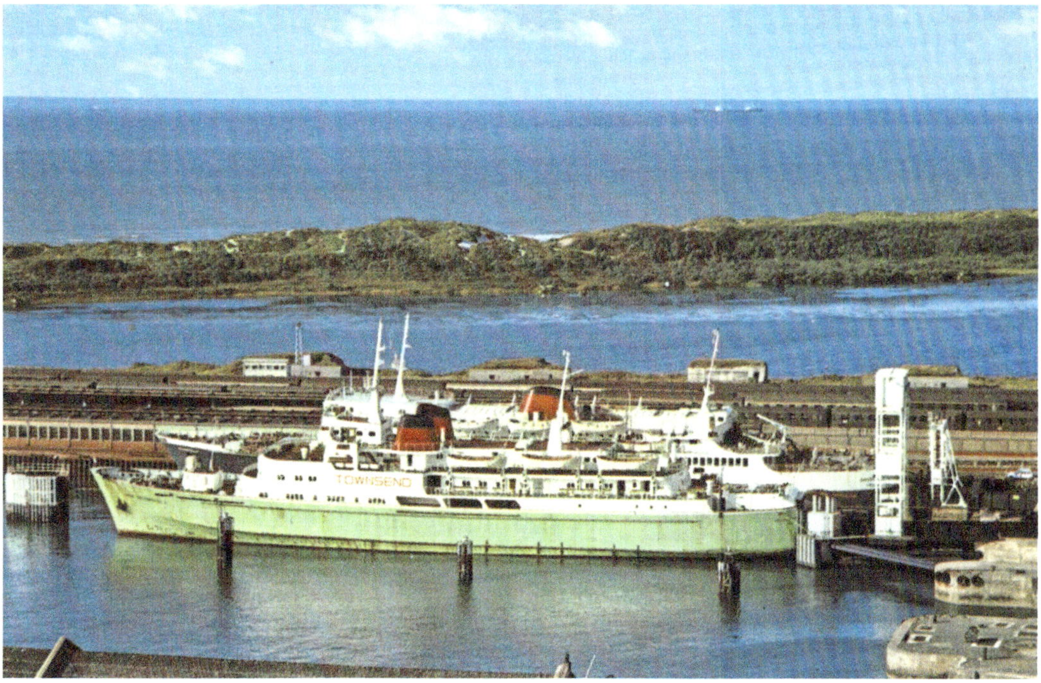

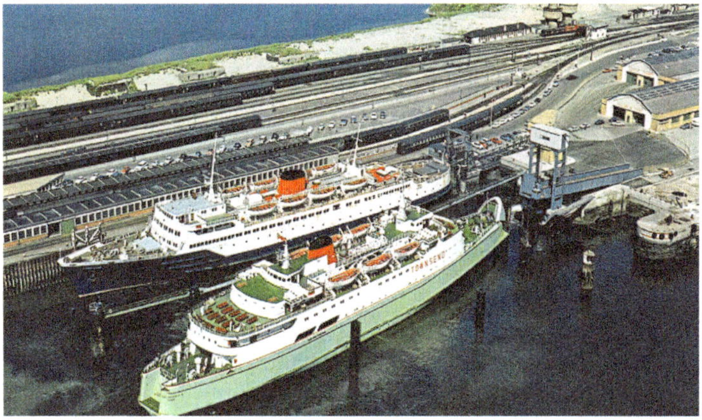

Above: *Compiègne* (1958, 3,467 grt) and *Free Enterprise III* (1966, 4,657 grt).

Below: _Vortigern_, 1969, 4,371 grt. 114.61 x 19.23 metres. 19½ knots.
b. Swan Hunter Shipbuilding Limited, Wallsend, Newcastle. Yard No. 10. Twin controllable screw, oil, two sixteen-cylinder Pielstick Vee engines, 4s.sa by Crossley Premier Engineering Company. British Railways Board.

She entered service on 31 July 1969 on the Dover–Boulogne route. In June 1970 she was struck and holed by a submerged object in the Channel and was relieved by *Maid of Kent* when she was sent to Southampton for repairs. In April 1978 she undertook a major overhaul at Smith's Dock, Middlesbrough, wherein an area was converted into a new 342-seat lounge. On 1 January 1979 she was transferred to Sealink UK Limited, operating on the Folkestone–Boulogne route.

At 05.24 on 4 March 1982, on a voyage from Folkestone to Ostend, she was stranded across a stone groyne near Ostend on a falling tide. She was re-floated two days later and entered dry dock at Amsterdam for repairs, which cost over £1 million. On 2 July she collided with Folkestone Pier and was sent to Dunkirk for repairs.

On 27 July 1984 she was taken over by Sea Containers Limited, Sealink British Ferries. She was arrested by the Admiralty Marshal at Portsmouth on 12 November over unpaid redundancy payments for members of the National Union of Seamen and was released the following day. On 10 January 1987 she relieved *St Brendan* at Fishguard and was chartered to Townsend–Thoresen in April for sixty days. On 1 June she was laid up on the River Fal briefly, but was brought into service once more, replacing *Versailles* and *Hengist*. The following year she replaced *Stena Sailer* at Holyhead and was sold to Lindos Shipping SA., of Piraeus, becoming *Milos Express* on 1 April. She was renamed *Express Milos* in 2000, *Nissos Lemnos* in 2003 and *Limon* in 2005. She was beached at Alang on 28 January 2005 and broken up.

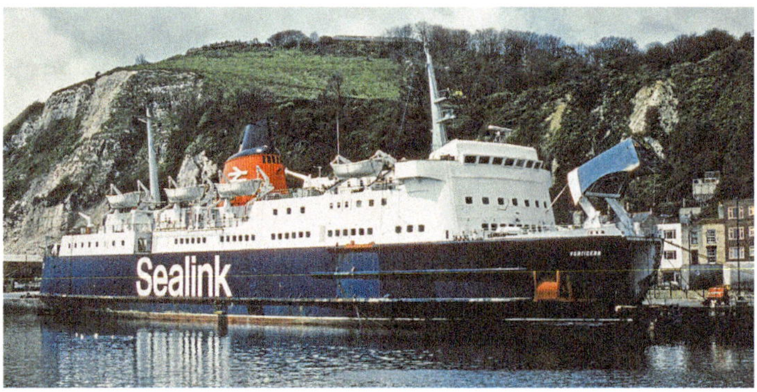

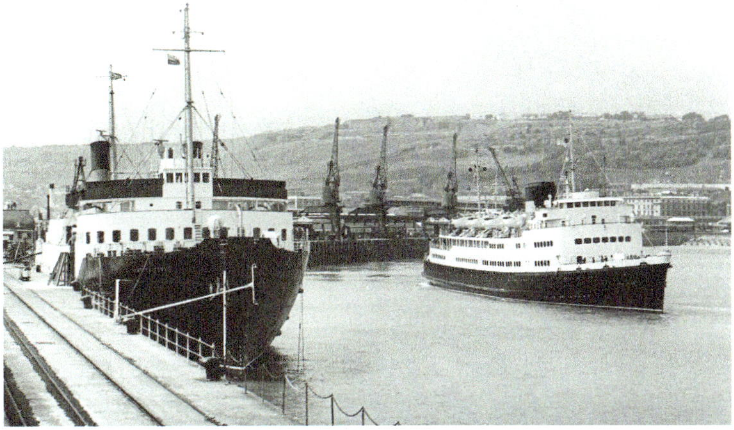

Hampton Ferry (1934, 2,839 grt) and *Reine Astrid* (1958, 3,795 grt).

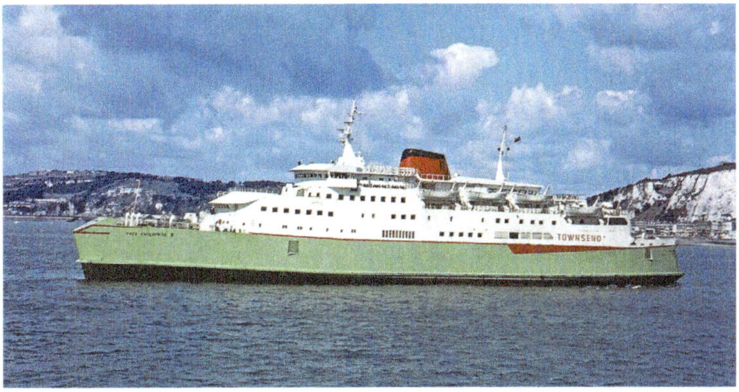

Free Enterprise V (1970, 5,044 grt).

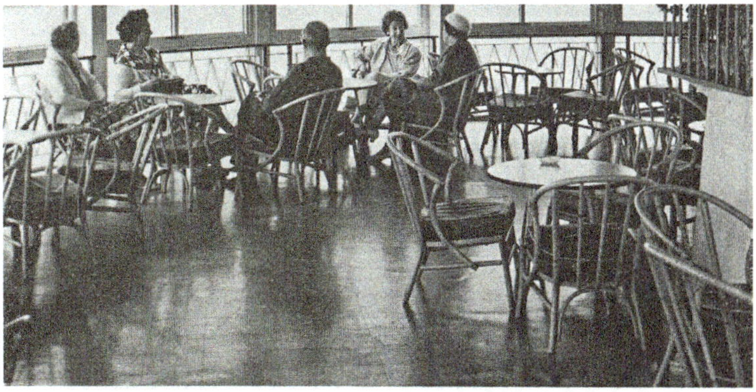

Prince of Wales Pier, Dover, in 1969.

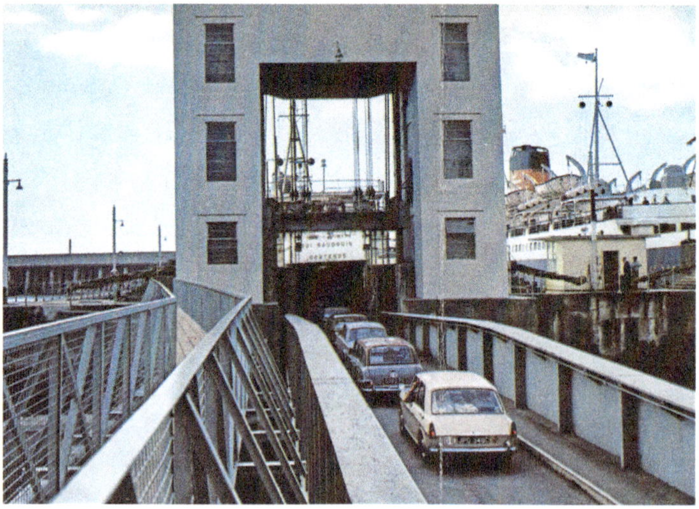

Left: Cars loading onto *Roi Baudouin* (1965, 3,241 grt) and *Maid of Kent* (1959, 4,413 grt).

Below: Dover brochures.

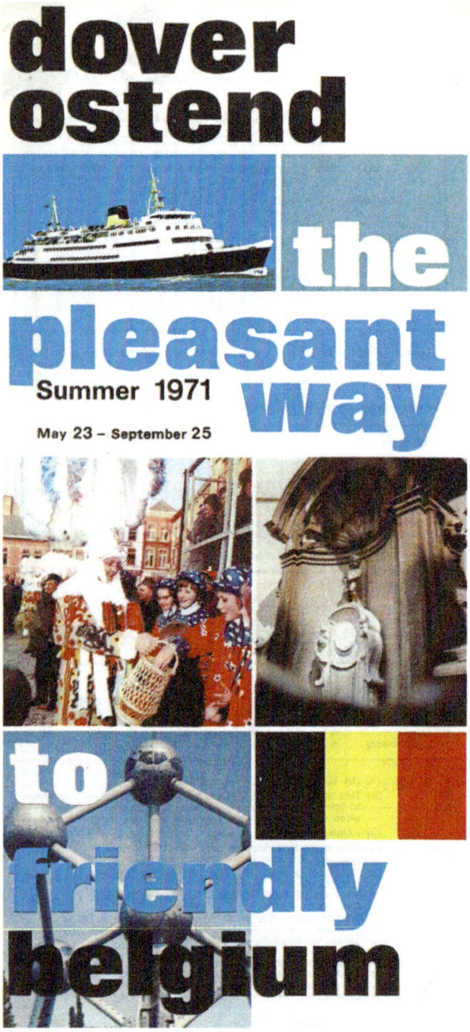

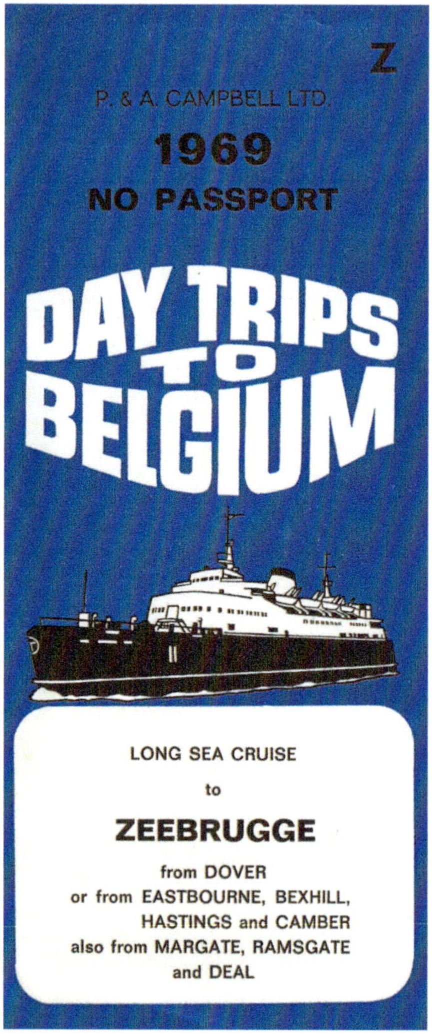

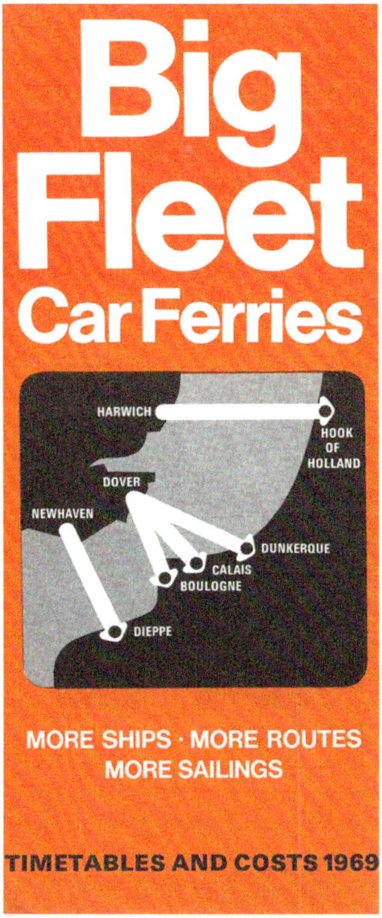

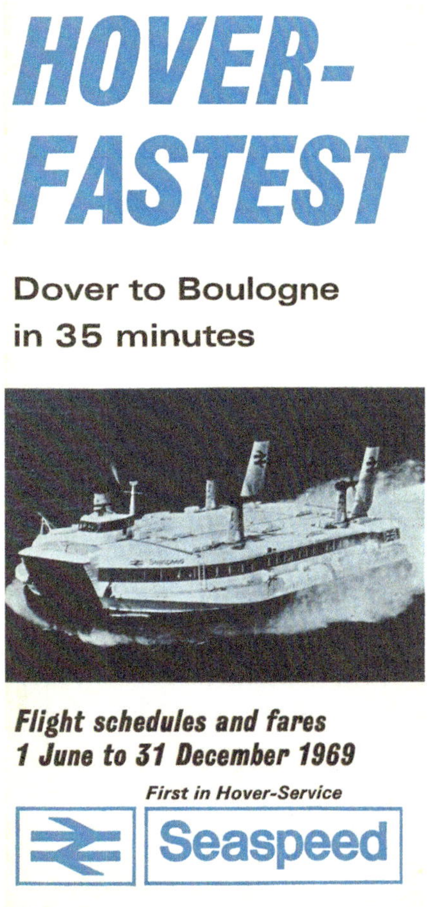

Right: Dover brochures.

Below: The launch of *Free Enterprise III* at the yard of NV Werf Gusto, Schiedam, on 14 May 1966.

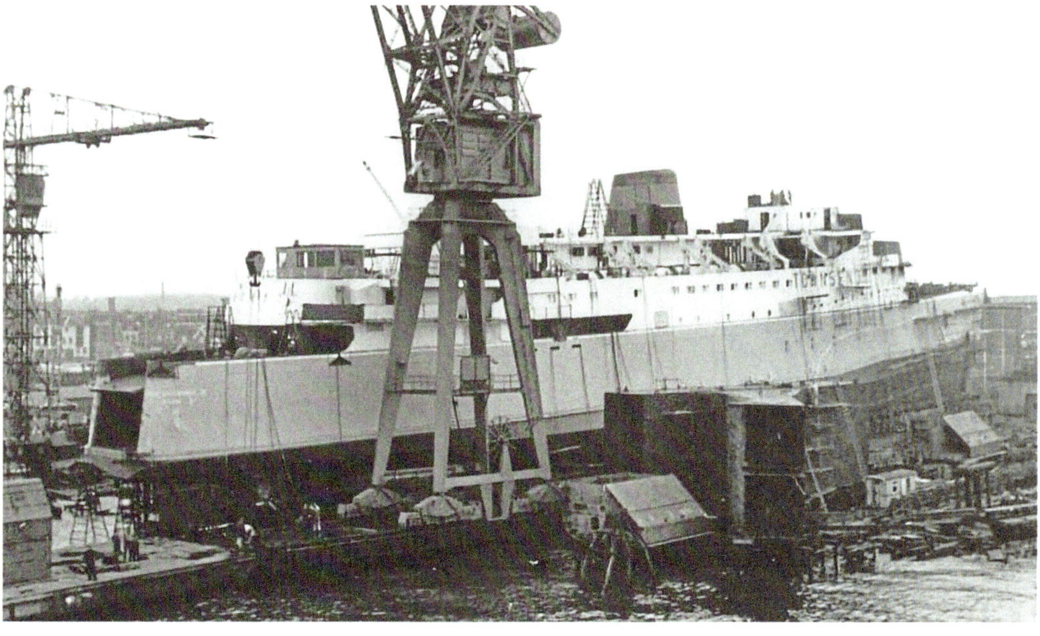

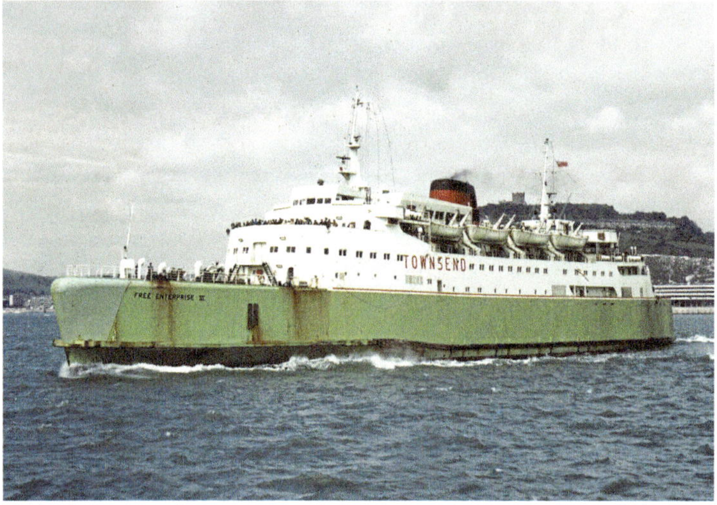

Free Enterprise III, **1966, 4,657 grt. 117.51 x 19.08 metres. 20 knots.**
b. NV Werf Gusto, Schiedam, Holland. Yard No. 324/c0538. Two twelve-cylinder and two six-cylinder Smit-MAN four-stroke single acting diesels, with hydraulic coupling geared to two screw shafts. Townsend Brothers, Ferries Limited.

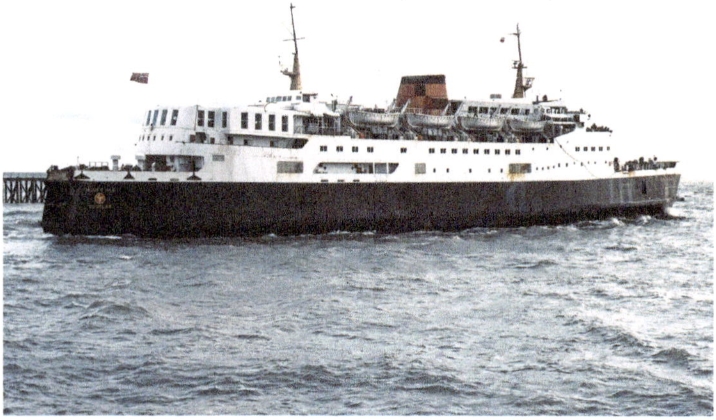

Free Enterprise III became *Mona's Isle* on 24 October 1984.

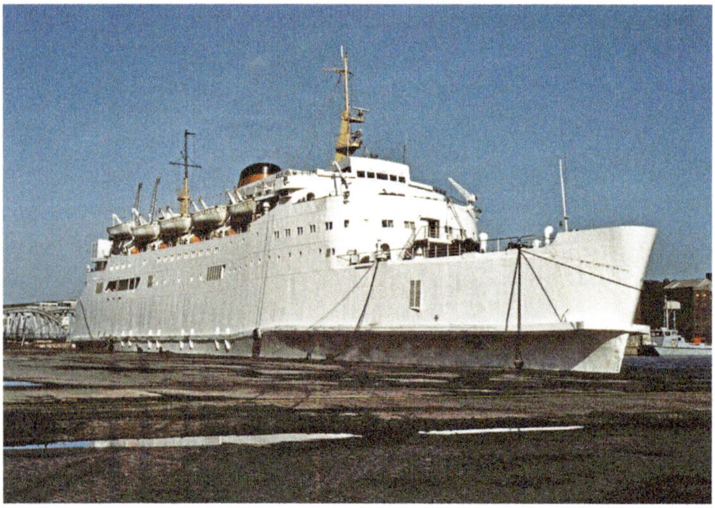

Mona's Isle was renamed *Al Fahad* on 25 March 1986 at Birkenhead.

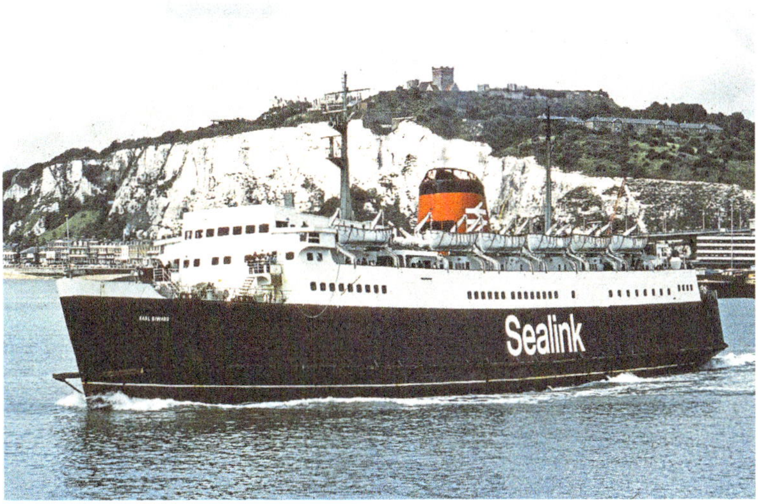

Dover became *Earl Siward* in 1977.

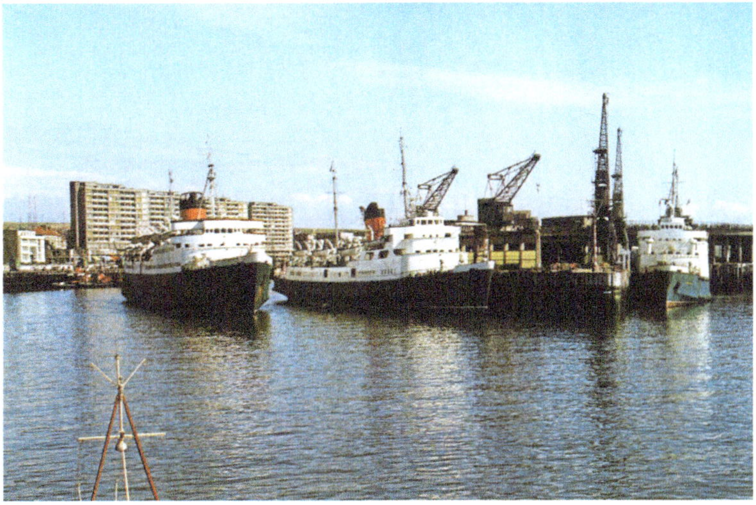

Cross-channel vessels at Boulogne.

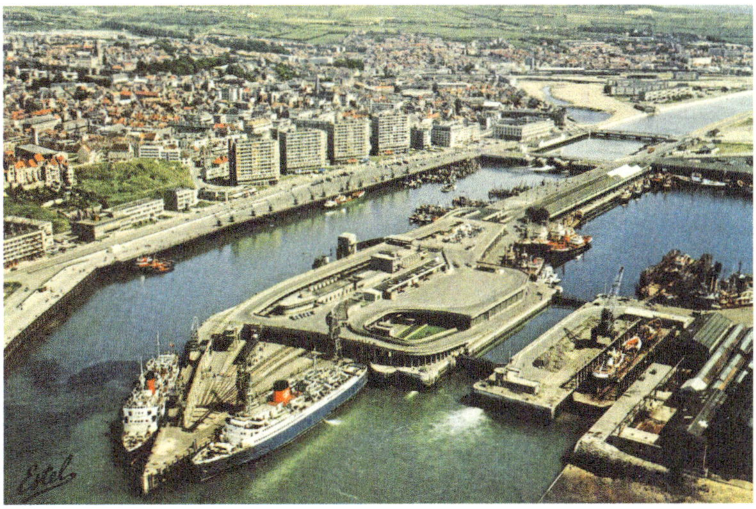

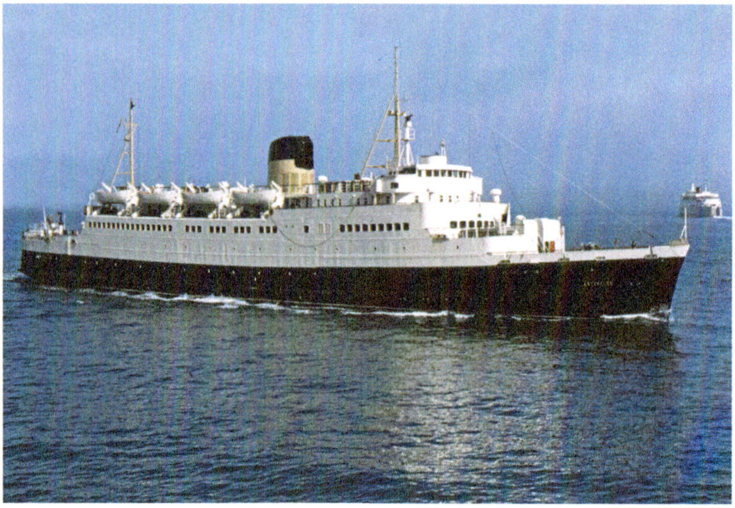

Artevelde (1959, 2,812 grt).

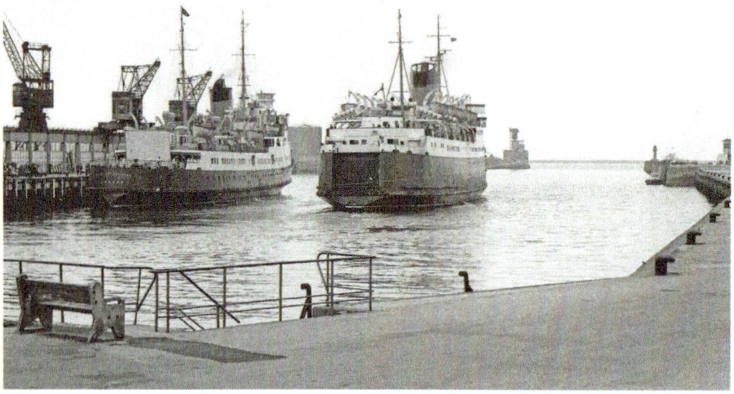

Maid of Orleans (1949, 3,776 grt) and *Maid of Kent* (1959, 4,413 grt).

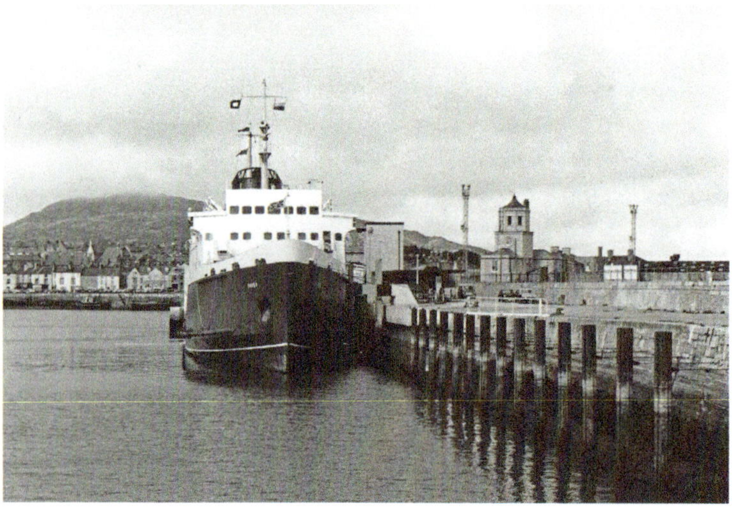

Dover (1965, 3,602) grt) covers at Holyhead while *Holyhead Ferry I* (1965, 3,879 grt) is away having her annual overhaul.

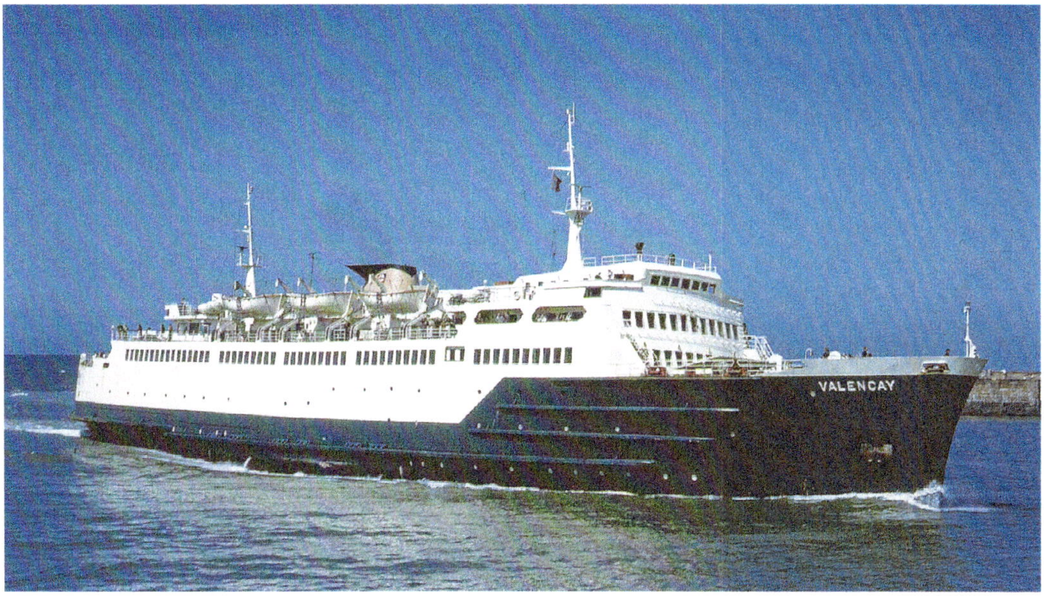

Above: *Valencay*, 1965, 3,430 grt. 105 x 17.1 metres.
b. Atlantique (Penhoët-Loire), St Nazaire, France. Yard No. E23. Twin reversible screws, two Pielstick Vee oil, two six-cylinder, 12,380 BHP by Les Chantiers de L'Atlantique. Soc. Nationale des Chemins de Fer Français.

She was launched on 6 February 1965 to be employed on cross-channel services from France to England. She was sold in 1984, becoming *Eptanisos*. She became *Pollux* in 2000 and then *Pollux I* in 2003. She was broken up at Gadani Beach in 2004.

Below: *Compiègne* (1958, 3,467 grt) reverses into her berth in Dover Harbour.

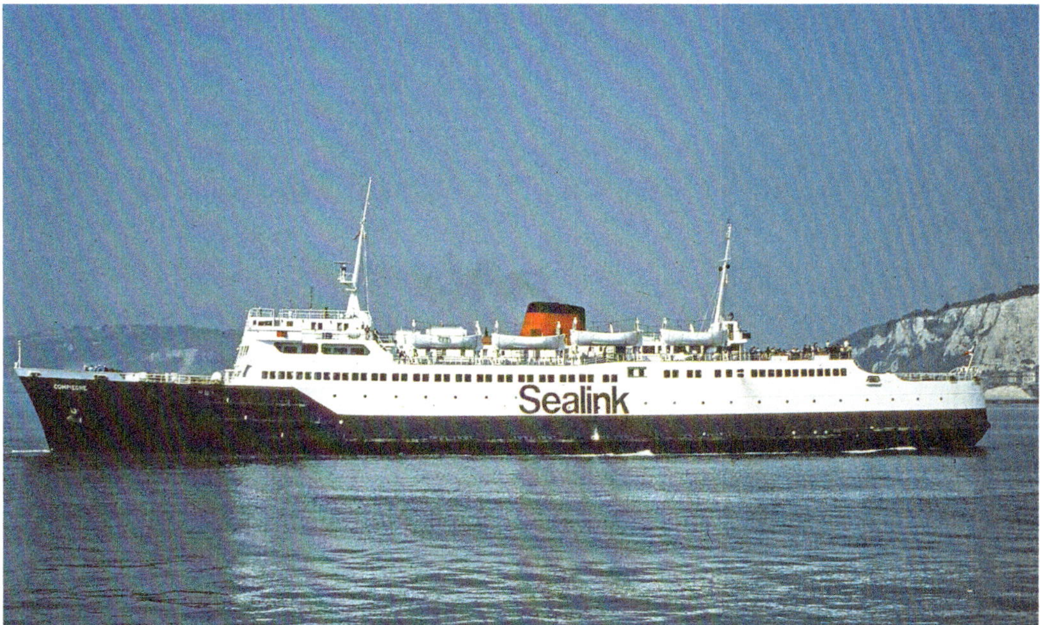

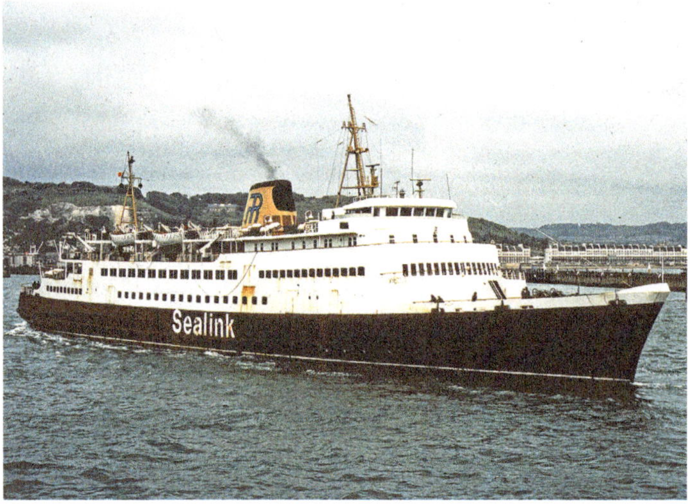

Prinses Paola (1966, 3,388 grt) at Dover.

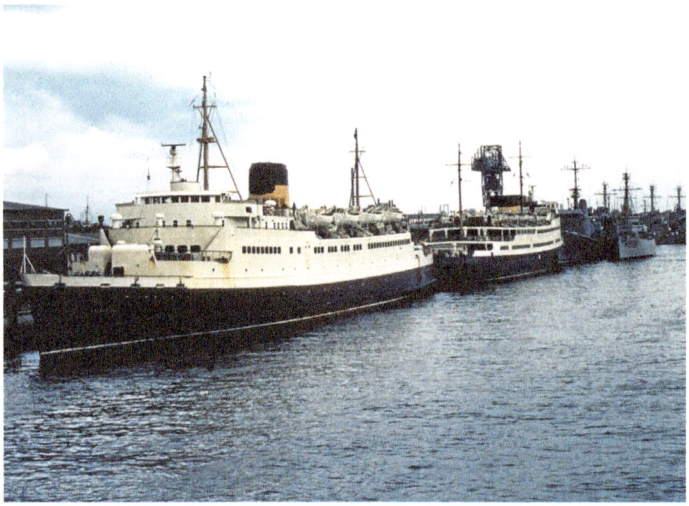

***Artevelde*, 1959, 2,812 grt. 116.9 x 16 metres. 21 knots.**

b. Cockerill-Ougree, Hoboken. Yard No. 794. Belgium Marine Administration.

Launched on 1 February 1958 for cross-channel services from Belgium to England, she was sold in 1976, becoming *Aegeon*, and suffered a serious fire at Drapetzona on 19 February 1996. She was beached and capsized at Atalanti Island.

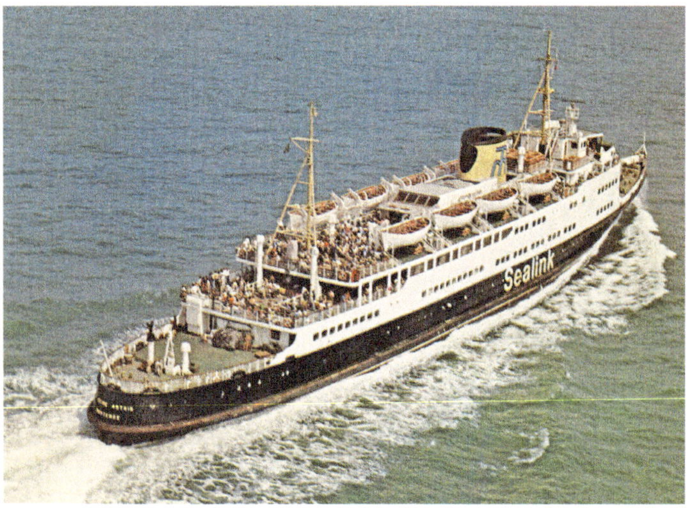

***Reine Astrid*, 1958, 3,795 grt. 114 x 15.2 metres. 23 knots.**

b. Cockerill-Ougree, Hoboken. Yard No. 785. Belgium Marine Administration.

Koningen Fabiola, 1962, 4,727 grt. 117 x 15.84 metres. 20 knots.
b. J. Boel & Zonen Shipyard, Temse, Belgium. Belgian Marine Administration.

She was named after the Queen of Belgium and was the first vessel ordered from Boel at Temse. She operated on Belgian Marine's Ostend–Dover passenger and car ferry service. She was sold and broken up in 2004.

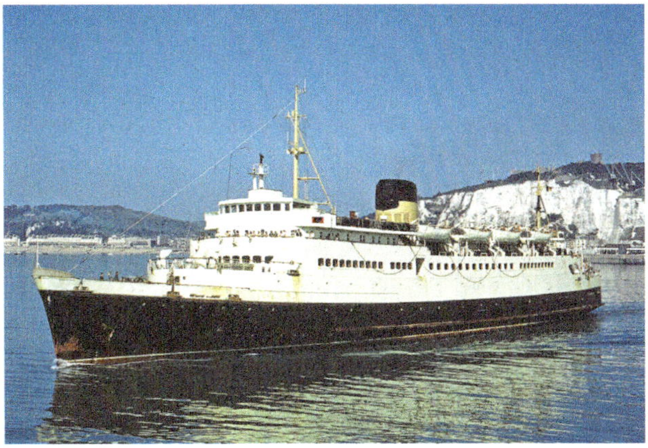

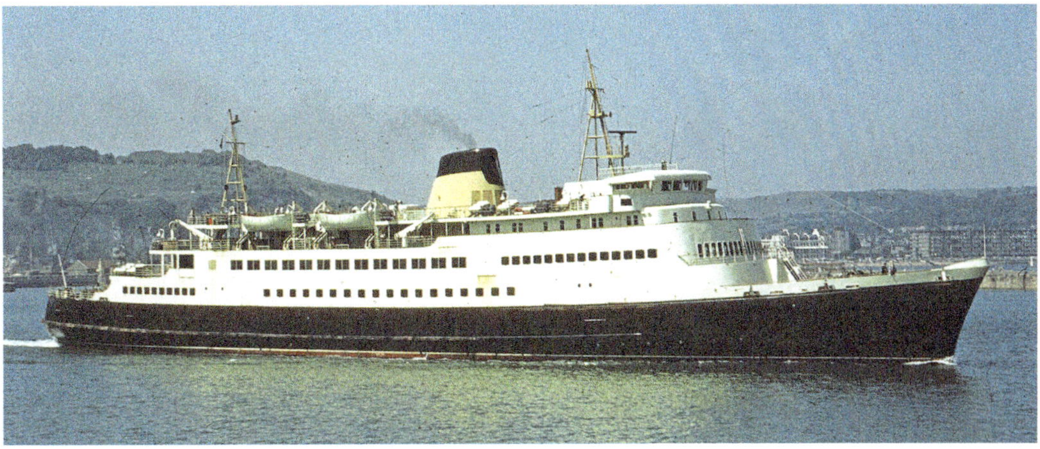

Prinses Paola (1966, 3,388 grt).

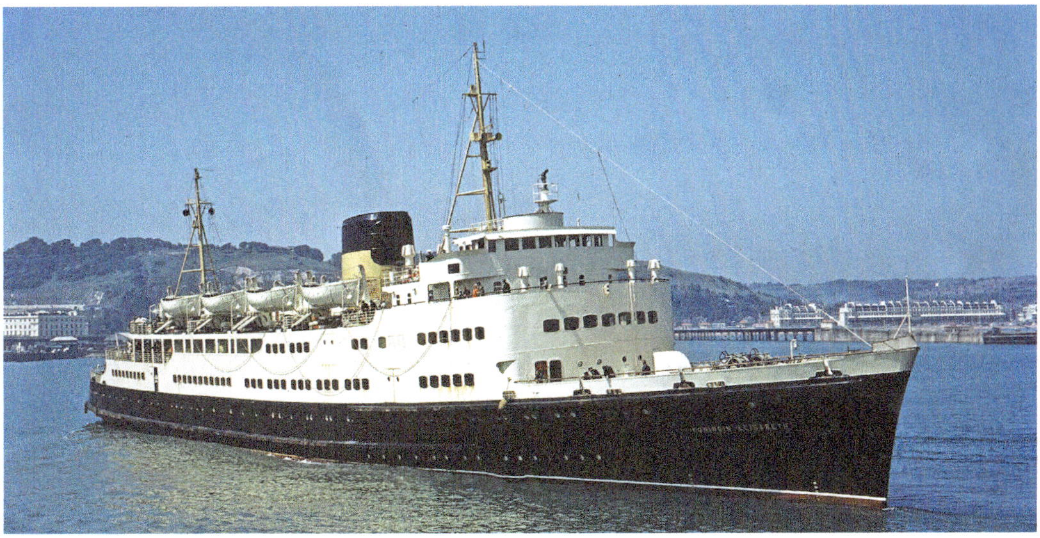

Koningin Elisabeth (1956, 3,389 grt) at Dover.

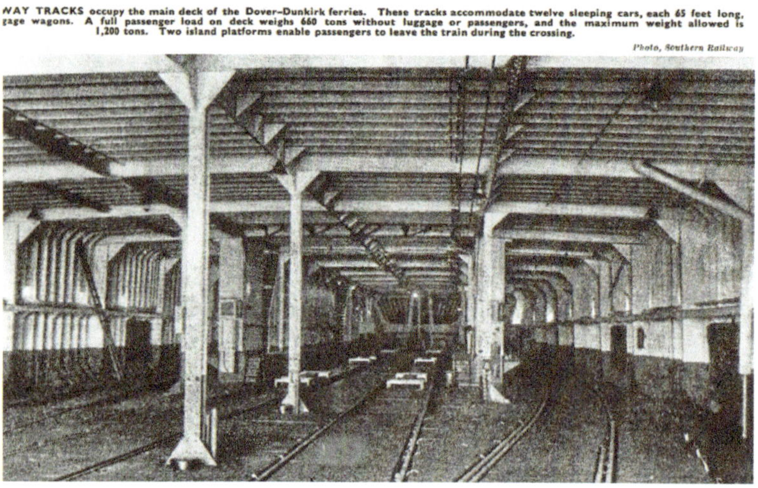

The main deck of the Dover–Dunkirk train ferry. The tracks accommodated twelve sleeping cars, each of which were 65 feet long.

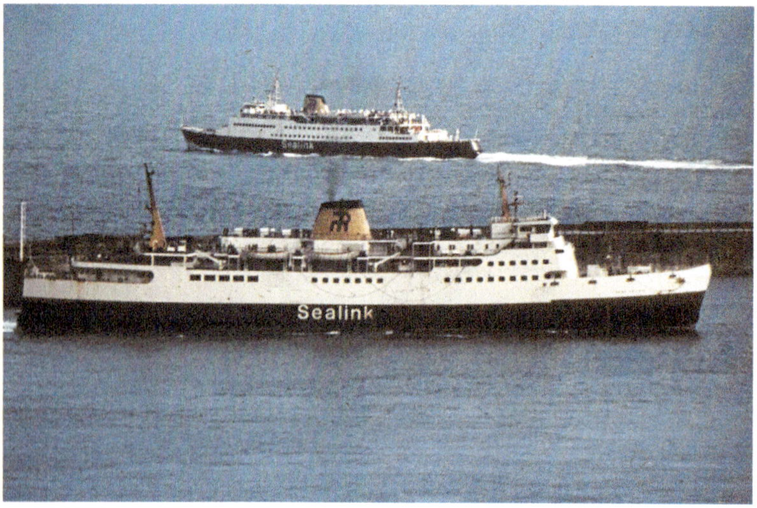

Prins Philippe (1973, 5,071 grt).

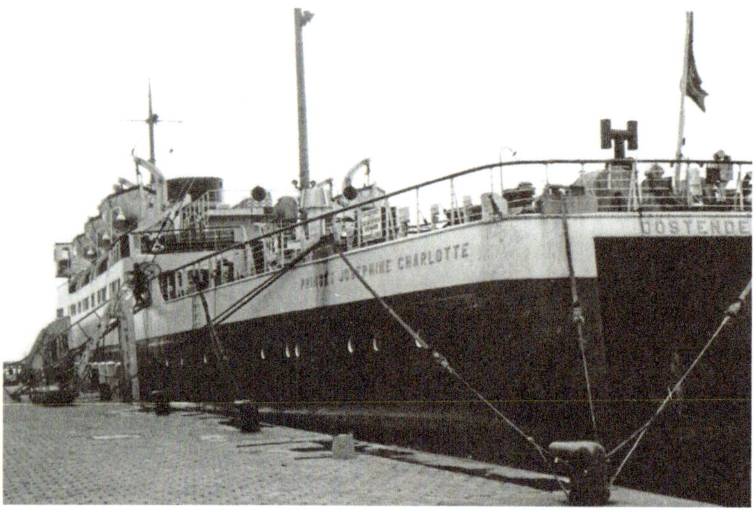

Princes Josephine Charlotte (2) (1949, 2,572 grt).

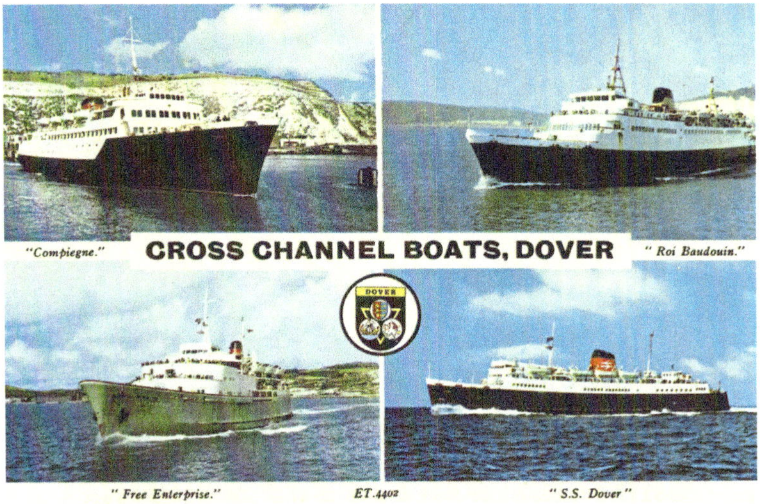

A cross-channel postcard for 1977.

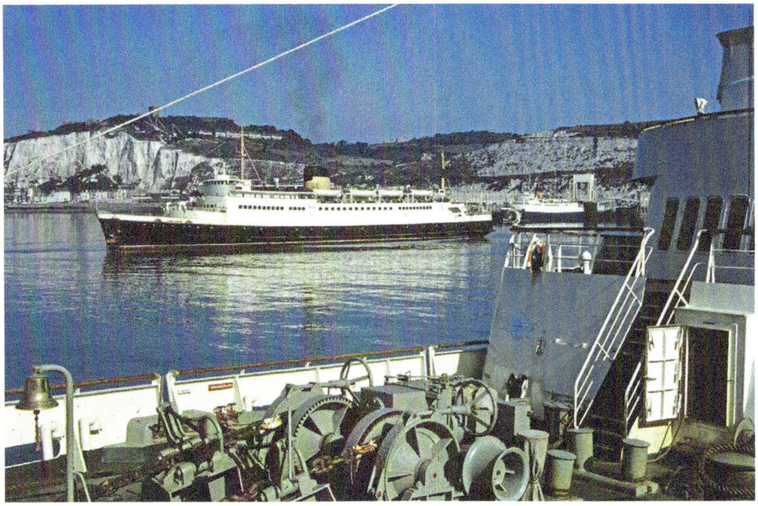

Koningen Fabiola (1962/ 4727 grt.)

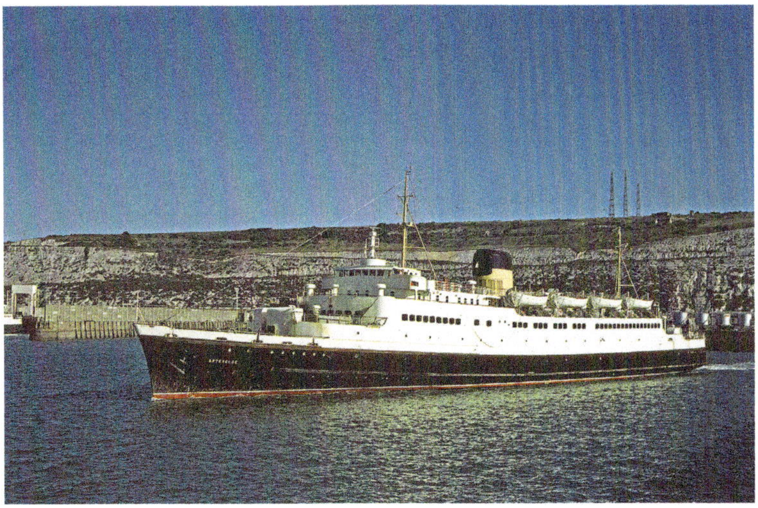

Artevelde (1959, 2,812 grt).

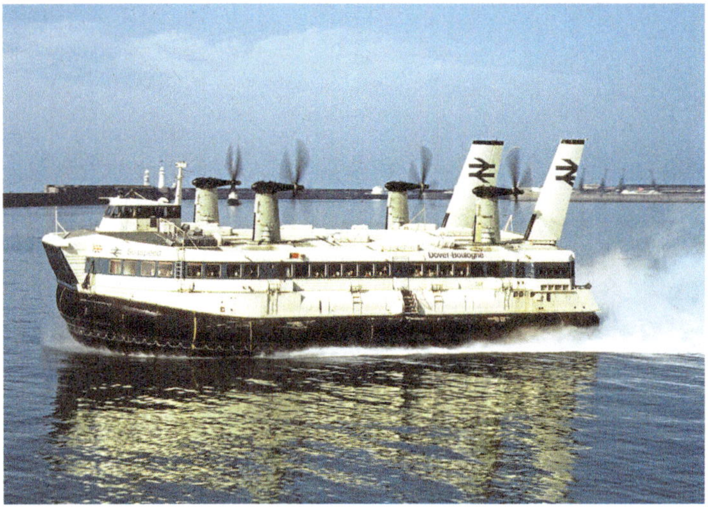

The *Princess Margaret* (1968, 280 grt) was built by the British Hovercraft Corporation Limited at East Cowes and was operated from Dover to Boulogne by Hoverspeed Limited. The company ceased operating in 2000 and the *Princess Margaret* and *Princess Anne* went to the Hovercraft Museum at Lee-on-the-Solent.

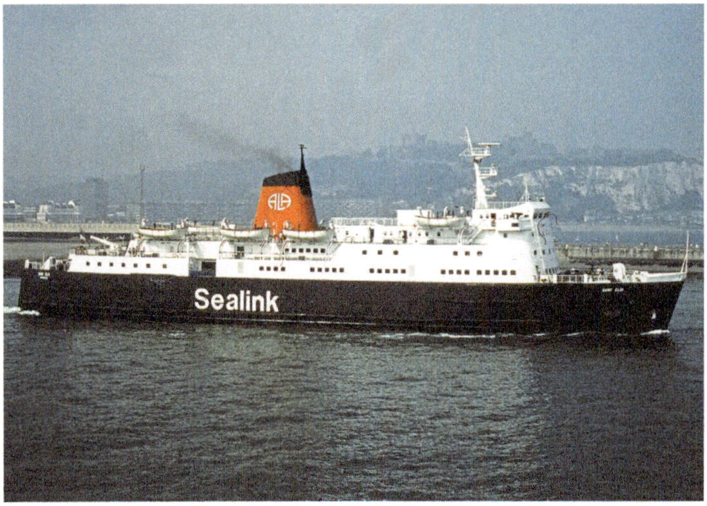

Saint Eloi (1975, 4,649 grt) at Dover.

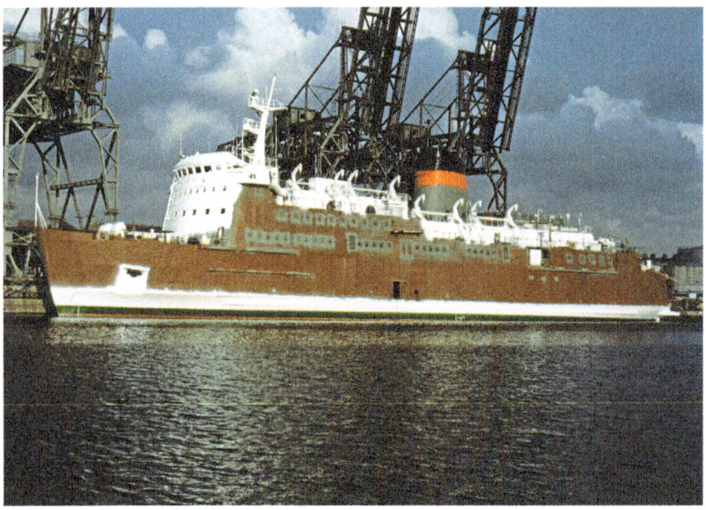

Saint Eloi became *King Orry* on 8 December 1990, operating on Irish Sea services for the Isle of Man Steam Packet Company Limited.

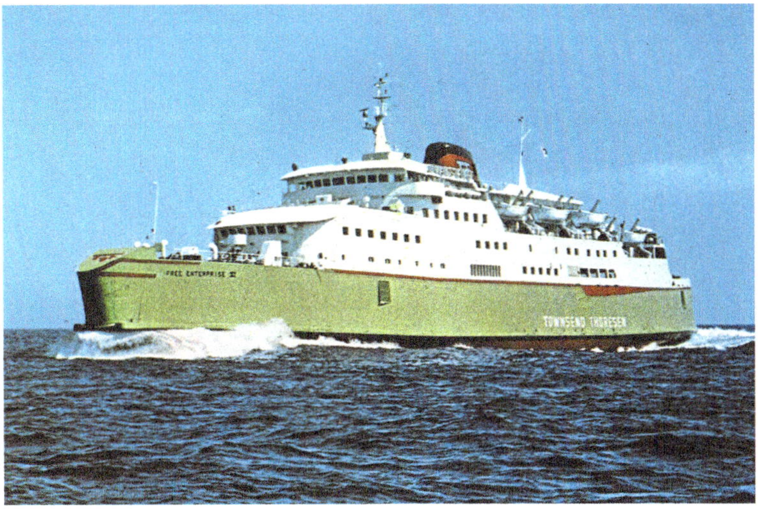

Free Enterprise VI (1972, 4,981 grt).

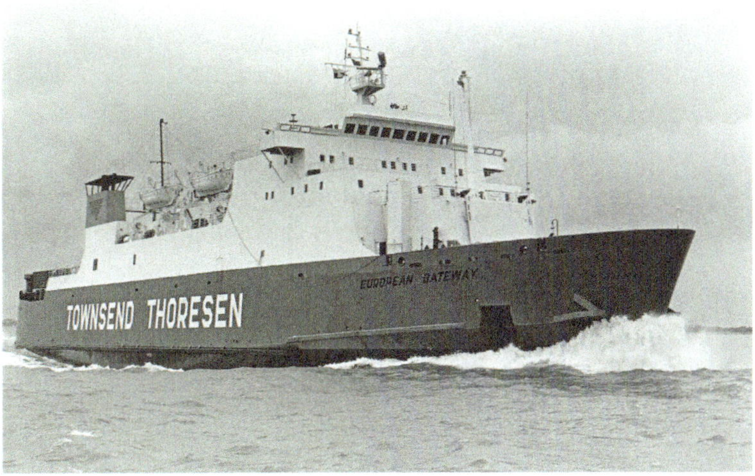

European Gateway (1975, 11,435 grt).

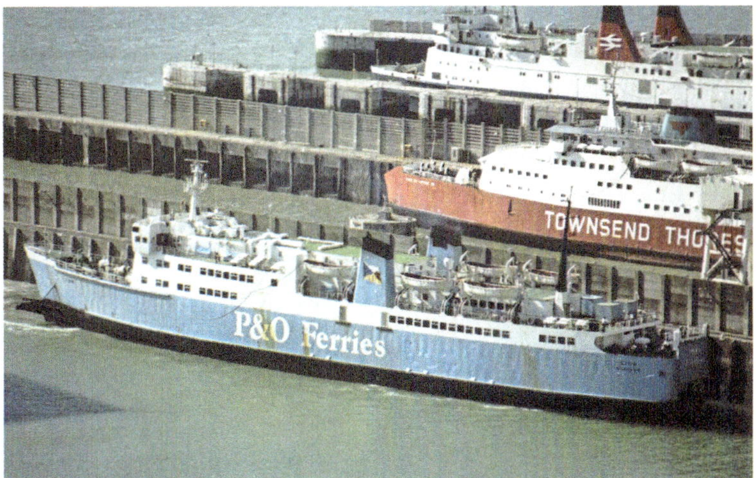

P&O Ferries' Dover–Boulogne service as operated by *Lion* (1967, 3,333 grt).

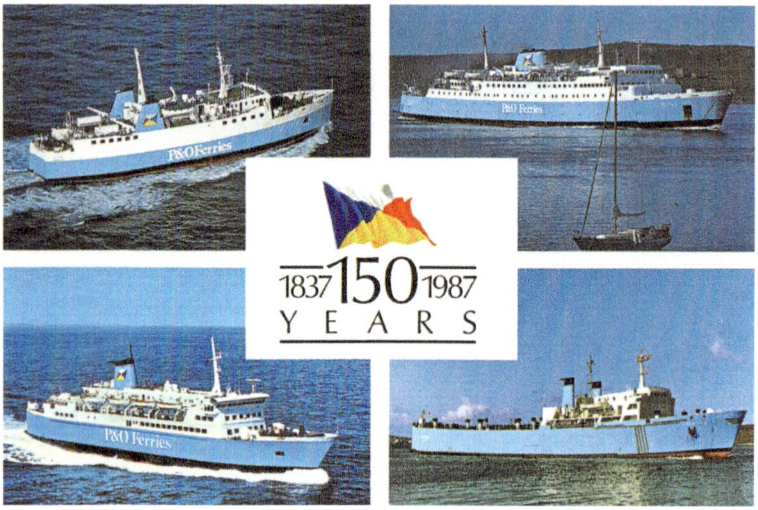

P&O 150 years postcard.

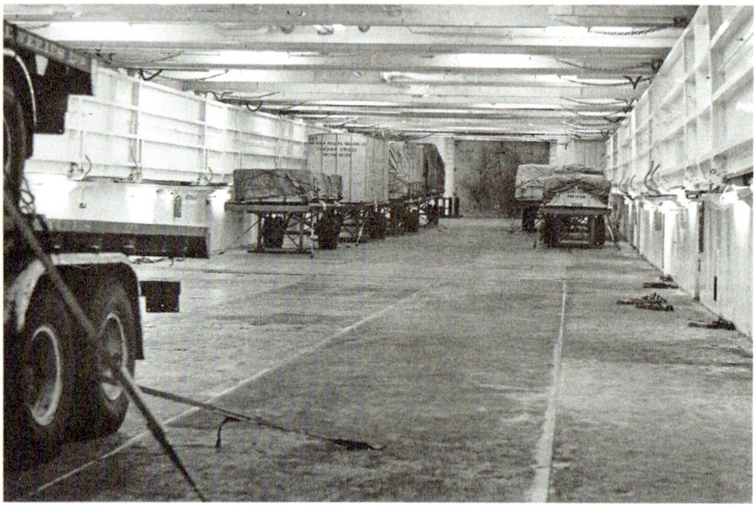

Car deck on P&O Ferries' *Lion*.

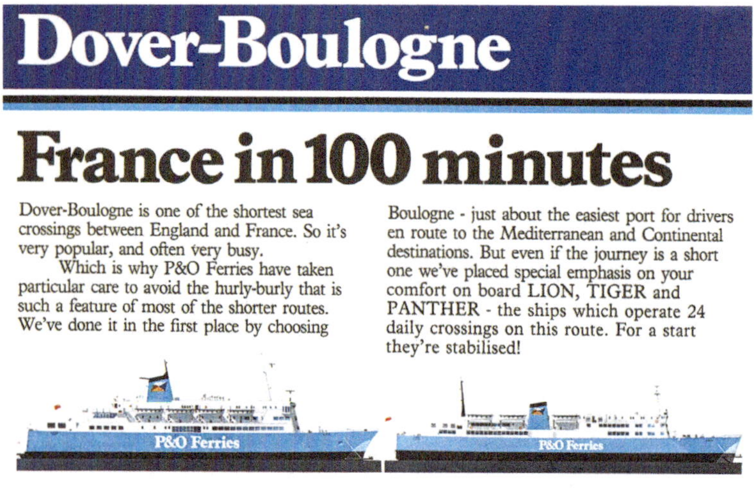

A P&O Dover–Boulogne advertisement for 1980.

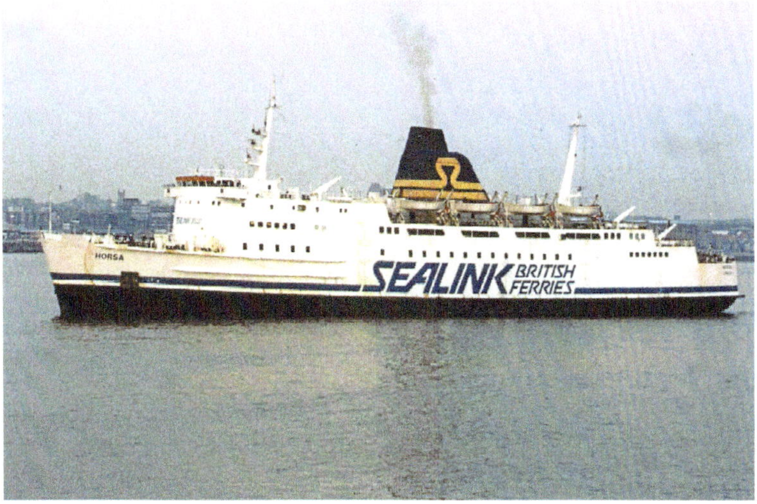

Sealink British Ferries' *Horsa* (1972, 5,590 grt).

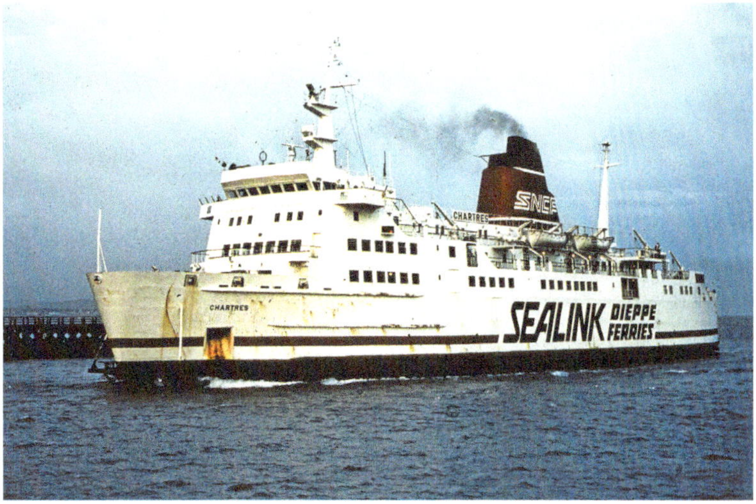

***Chartres*, 1973, 4,800 grt. 115.4 x 19.23 x 6.18 metres. 20½ knots.** b. Dubigeon-Normandie S A., Nantes. Twin screw, two sixteen-cylinder Pielstick Vee oil, 4s.sa, 16,000 BHP by Chantiers de l'Atlantique. Soc. Nationale des Chemins de Fer Français.

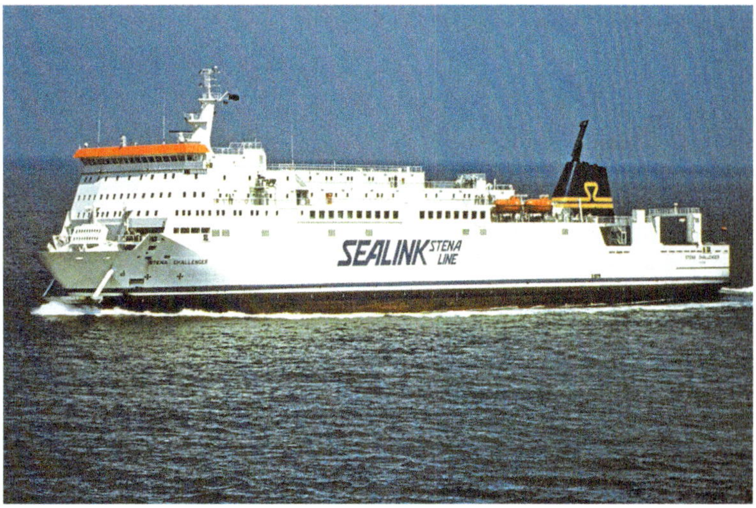

Stena Challenger (1991, 18,523 grt).

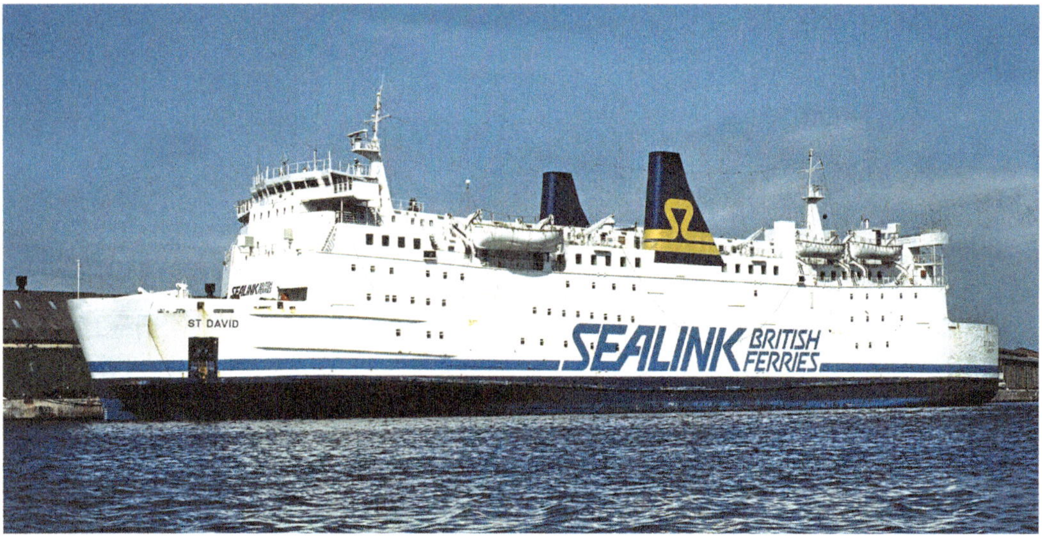

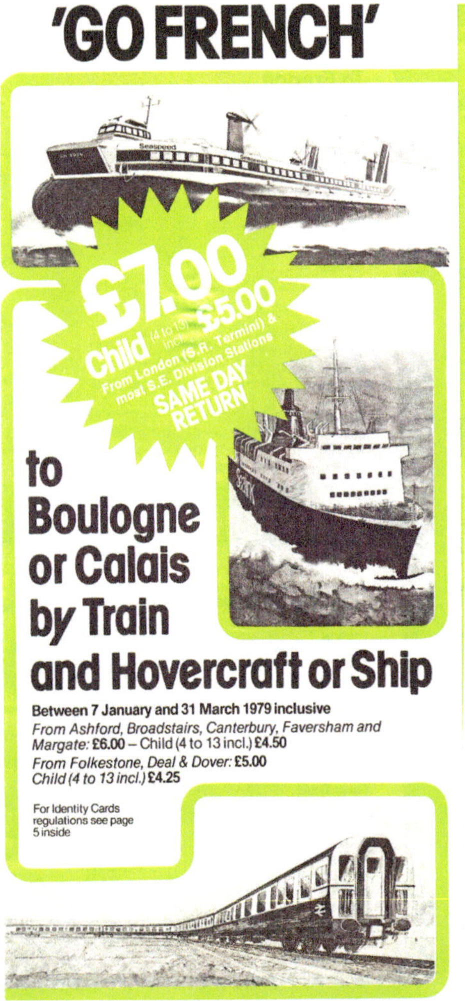

Above: *St David* (1981, 12,619 grt).

Left: A brochure for 1979.

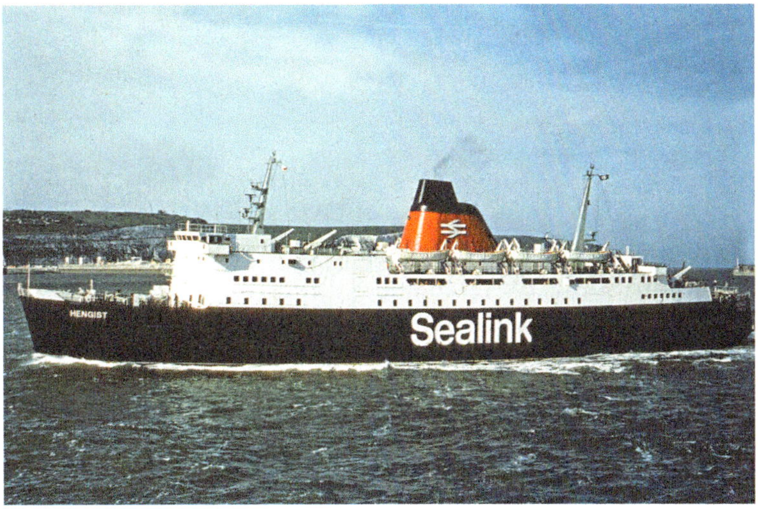

Hengist (1972, 5,590 grt).

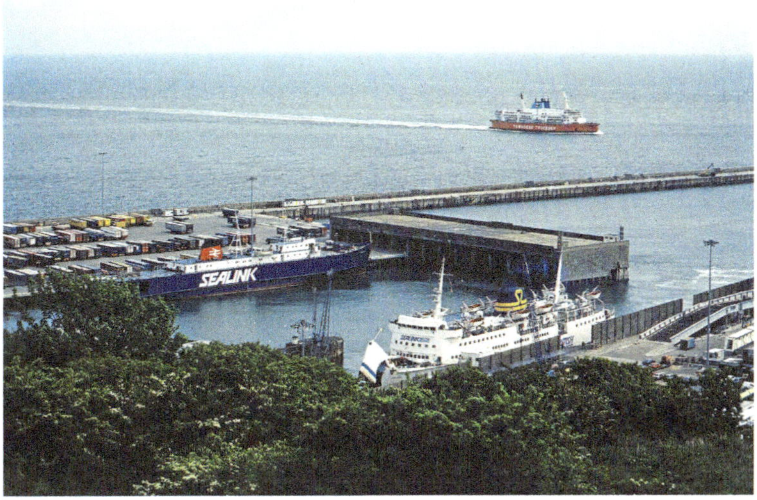

Dover Harbour.

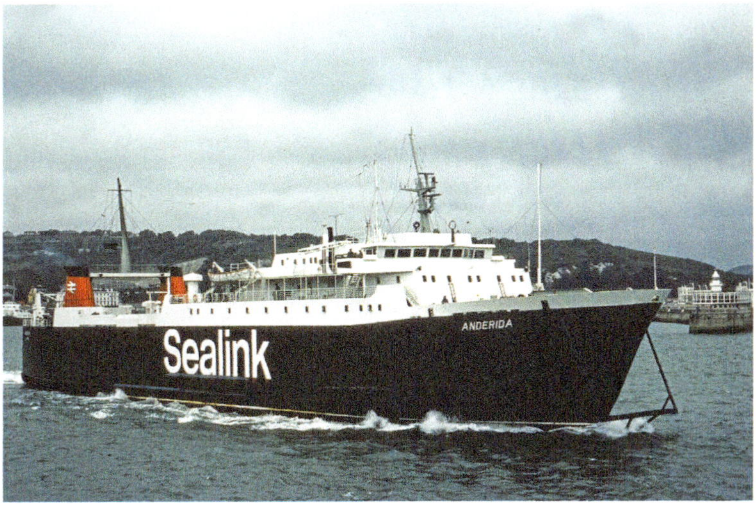

Anderida, 1972, 1,601 grt. 106 x 16.08 metres. 17 knots.
b. Trosvik Verksted A/S., Kristiansund. Yard No. 95. Sealink Limited.

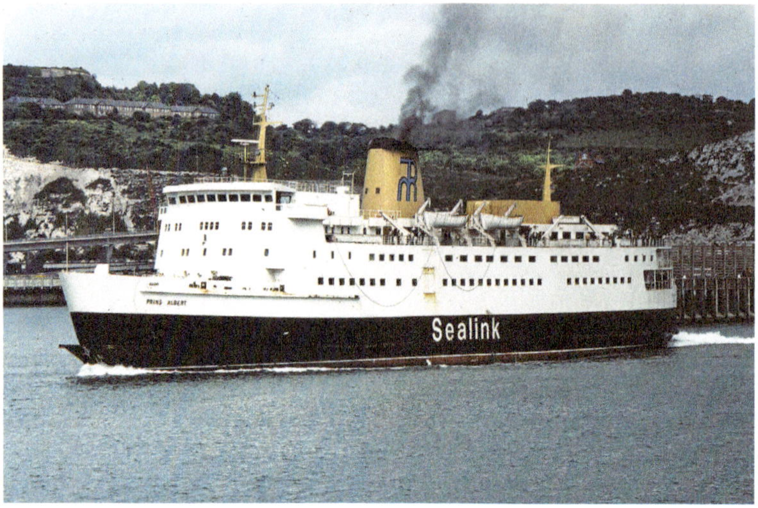

Prince Albert (1978, 6,019 grt).

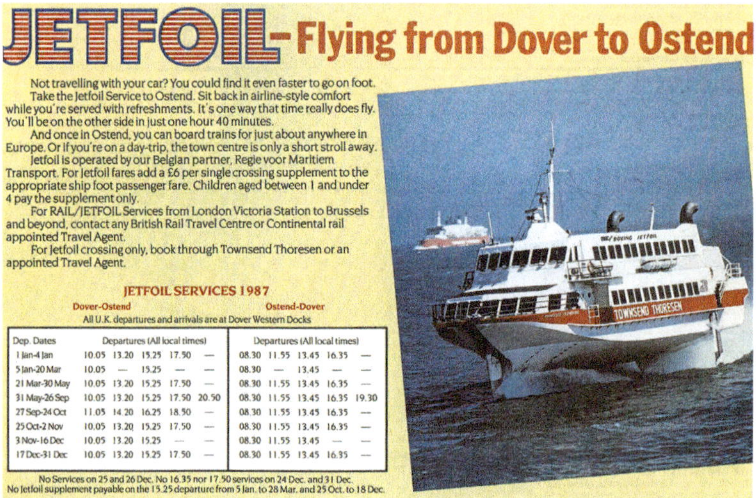

A Townsend Thoresen Jetfoil advertisement for 1987.

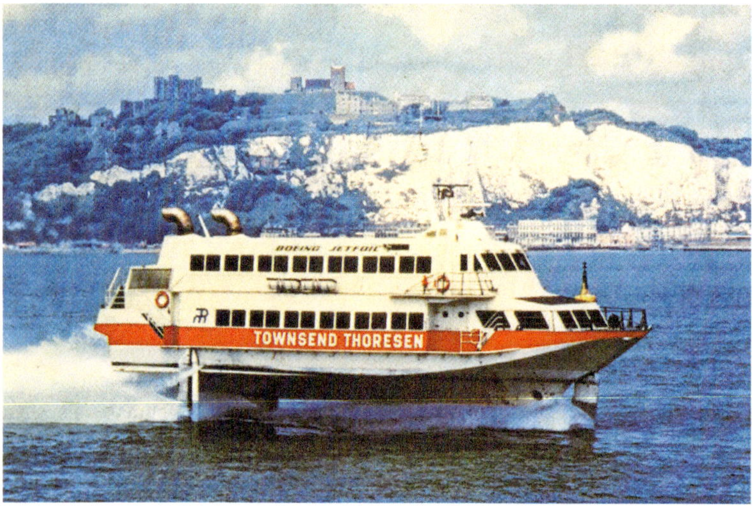

Princesse Clementine (1981, 329 grt).

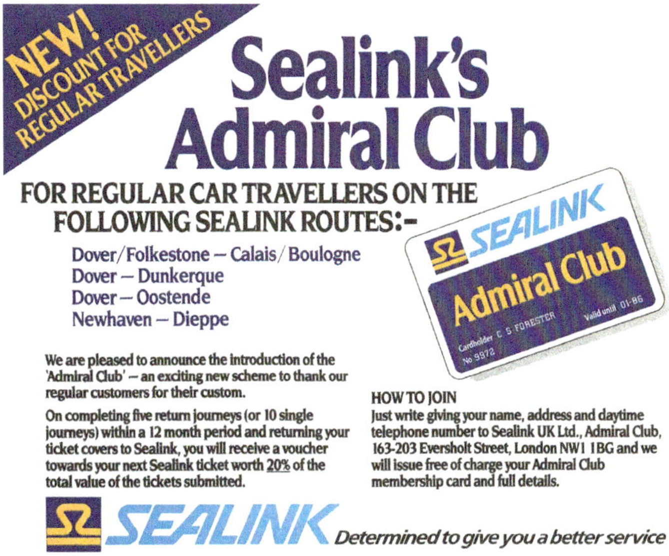

A 1985 advertisement for Sealink's Admiral Club.

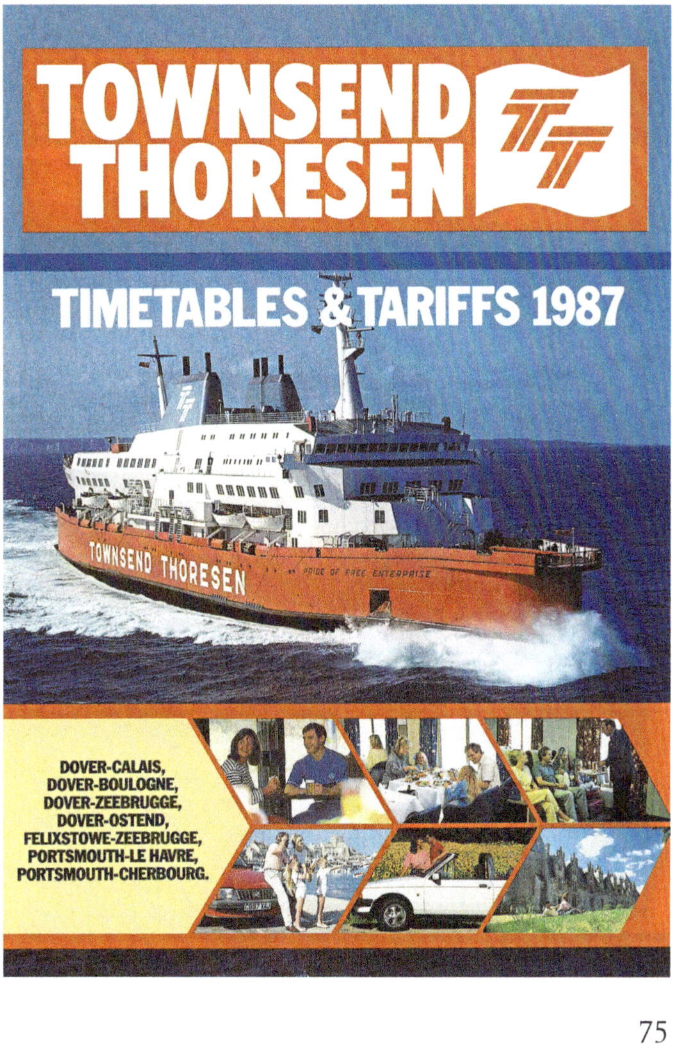

The Townsend Thoresen timetable for 1987.

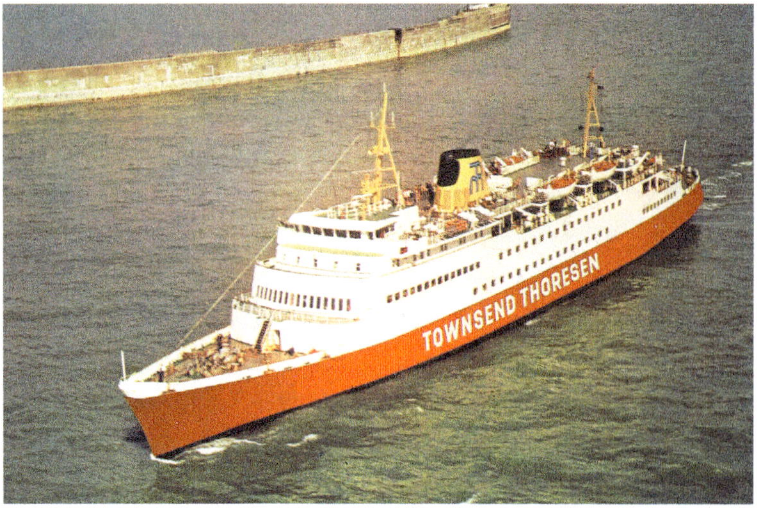

Prinses Paola (1966, 3,388 grt).

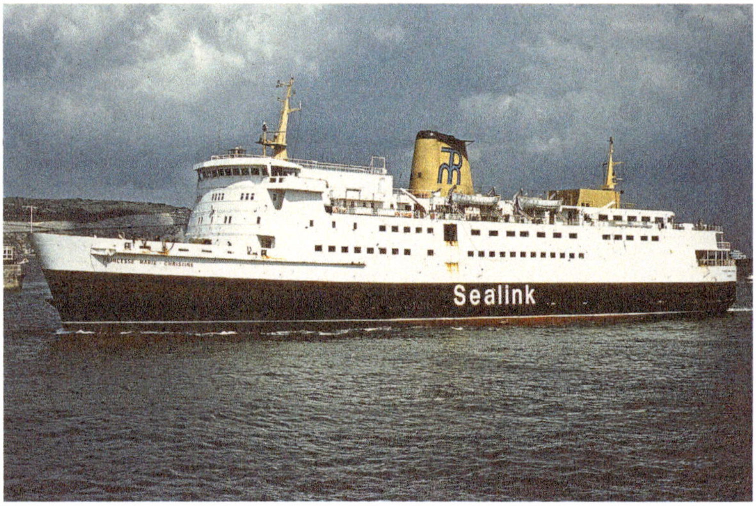

***Princesse Marie Christine*, 1975, 5,543 grt. 118.42 x 19.99 metres. 22 knots.**
b. Cockerill Yards, Hoboken. Yard No. 878. Belgium Marine Administration.

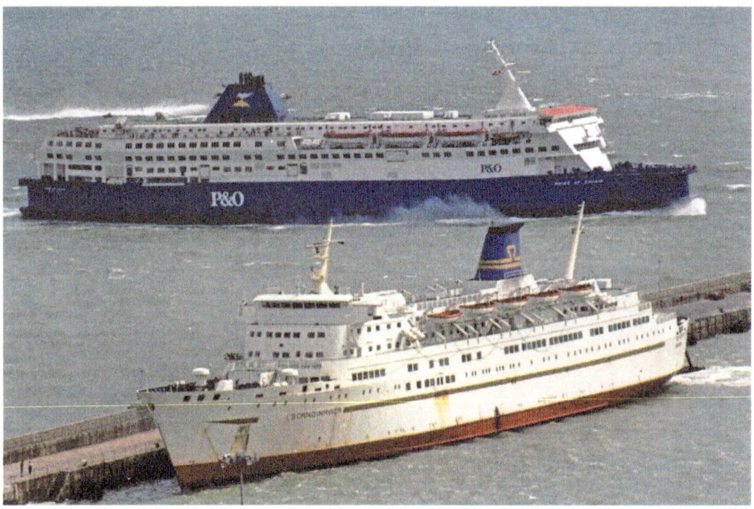

Pride of Calais (1987, 26,433 grt) and *Scandinavica* (1974, 8,753 grt) at Dover.

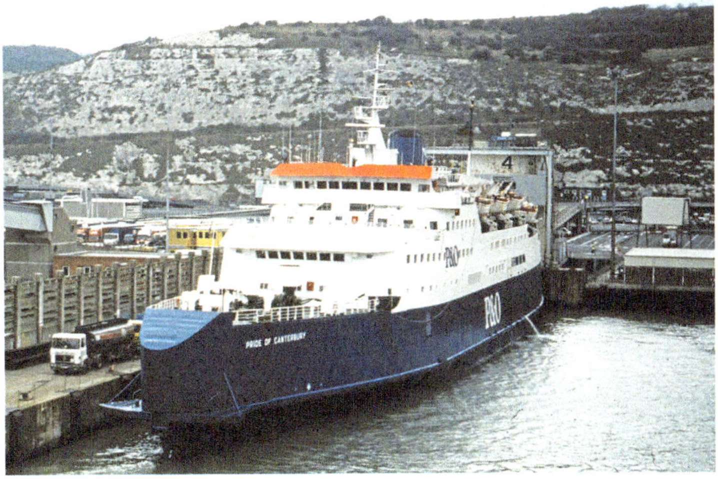

Pride of Canterbury (1974, 4,985 grt).

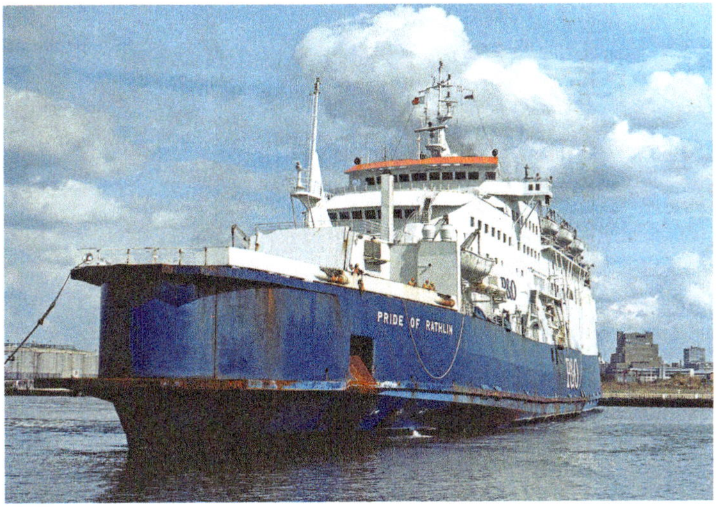

Pride of Rathlin, 1973, 4,981 grt. 117.5 x 19.5 metres.
b. IHC Gusto, Schiedam.

Launched on 22 October 1972 as *Free Enterprise VII* for the company's cross-channel services from Dover, she was renamed *Pride of Walmer* in 1988, *Pride of Rathlin* in 1992 and *BSP III* in 2000. She sank on 11 July 2015.

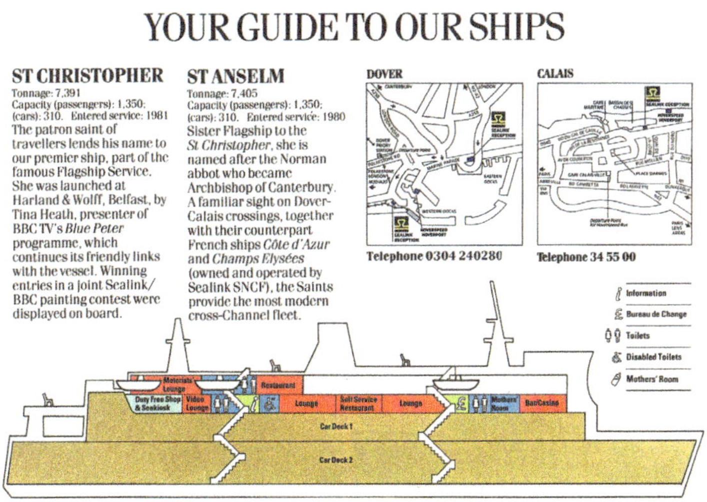

A Sealink advertisement for 1989.

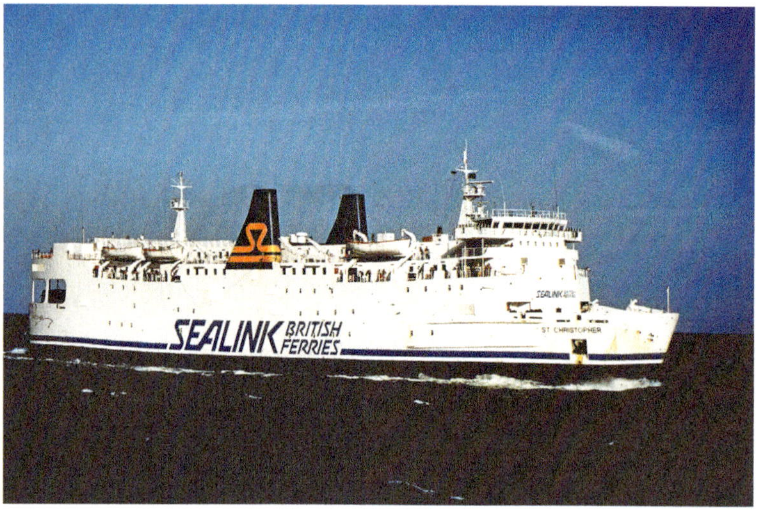

St Christopher (1980, 7,399 grt).

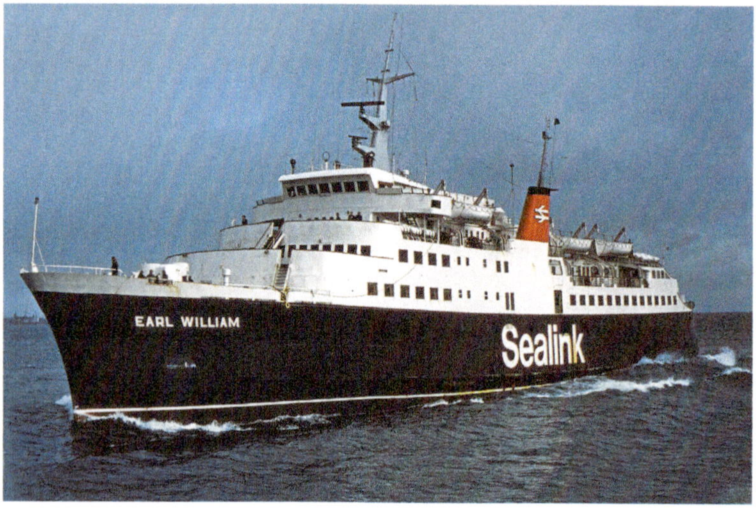

Earl William (1964, 3,984 grt).

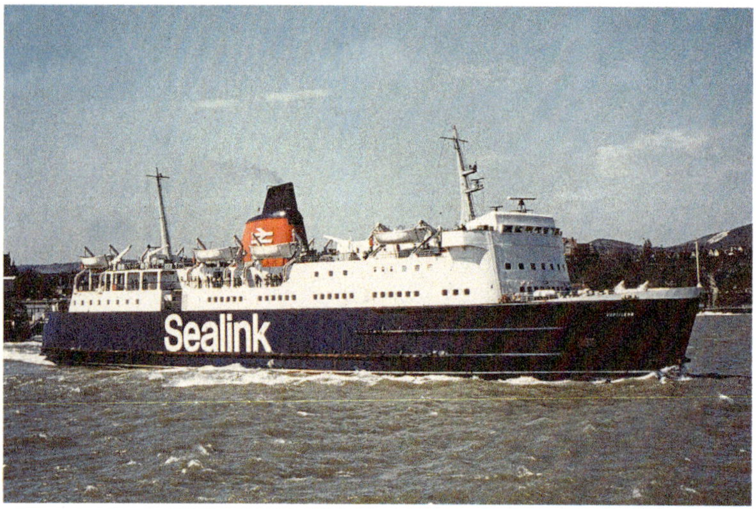

Vortigern (1969, 4371 grt).

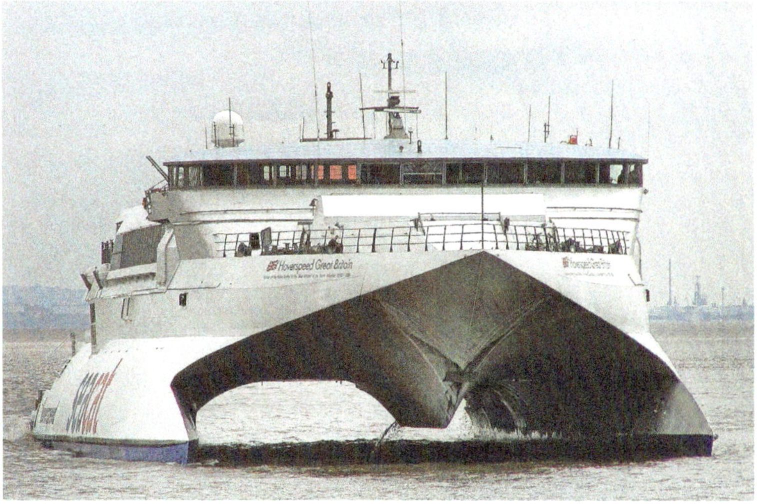

Hoverspeed Great Britain (Incat 025) (1990, 3,003 grt).

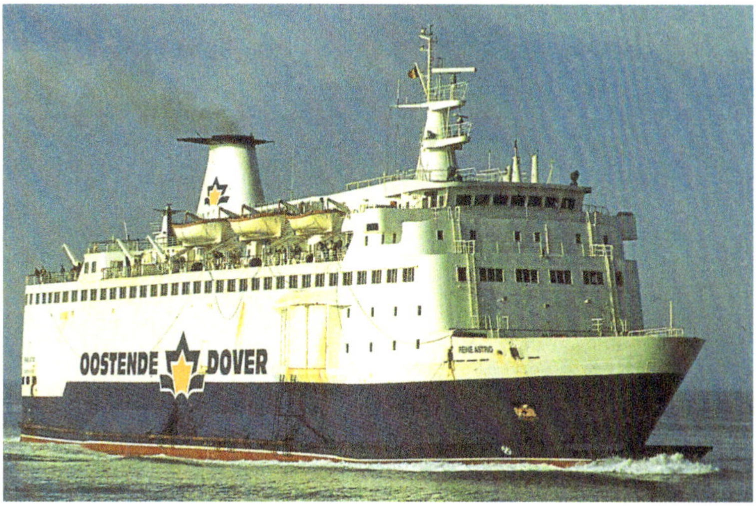

Reine Astrid (1975, 5,443 grt).

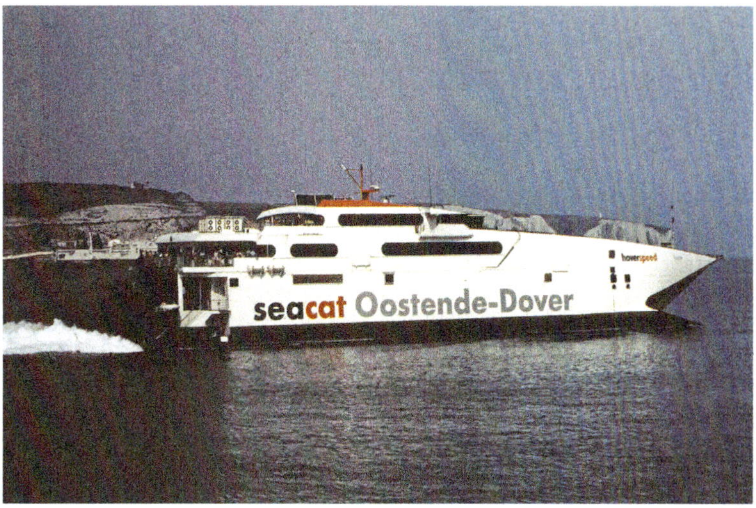

Rapide (Incat 038) (1996, 4,112 grt).

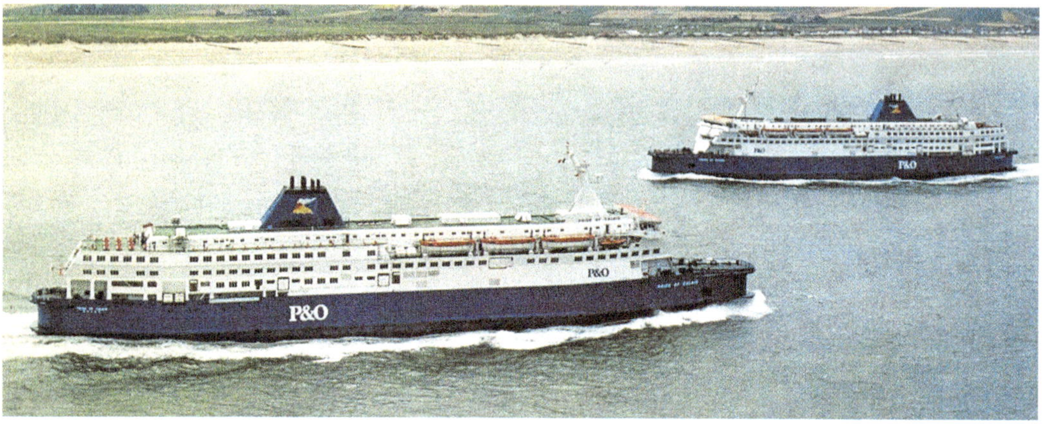

Pride of Dover (1987, 26,433 grt) and *Pride of Calais* (1987, 26,433 grt).

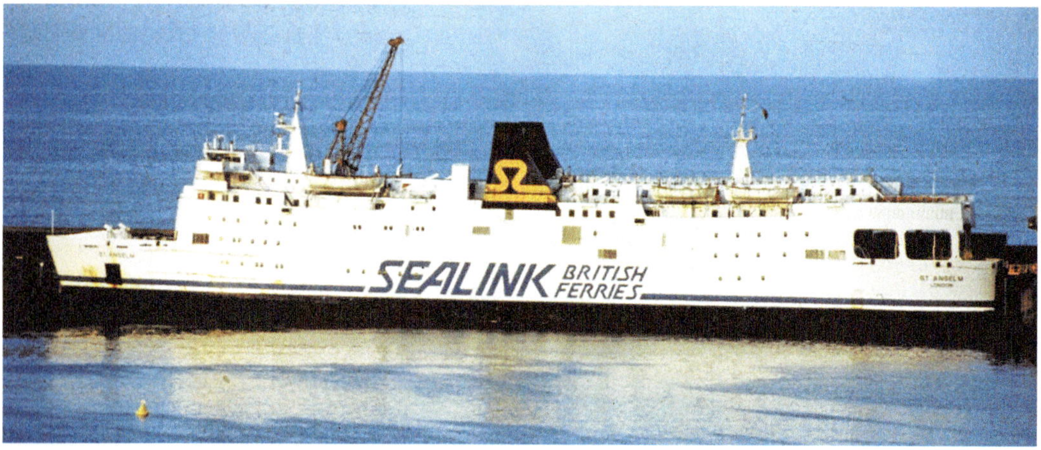

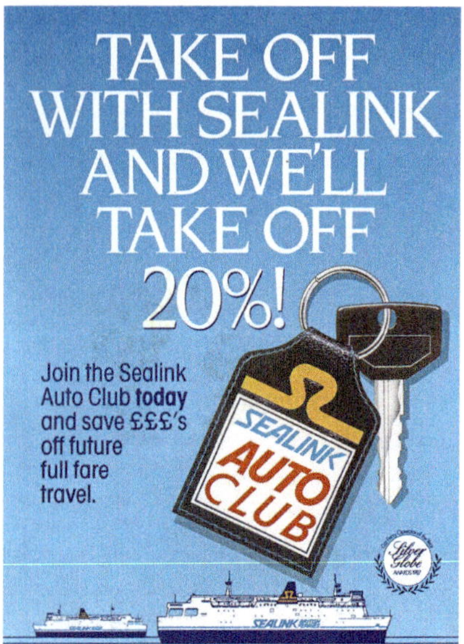

Above: *St Anselm* (1980, 7,399 grt).

Left: The 1988 Sealink Auto Club brochure.

DOVER'S OPERATORS

SEALINK

Calais

Crossing time
Calais 1 hour 30 minutes

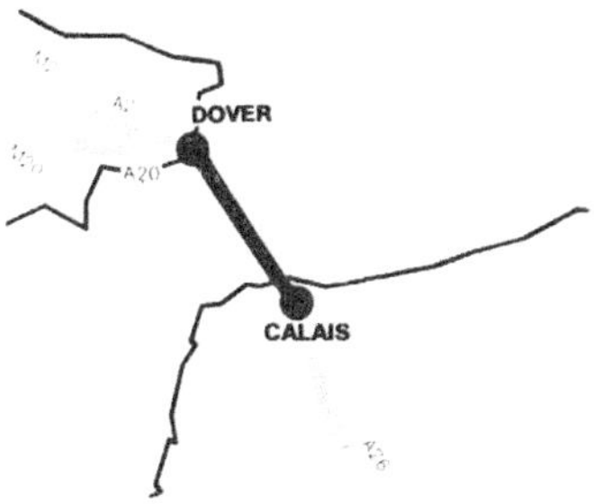

Up to 18 crossings daily

P&O European Ferries

Boulogne, Calais, Ostend Zeebrugge

Crossing times

Boulogne	1 hour 40 minutes
Calais	1 hour 15 minutes
Ostend	3 hours 45 minutes
Zeebrugge	4 hours

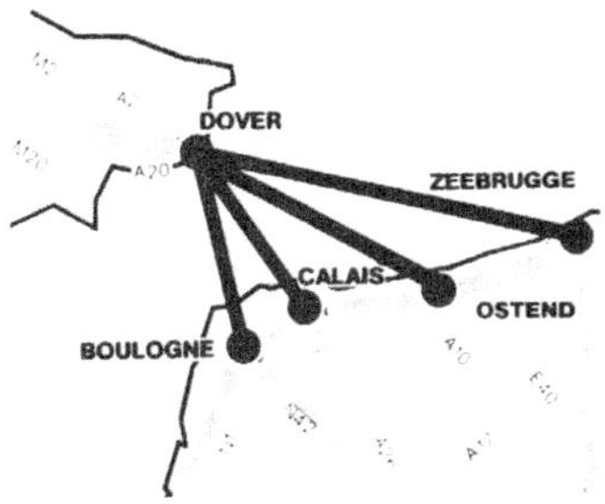

Boulogne: Up to 6 crossings daily
Calais: Up to 15 crossings daily
Ostend: Up to 7 crossings daily
Zeebrugge: Up to 6 crossings daily

HOVERSPEED

Boulogne and Calais

Crossing times

Boulogne	40 minutes
Calais	35 minutes

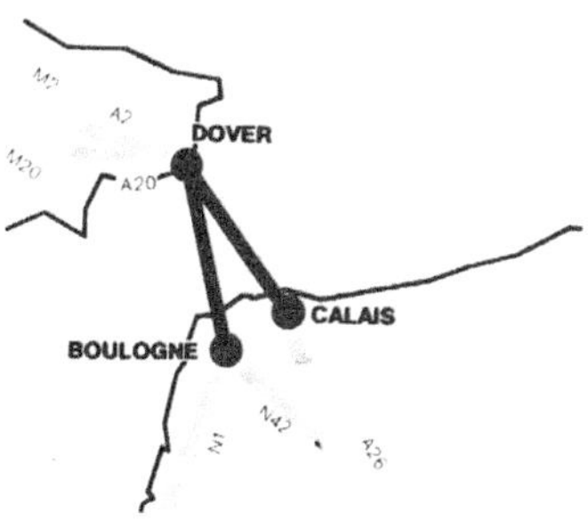

Boulogne: Up to 6 crossings daily
Calais: Up to 23 crossings daily

Jetfoil P&O European Ferries

Ostend

Crossing time 1 hour 40 minutes (Foot passengers only).

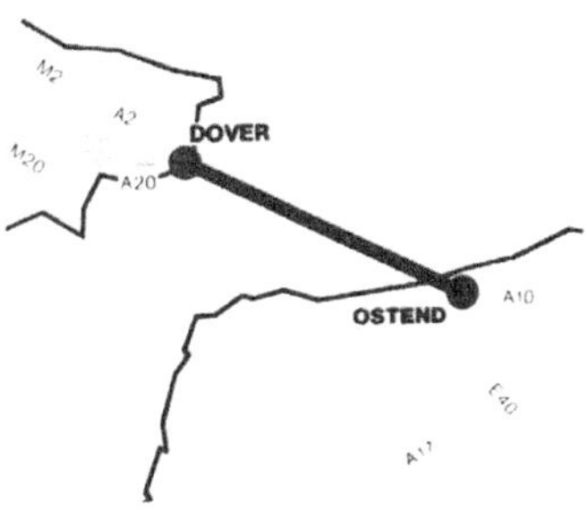

Jetfoil: Up to 5 crossings daily

Dover operators as of 1989.

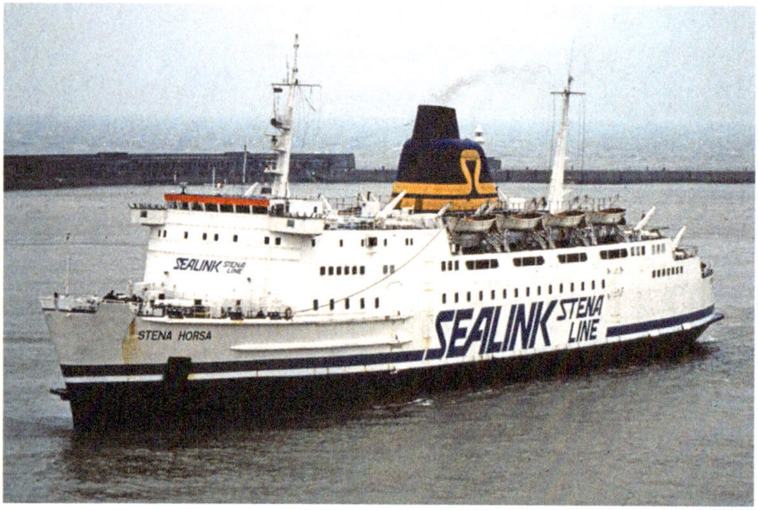

Stena Horsa (1972, 5,590 grt).

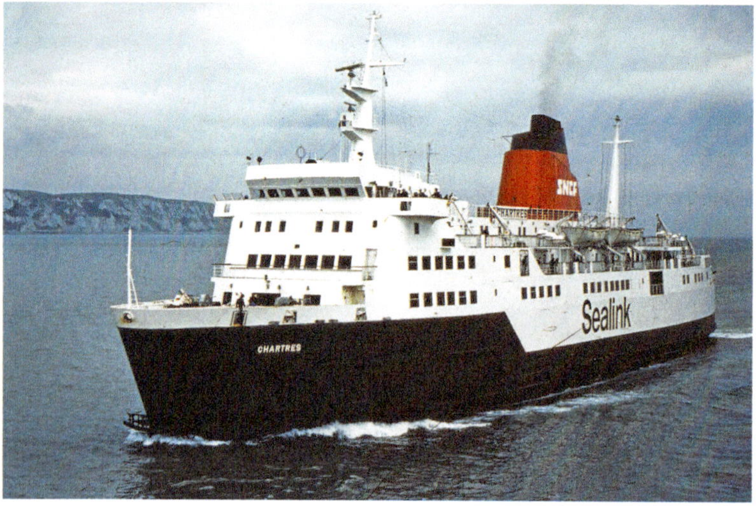

Chartres (1973, 4,800 grt).

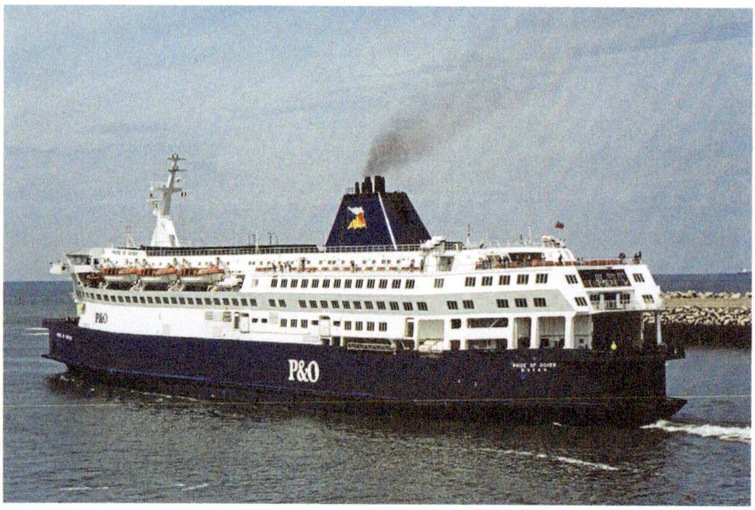

Pride of Dover (1987, 26,433 grt).

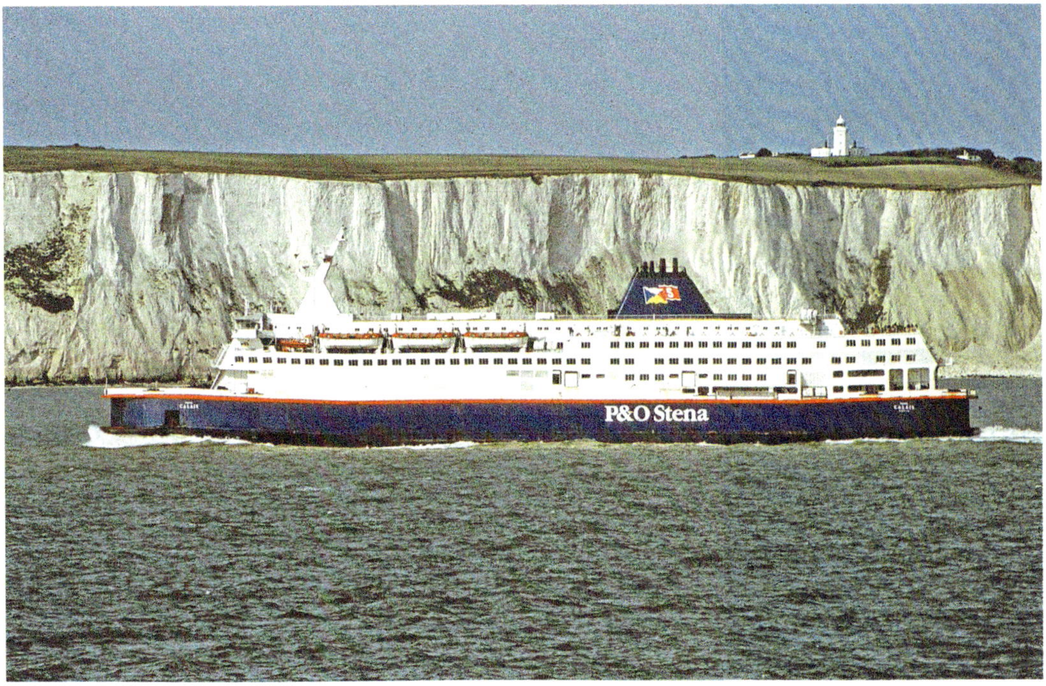

Above: *Pride of Calais* (1987, 26,433 grt).

Below: *Fiesta* (1979, 25,318 grt).

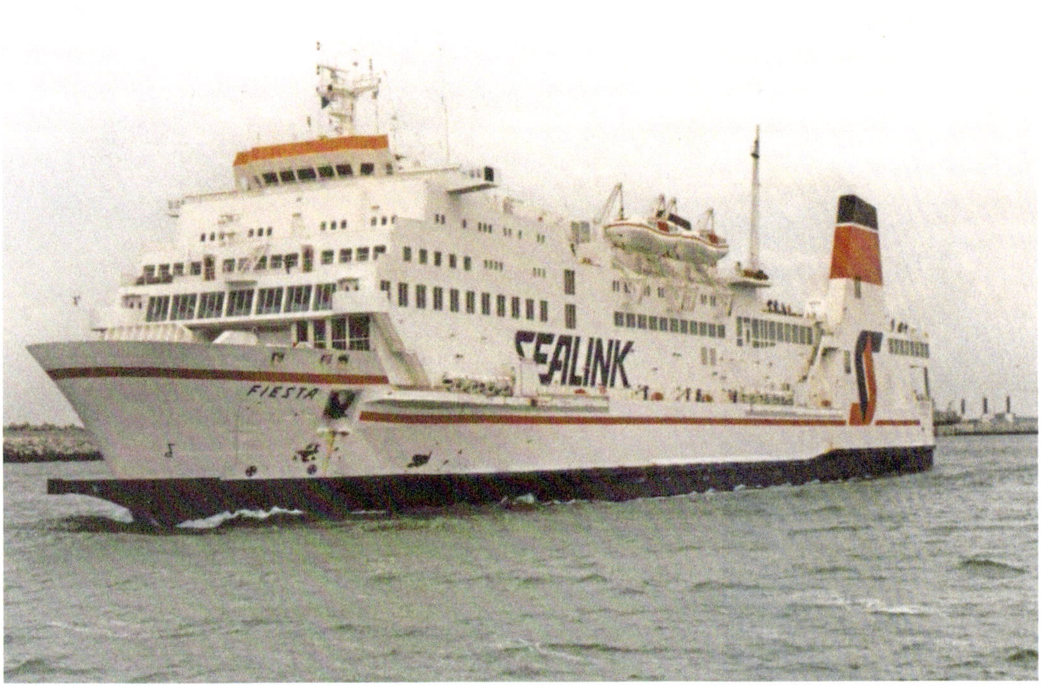

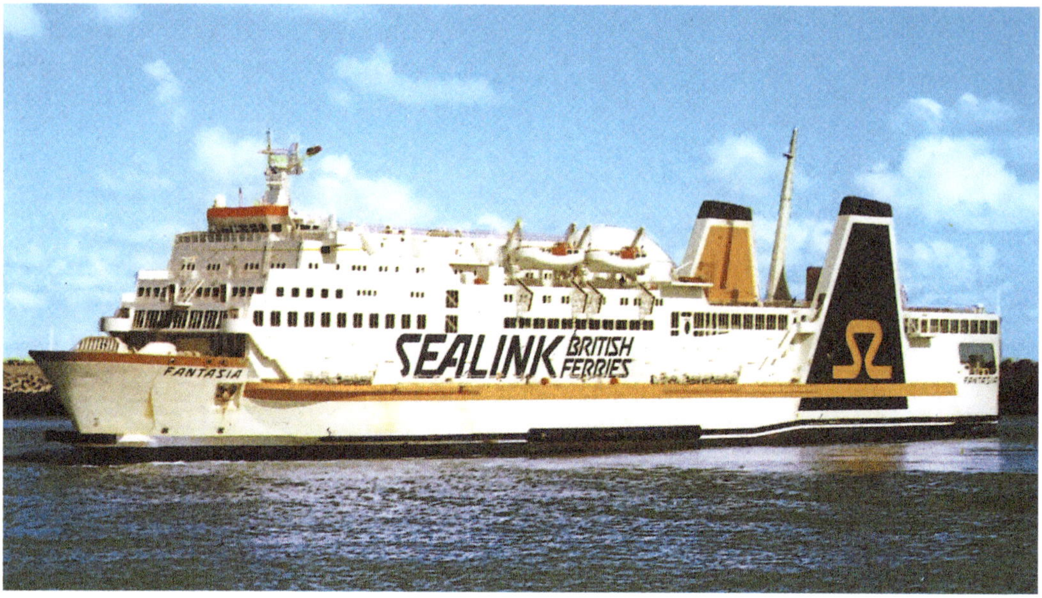

Above and below: *Fiesta* became *Fantasia* in February 1990.

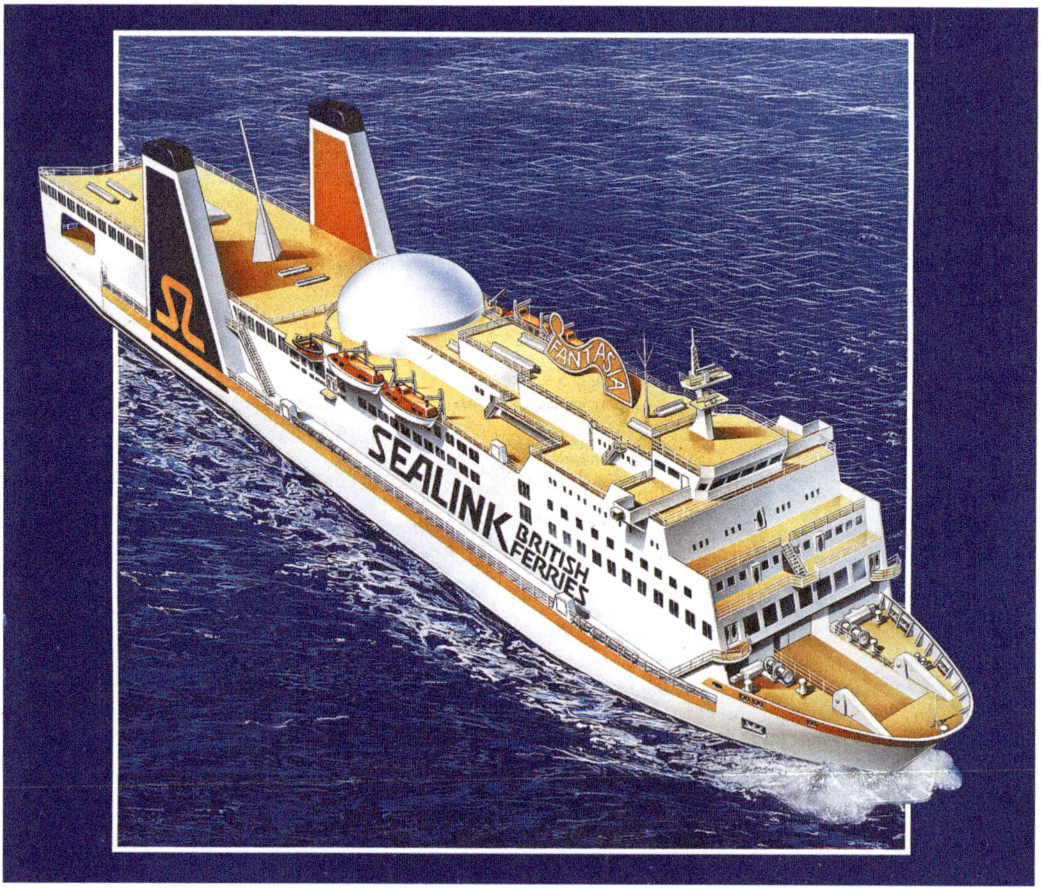

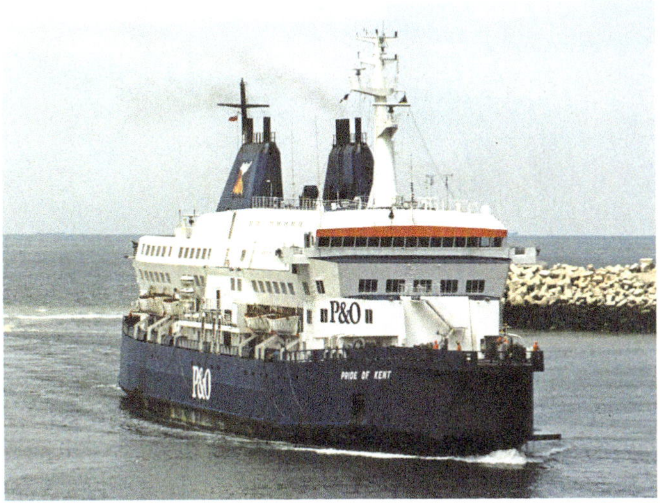

Pride of Kent (1979, 7,951 grt).

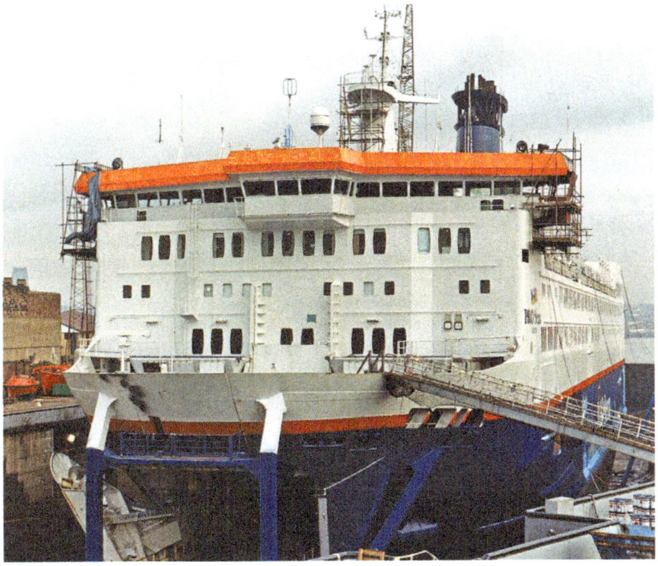

P&OSL Provence, 1983, 15,811 grt. 152.2 x 28.5 metres. 19 knots.
b. Ch. du Nord et de La Méditerranée, Dunkirk Yard No. 310. P&O Stena Line.

Launched as *Stena Jutlandica* on 22 December 1980, she became *Stena Empereur* in 1996, *P&OSL Provence* in 1998, *PO Provence* in 2002, *Pride of Provence* in 2003, and then both *Alkmini A* and *Pride of Telemark* in 2005. She was beached at Alang on 27 October 2011 and was broken up by Chaudhary Industries.

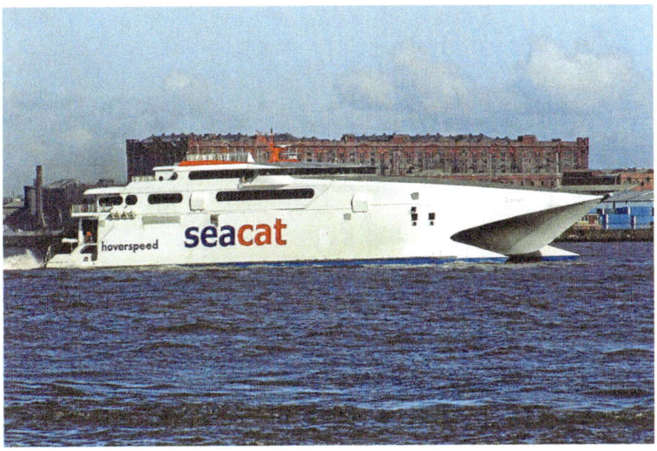

Seacat Diamant, 1996, 4,305 grt. 81.2 x 26 metres.
b. Incat Limited, Hobart, Tasmania. Yard No. 041. Sea Containers Limited.

Built as *Holyman Express*, she became *Holyman Diamant* in 1997, *Diamant* in 1998, *Seacat Diamant* in 2004 and *Jaume III* in 2007.

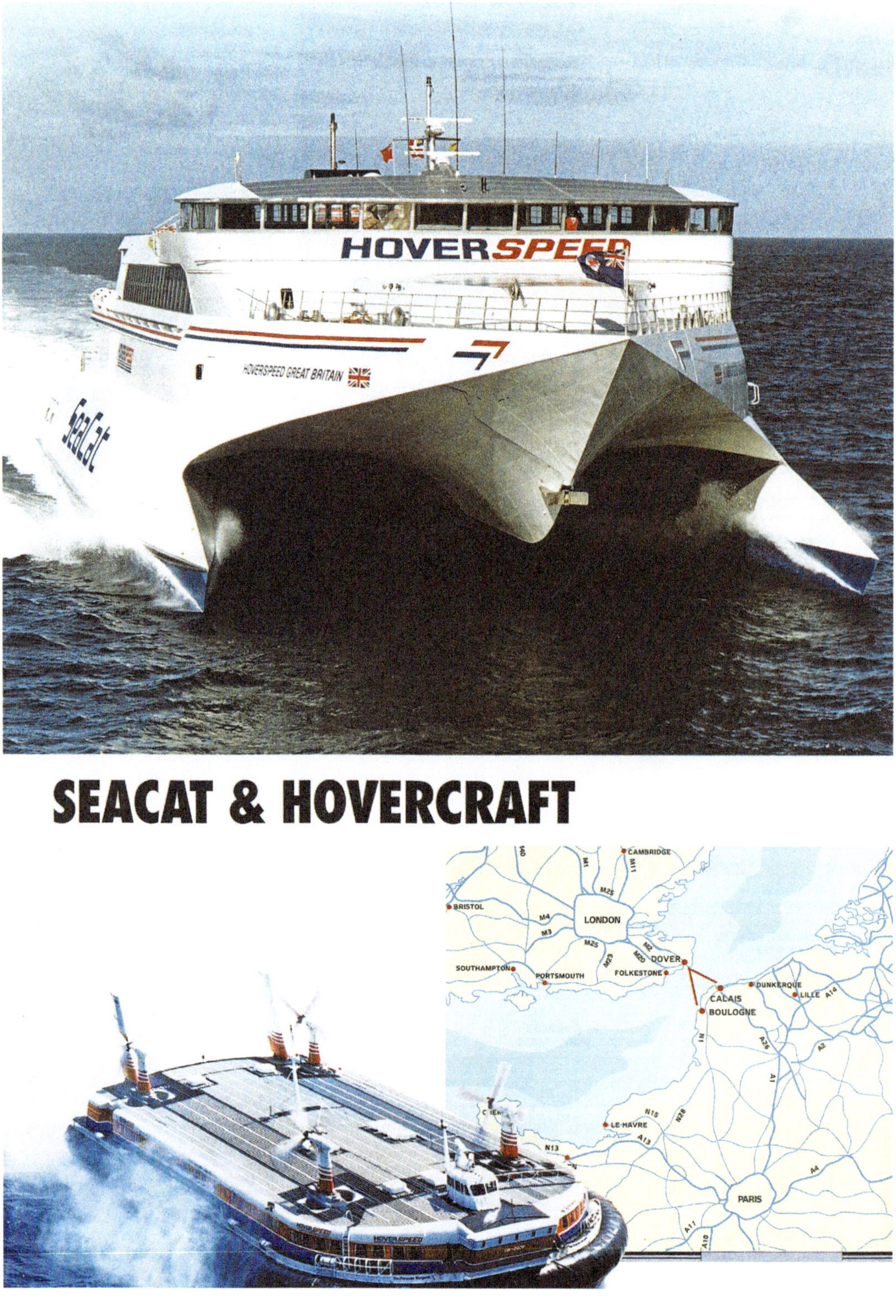

A Hoverspeed advertisement for 1991.

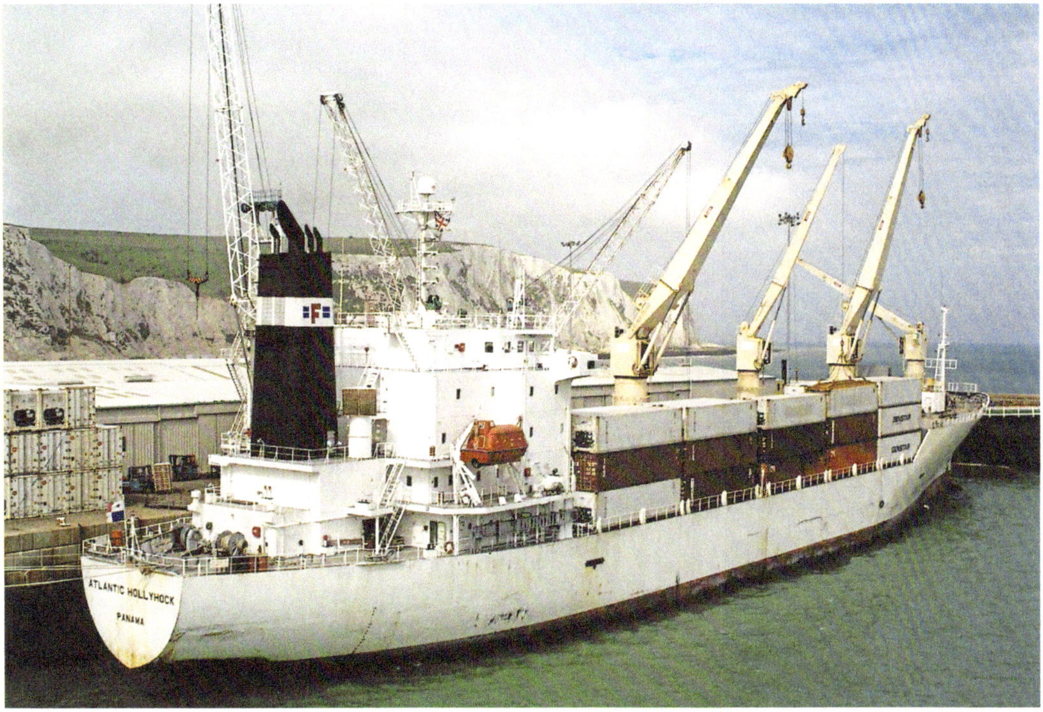

Above: *Atlantic Hollyhock* (1999, 9,649 grt). (Chris Brooks)

Below: *Argentina Star* (1992, 10,629 grt). (Chris Brooks)

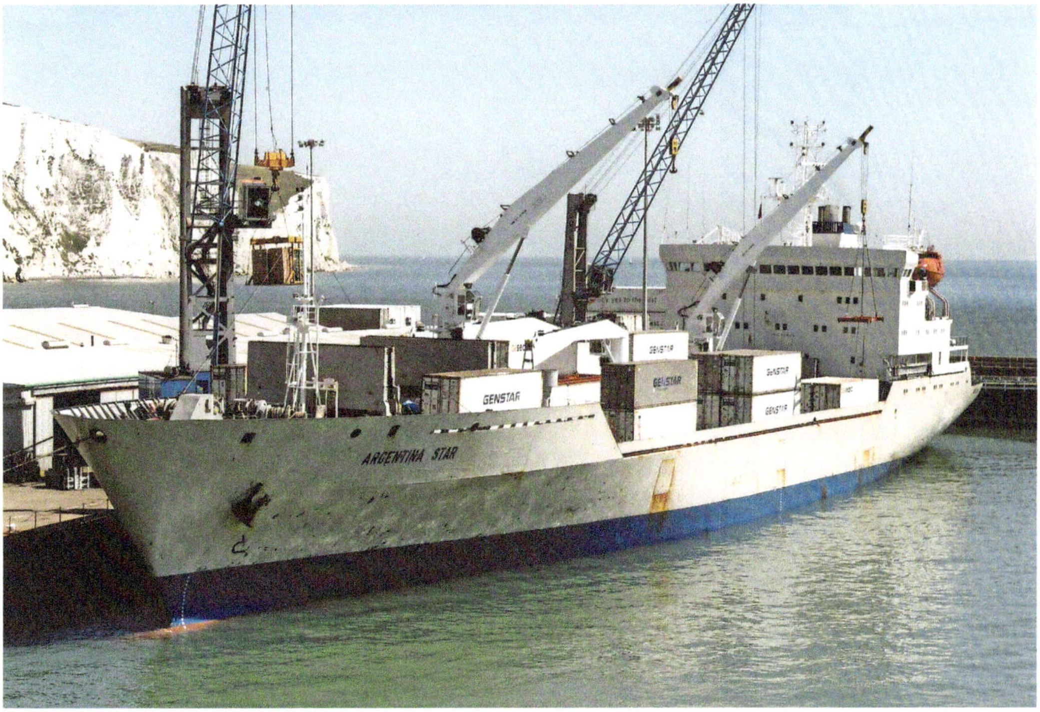

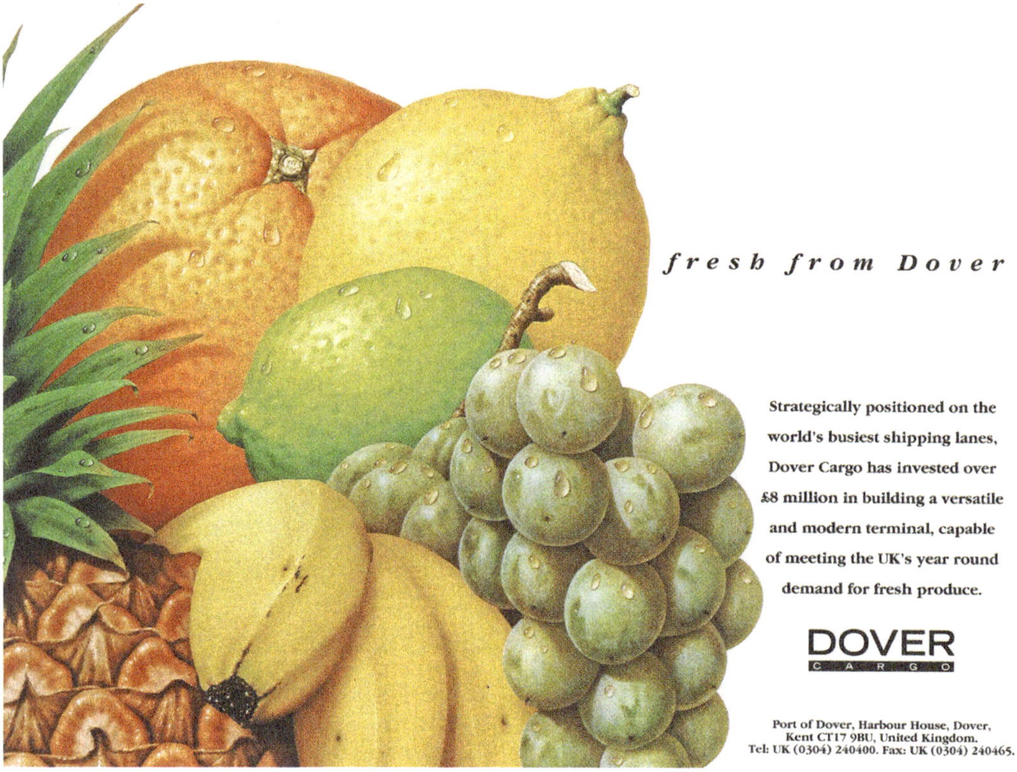

Above: A Port of Dover advertisement for 1994.

Below: Port of Dover tugs.

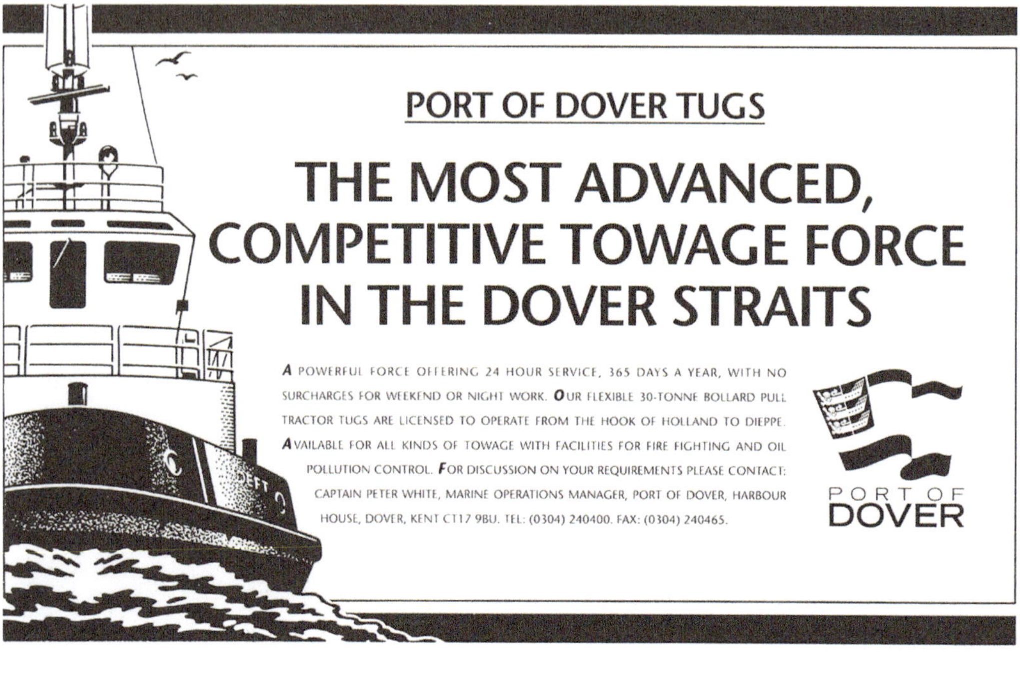

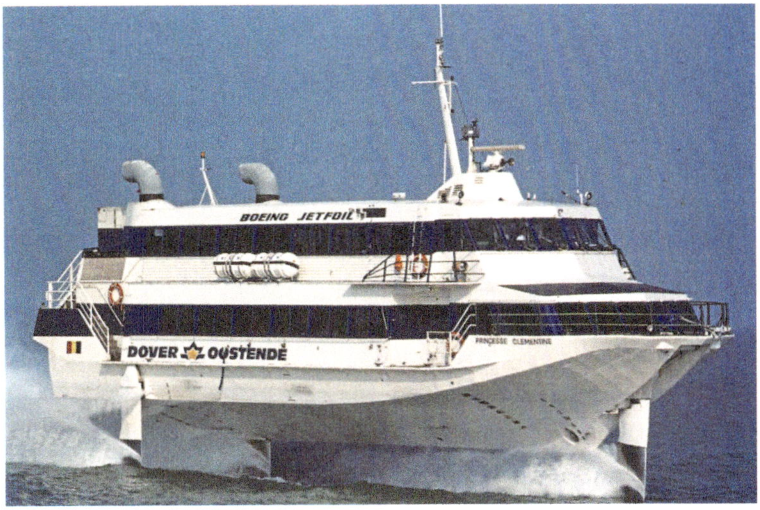

Princesse Clementine (1981, 329 grt) on the Dover–Ostend service.

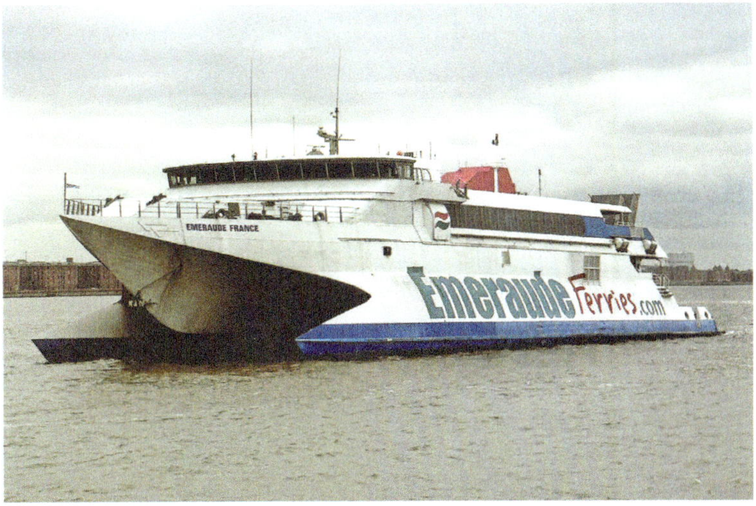

Emeraude France (Incat 023) (1990, 3,003 grt).

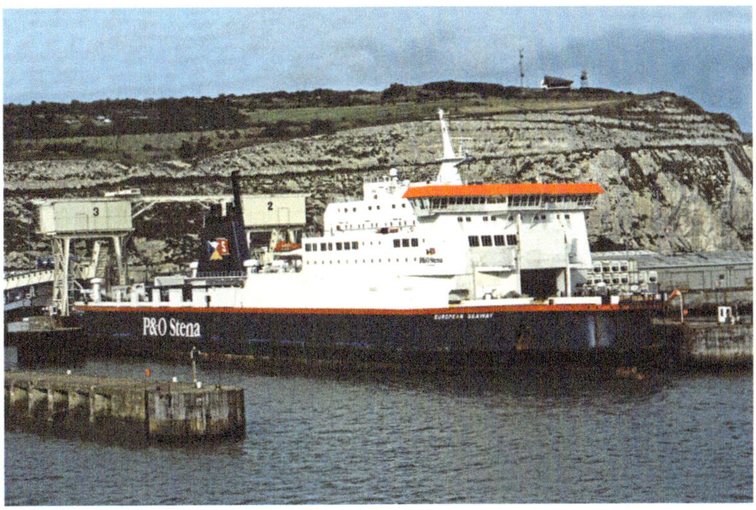

European Seaway (1991, 22,986 grt).

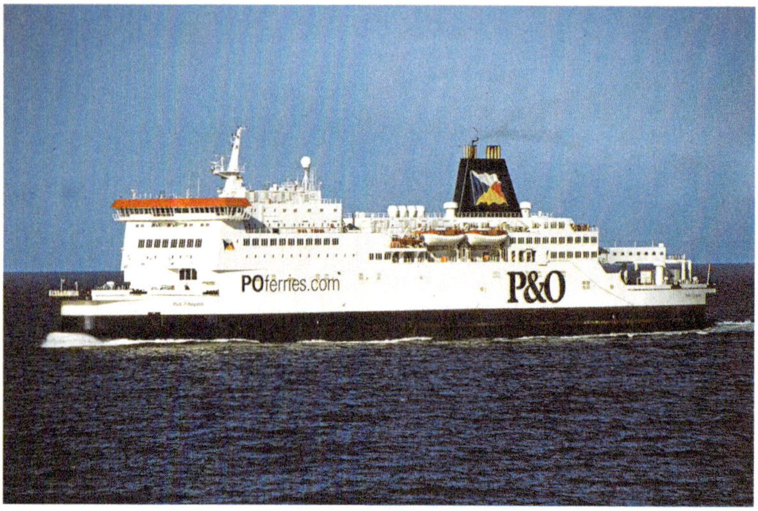

Pride of Burgundy (1993, 28,138 grt).

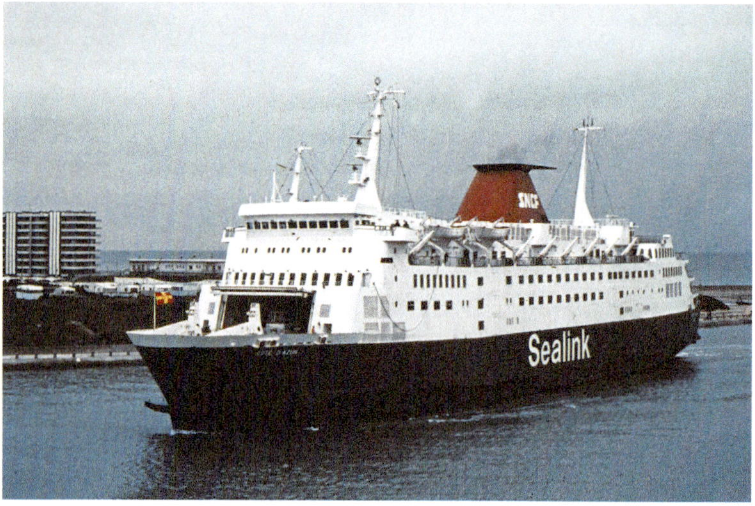

Cote D'Azur (1981, 8,862 grt).

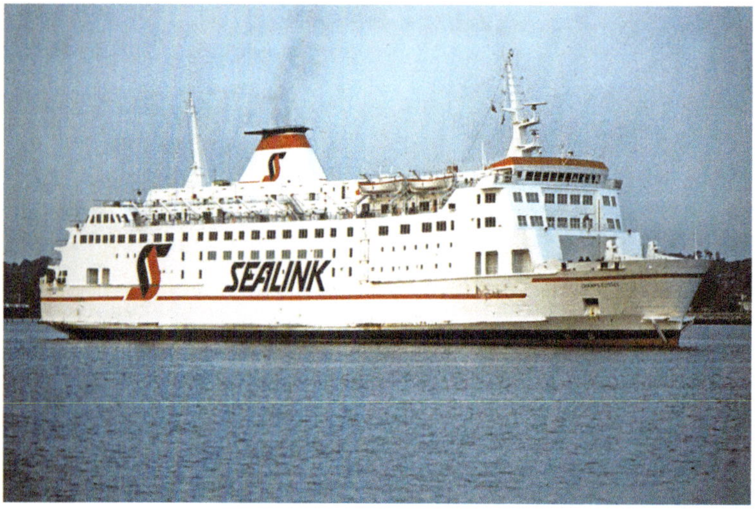

Champs Elysées (1984, 9,069 grt).

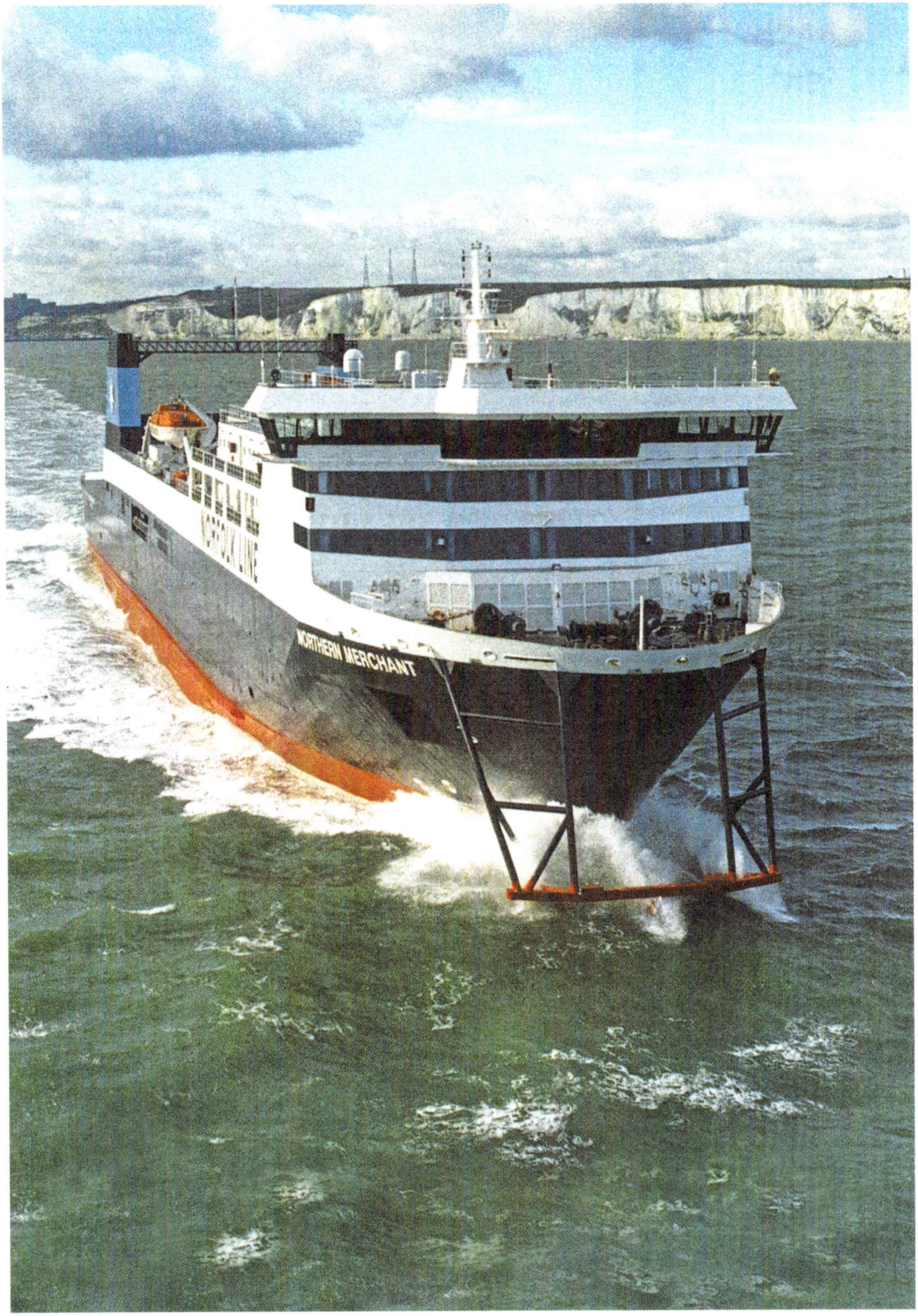

Northern Merchant (2000, 22,152 grt).

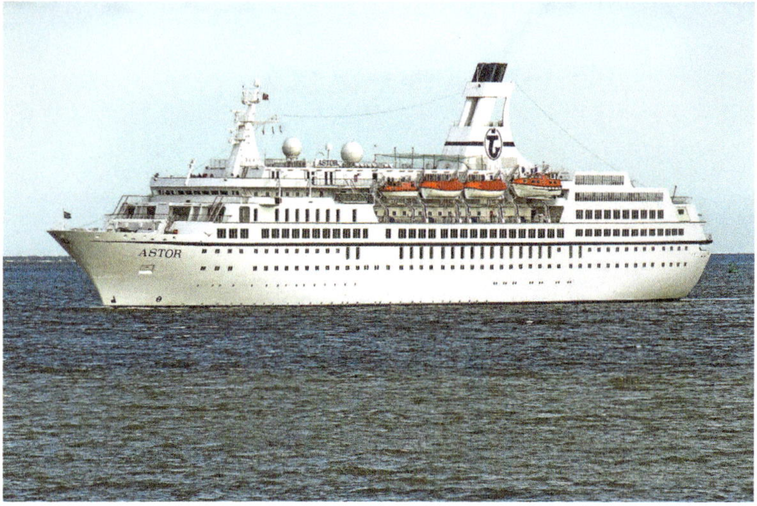
Astor (1987, 20,606 grt).

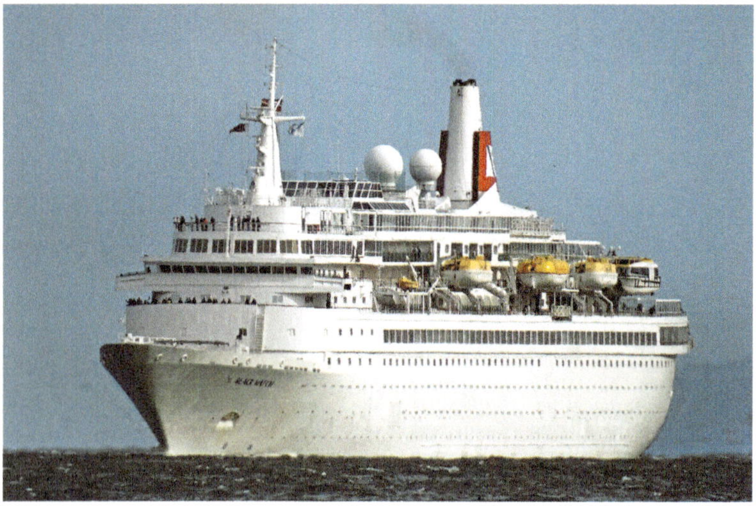
Black Watch (1972, 28,613 grt)

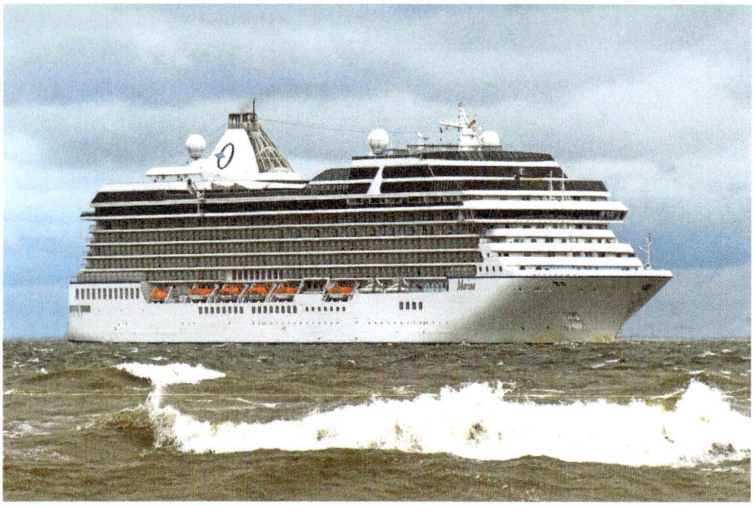
Marina (2011, 66,084 grt).

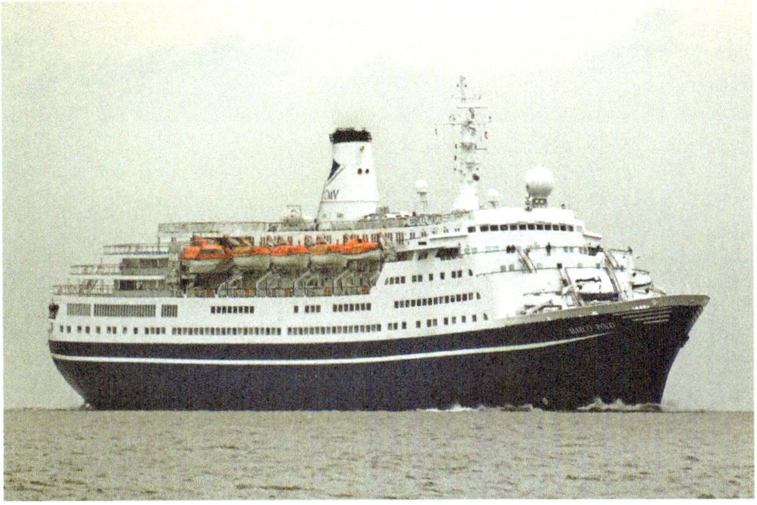

Marco Polo (1965, 22,080 grt).

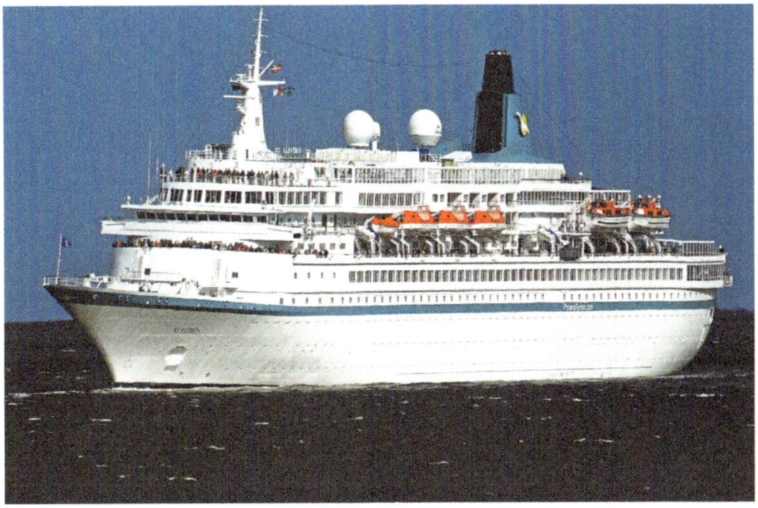

Albatros (1973, 28,518 grt).

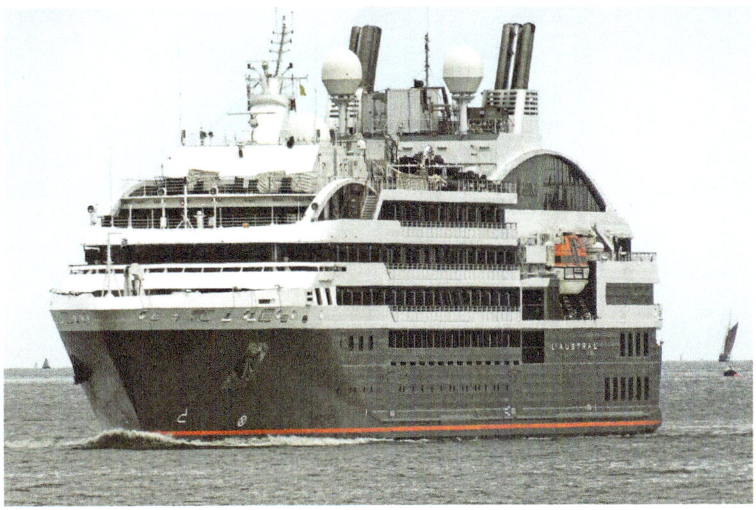

L'Austral (2010, 10,944 grt).

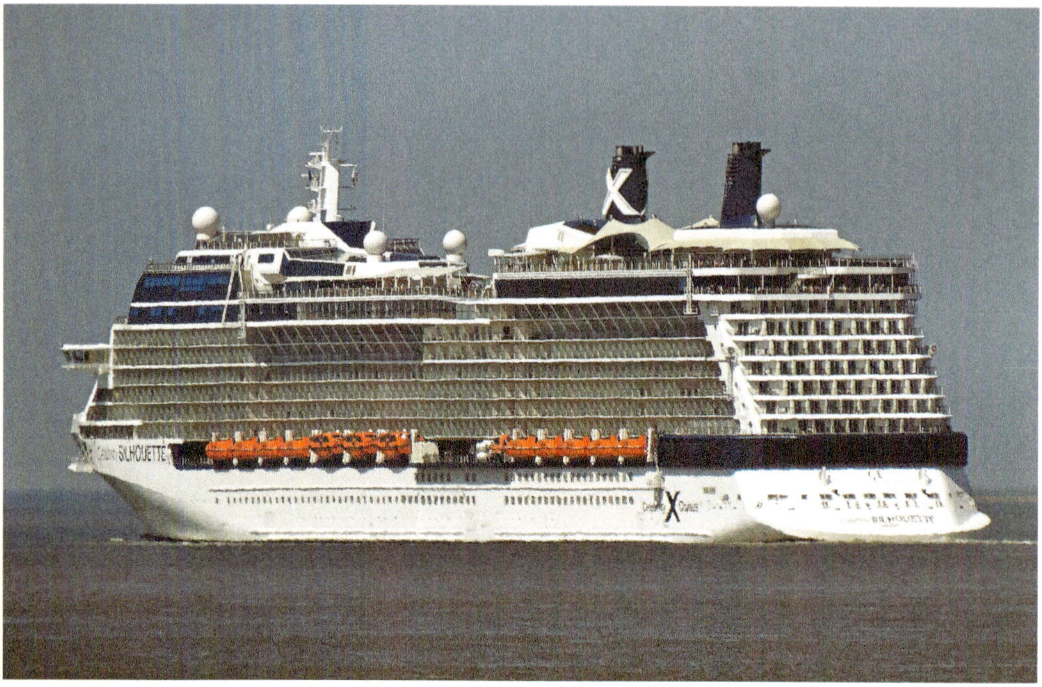

Above: *Celebrity Silhouette* (2011, 122,210 grt).

Below: *Disney Magic* (1998, 83,338 grt).

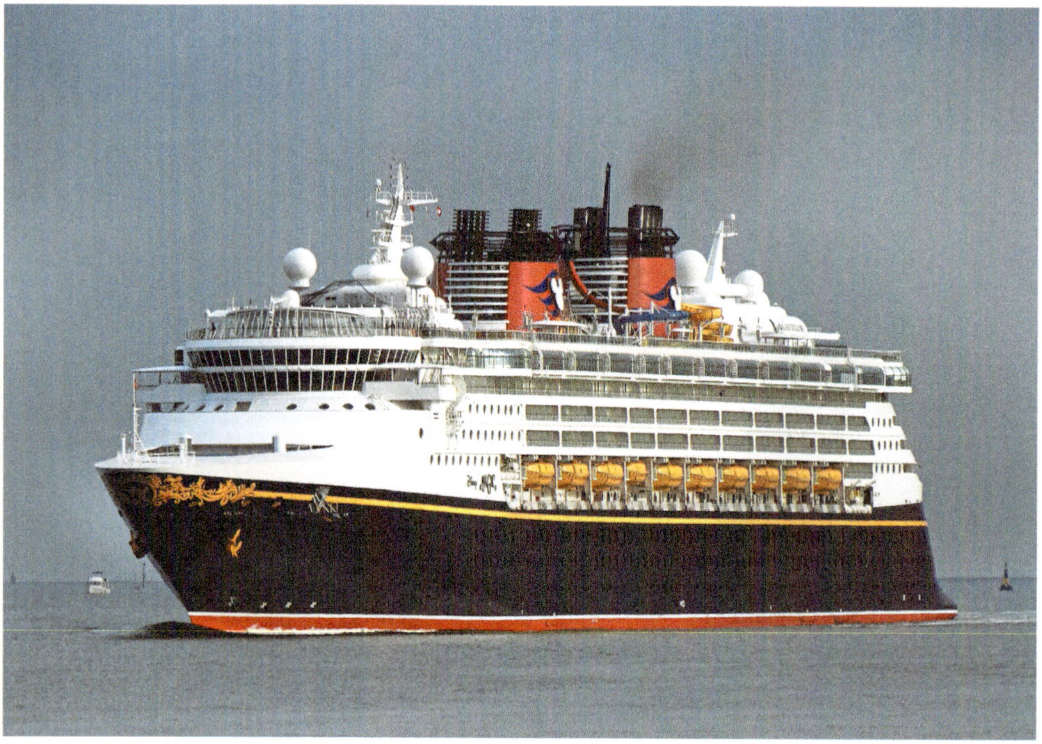

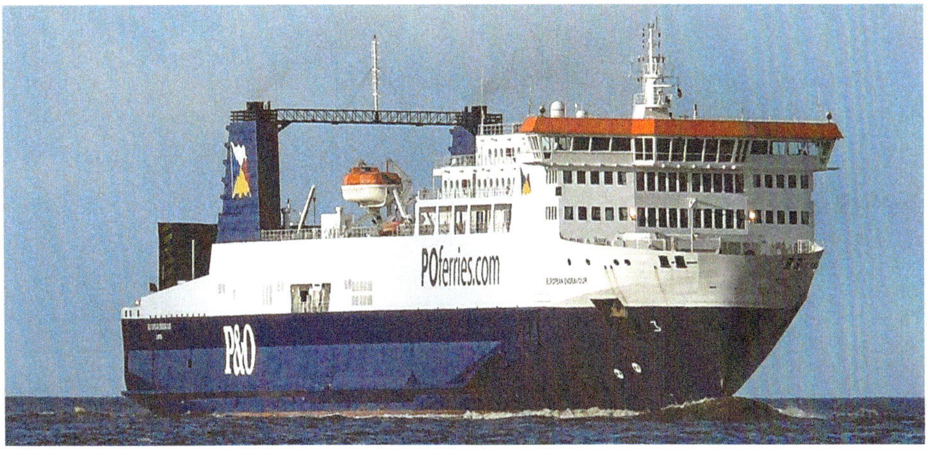

European Endeavour (2000, 22,152 grt).

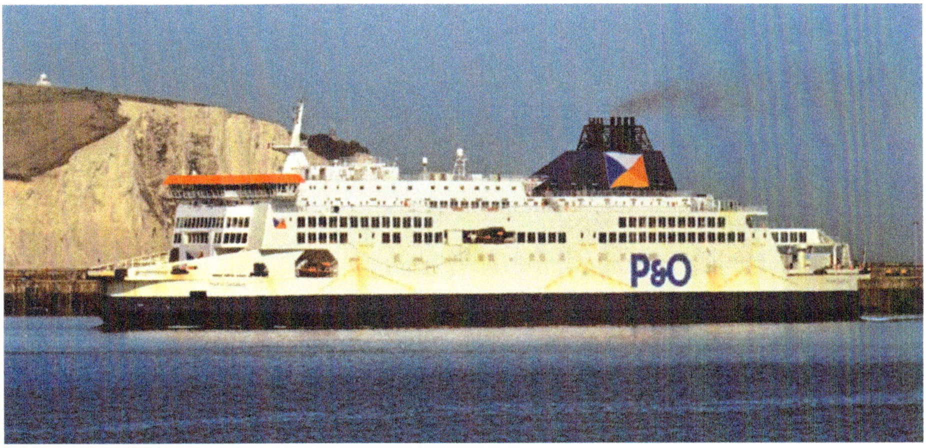

Pride of Canterbury (1991, 30,635 grt).

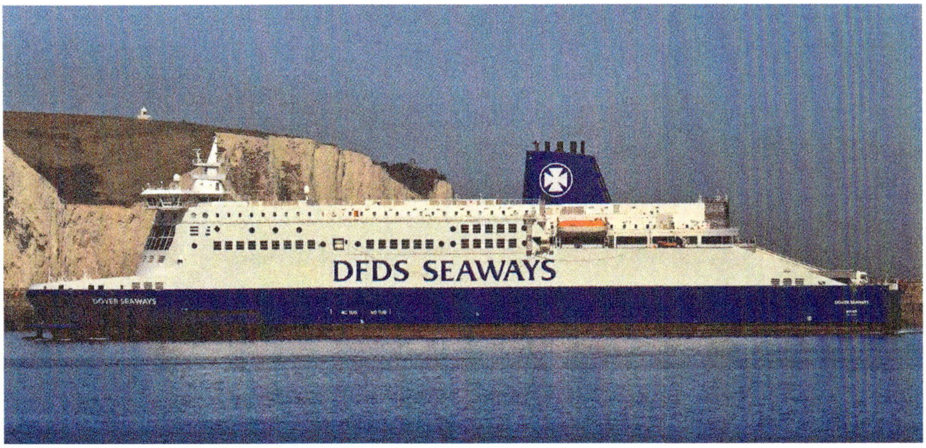

Dover Seaways (2006, 35,923 grt).

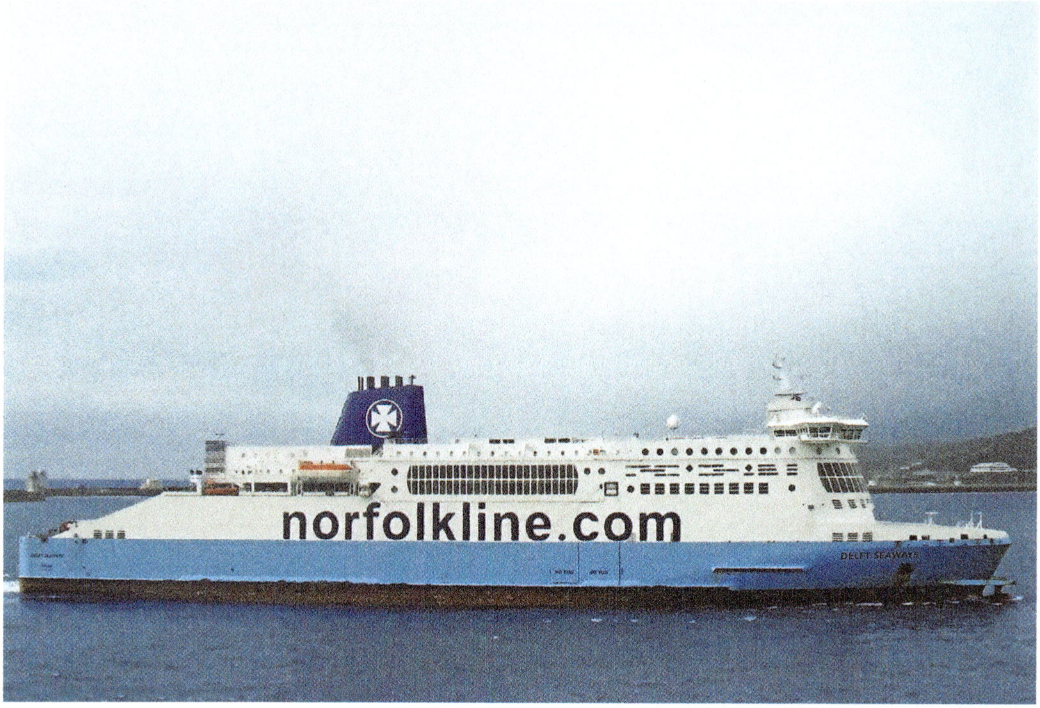

Above: *Delft Seaways* (2006, 35,923 grt).

Below: *Spirit of France* (2012, 47,592 grt).

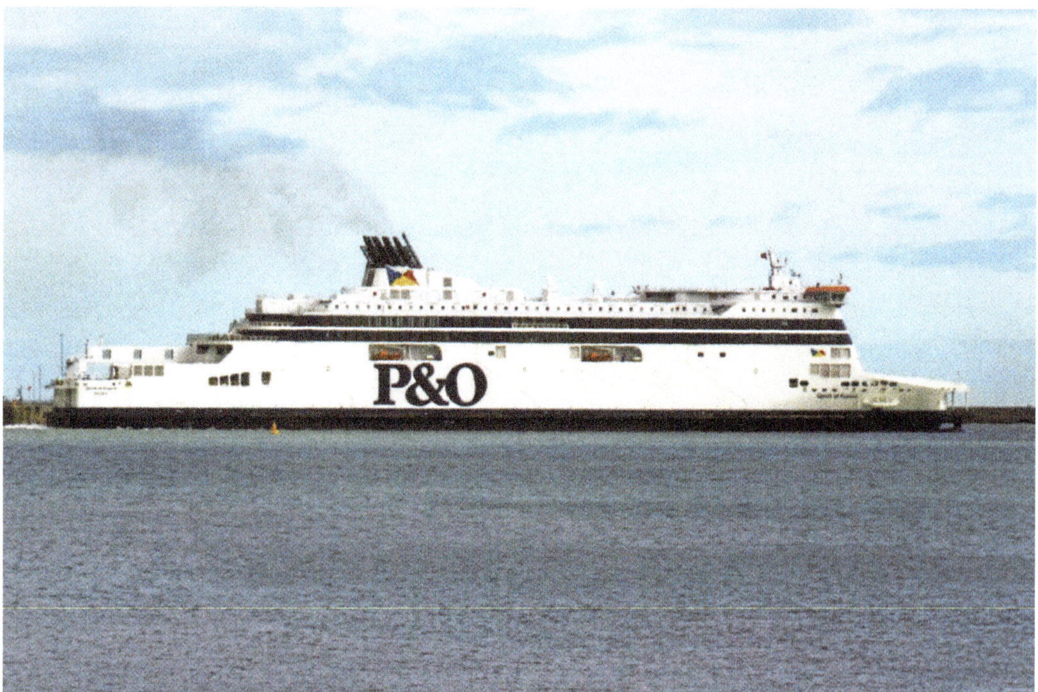